WELCOME TO RECOMENDO: THE EXPANDED VERSION

This book features our best 1,000 recommendations, selected from all the brief suggestions we've sent out over the past four years. Each Sunday morning we email 6 brief suggestions in a free email newsletter called Recomendo; we've rounded up the best thousand items here. This edition is improved and expanded from a first edition of this book we did two years ago.

How to use this book

Because they were first sent as email, each original item had a web link. Now that they have been transferred to paper that link shows up as a QR oode. To reach the link, hover your phone camera over the code. The newest phone models will see the code automatically in

camera mode. If your phone is older, you may need to open a QR code app first. The best, simplest, easiest QR reader app we recommend is called QR Scanner by Kaspersky. It's free and comes in iOS and Android versions. To download, visit: usa.kaspersky.com/qr-scanner, or use the QR code above.

Alternatively, you can google the item name in a recomendo most times to find it; but that does not always work.

To get recomendos in the future

If you like what you see here, you can sign up for the free Recomendo newsletter. You'll get 6 short text items on one-page each week. Sign up at recomendo. com to join almost 50,000 other happy subscribers. Or use this QR code. Share with your friends by forwarding an issue you like.

To get the complete past stuff

You can find all the past issues in their original form at recomendo. com.

To buy extra copies of this book

RECOMENDO
THE EXPANDED EDITION

1,000 brief reviews of cool stuff

By Claudia Dawson, Kevin Kelly, and Mark Frauenfelder

This book is printed on demand. Copies cost $12.99 from Amazon with Prime delivery. We honestly believe this book makes a great inexpensive gift; just about everyone will find a bunch of useful recommendations.

Check out our visual Recomendos

In addition to our weekly newsletter, every couple weeks the three of us record a very brief video of something new we recommend. We call it Recomendo Shorts and you can check them out on Youtube here.

Tell us your own recommendations

After reading this book you might know about a great tool, tip, hack, gadget, destination, or media creation that you'd like to recommend to us. Just fill out this form here.

Wait, there is more!

We run the Cool Tools site, which has been reviewing useful tools for individuals and small groups making things since 2003. In addition, we also produce a weekly podcast (Cool Tools Podcast) where we ask a notable maker about their four favorite tools. All this goodness issues from cool-tools.org.

Disclosure

Some of the recomendos in this book are items you can buy. When we list an item that Amazon sells, the QR code will link to the Amazon item with an affiliate code that gives us a small referral fee. This fee pays for the Recomendo site and newsletter, and the cost of producing this book. But none of our reviews have been paid for by others, or rely on free samples, or are product placements. The three of us authors spend our own money to purchase the items we suggest. Our recommendations are genuine and sincere.

— Kevin Kelly (@kevin2kelly)
Mark Frauenfelder (@frauenfelder)
Claudia Dawson (@clauddaws)

Credits

This book was written by Kevin Kelly, Mark Frauenfelder, and Claudia Dawson. Claudia produced the entire book, laid out each page, and created the index. She also manages the website. The illustrations were collected by Faisal Ahmed. Christina Kuhl proofread the book. Kevin designed the covers and the page layout. The book is set in Chivo font.

Copyright

Recomendo:
The Expanded Edition
1,000 brief reviews of cool stuff

Copyright 2020
by Claudia Dawson, Kevin Kelly, Mark
Frauenfelder
Cool Tools Lab, LLC.
All rights reserved.

First edition

ISBN-13: 978-1-940689-04-3

CONTENTS

SHOPPING

Superior shopping bags

We live in an area where you must bring your own bag to the store. That usually meant recycled paper bags, or floppy cloth bags. At the suggestion of a guest on our Cool Tools podcast, we started using these fantastic Planet E collapsible "bags" that unfold into a rigid cloth box. They are roomier, much easier to pack and unpack, and can carry a lot of weight without distorting their shape. They are lower and wider, more stable so they won't fall over, and easier to move into the car. They fold flat, seem indestructible, and are made of recycled plastic bottles. We'll never go back to other kinds of bags. — KK

Basic gift-wrapping videos

I always need a refresher course when it comes time to wrapping gifts, and there are a lot of instructional videos on YouTube, but most are too complicated for me. This basic gift wrapping video is helpful and I learned that all this time I was forgetting to fold over the edges before I taped them down. — CD

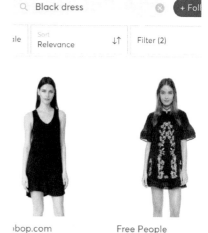

Subscription box spoilers

My Subscription Addiction spoilers section is my go-to bookmark when I can't physically wait to get monthly makeup box from Sephora. But this site is so much more than that. It's a massive directory of subscription boxes you can search by gender, categories, and countries. As well as reviews, there are promo codes and a free forum for swapping items. — CD

Tailored shopping

bop.com

Free People
$168

When I have an idea of what I want, but don't want to go searching for it at the mall, I use my ShopStyle app (iOS, Android). I can filter my search according to keyword description, color, size, price, brand, department store, etc. The "Tailored Shop" updates daily and personalizes a store based on past searches and favorites — perfect for virtual "window shopping." — CD

Lowest Amazon prices

Prices on Amazon oscillate week to week far more than you might think. Paste an Amazon url into Camelcamelcamel.com to see the chart of an item's price history. If you are not in a hurry, you can use the chart to set a plausible low target price and Camel will send you an alert and buy button when (if) it reaches that price. — KK

Amazon $5 credit for late delivery

If you're a member of Amazon Prime, you get guaranteed delivery dates for your Prime purchases. I recently learned you can get a $5 credit if a delivery is late. Just go to Amazon's Live Chat and tell the representative that you have a late delivery and want a credit. It's worked for me all four times I've tried it. — MF

Amazon's Interesting Finds

Amazon's Interesting Finds will give you pages of really cool, surprising stuff. Like the Milk Drop Bowl above (no longer available). I don't know how they are curating it, but I particularly like the Fun option. — KK

Shop Kickstarter projects

Amazon now has a section where they sell originally Kickstarted projects. Bottom-up retailing. — KK

Finding the best products online

Google's algorithm is not working as well as it once did for product recommendations. It could be that spammy websites have gotten better at gaming the algorithm, pushing their search results to the top. My friend Rob Beschizza shared a wonderful tip. He tweeted, "a search for 'best cordless hedge trimmer' gets 400 identical top lists of Amazon referral links with smarmy PR copy. But 'best cordless hedge trimmer reddit' gets the best cordless hedge trimmer." Try it, it works for any product! — MF

Get fast quotes

I take full advantage of the Request a Quote option on Yelp. Once you type out your request, Yelp gives you the option to submit the same message to similar businesses nearby. I click the max amount available (up to 10), and

find that most people start responding right away! I've used this recently to find the cheapest and fastest phone screen repair. — CD

Engineering gift guide

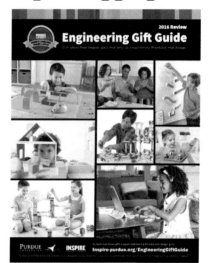

When it comes to giving gifts to the kids in my life, I prefer to not buy toys that are trending now but will become junk in a few months. For the holidays, I'm planning on buying from the Engineering Gift Guide from Purdue, which has a lot of inspiration-inducing gifts for boys and girls ages 3-18. — CD

Best holiday gift guide

For my tastes, the best holiday gift guide is the annual catalog of cool books, games, toys, and DIY tools put together by The Kid Should See This website. Ordinarily the site hosts the best video clips your kids should see, but during the holidays they compile this long and annotated list of cool stuff that is aimed at active kids, but also works for adults with young minds. — KK

Automatic product comparisons

When researching a product online, type in the item in Google and then add "vs". Google will auto-complete with the most popular, and highly rated, alternatives, and the top link will educate you quickly. Then "vs." autocomplete the new item and you'll have a good sense of the field. — KK

Getting good stuff on Craigslist

This brief, succinct blog post has great advice on how to find what you want (at least with used furniture) on Craigslist. For instance, don't forget to search for common misspellings of your target. These tips match my experience in buying used tools on Craigslist. — KK

Shopping research

When I'm in shopping mode I check out BestReviews. Modeled after Wirecutter and Cool Tools, it tests, compares and recommends a huge variety of products, from ATV ramps, to kiddie pools, to pressure washers. It carries no ads, relying on Amazon links for revenue. While its range is vast, the depth of reviews is uneven, but I find their simple summaries of the best stuff worthwhile to check out. — KK

Student Prime membership

College students can get Amazon Prime (free shipping, streaming, cheap music) for free their first 6 months of being a student and 50% off thereafter. Check out Prime Student. — KK

Estate sale marketplace

I have great childhood memories of going to estate sales with my mother in rich neighborhoods. Everything but the House is estate sale hunting without the effort. It's like a more refined eBay. I've already spent way too much time bookmarking things and imagining the history of each item. — CD

Spotting fakes on Amazon

We've previously recommended Fakespot, a website that grades Amazon products for their shill, fake review, or fraud factors. These grades are not foolproof, but are extremely useful. What's new is their Fakespot extension for the Chrome browser, which overlays your Amazon pages with their grades for all the related and recommended products shown on a page. This means you don't have to leave the Amazon page to see the grades, and it also means you will see product grades before you click on them. It's behavior changing. — KK

Shopping must

A great hack to know during shopping days is to always check out RetailMeNot before purchasing anything online, outside of Amazon. There is a high chance I'll find a discount coupon for a retail purchase I am considering. RetailMeNot will give you the coupon code, and the rate of success others have recently had in using it (the codes are crowdsourced). Discounts of 10, 20, or 30% are not uncommon in my experience. I don't shop without it. — KK

Instant discount coupons

Honey is an online coupon service much like the website RetailMeNot. But instead of going to Retailmenot to get a discount code for an online shop (which works very well), Honey lives as an extension in your web browser and automatically pops up on the page when you go to a shopping site. It can also track prices. In my experience about 1 in 10 times Honey has a code I can actually use, but since it costs no money and zero effort to use, it is very much worth it. — KK

Summarize Amazon reviews

TheReviewIndex finds recurring patterns in Amazon Reviews and then makes sense of it for you. It displays positive/ negative ratings for things like "ease of use," "quality," "reliability," and much more depending on the item. You can click through further to see snippets from user reviews pertaining to one particular aspect of the product. Right now the website only supports Electronics, Gadgets and Appliances. Worth bookmarking to make your shopping decisions a little easier. — CD

Nerdy kit gifts

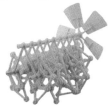

I spent a weekend assembling some cool kits that would make fun gifts for nerdy people like me. Mostly laser-cut parts with lots of gears or moving parts. My recommendations of the best kits are here. But the neatest cool and unusual kit is this small version of the 24-footed Strandbeest, which walks powered by a blast of air. At only $15, it's a bargain. — KK

Download past Amazon purchases

As a freelancer, I need to keep track of office supplies and other items that are tax deductible. I buy almost everything on Amazon, and I recently learned that you can download your past purchases as spreadsheet files. This is going to save me a lot of time because I can filter out things like food, clothing, toys, etc. — MF

List of sustainable companies

Takecare.io is a curated list of sustainable alternatives for consumer goods and other innovative companies. It's a crowdsourced list, so it's growing all the time. Scroll through and check it out. — CD

Shark Tank contestants

This page lists every contestant who's been on *Shark Tank*, along with a link to their website. Useful if you want to find out more about one of the products or services pitched on the show. — MF

KITCHEN

A better multicooker than the Instant Pot

The Instant Pot multicooker has become an internet sensation, with recipe books and  YouTube videos devoted to it. I also was a fan of my Instant Pot until it died last month and I switched to a Zavor Lux 6-Quart Multicooker ($160). It's superior to the Instant Pot on at least three counts. First, the top lid doesn't get so hot that it will burn you if you touch it. Second, it heats much faster, which makes a huge time difference when pressure cooking a meal. Third, the silicone gasket on the lid is braced so it doesn't sag like it does on the Instant Pot, which is a common issue and prevents the Instant Pot from achieving a high enough pressure. The Zavor costs a bit more than the Instant Pot, but it's worth it. – MF

Granite-coated non-stick cookware

For years, my family has been using Le Creuset cast iron pans. The large one is almost too heavy for my wife to deal with. Also, they take a long time to heat up. While we are not ready to get rid of them, I recently discovered Carote non-stick frying pans. They're coated with some kind of natural granite material and they have a bakelite handle that stays cool (unlike the Le Creuset handles that get extremely hot). The aluminum Carote heats up quickly, and it is the best non-stick frying pan I've ever had. Everything just slides right out of it and it's very easy to clean with water and a paper towel. You can try out the 8-inch frying pan, which costs under $15, to see if you like it before buying a larger pan. — MF

Teflon frying pan alternative

A surprisingly workable alternative to a Teflon frying pan is a ceramic coated pan. We use a GreenPan (it's actually white ceramic inside) that unsticks as well as old Teflon. The cheap Teflon pans we use only last about 4 years. Our GreenPan is 5 years old and shows no wear. The 10-inch GreenPan is $25. — KK

My new favorite peeler

I've tried a lot of vegetable peelers, and the OXO Good Grips Pro Y-Peeler is now my favorite. It feels solid in my hand, and it has a long blade to speed up peeling. It's great for peeling sweet potatoes. — MF

Best ice cream scoop

This OXO Ice Cream Scoop ($13) makes serving dessert painless. The pointed scoop makes it easier to break into frozen ice cream and the eject trigger drops it right in your bowl. I like to run it under warm water right before I scoop to soften the ice cream. — CD

Small deep fryer

I don't deep fry food every day, but when I'm in the mood for some sweet potatoes fried in coconut or avocado oil, I am glad I have this $25 Fry Daddy deep fryer. It's small so it doesn't need a lot of oil and it heats up quickly. I keep the oil in the fryer and put the lid on once it has cooled down and use the same oil the next time I use it. — MF

Ground beef chopper

This OXO Good Grips Ground Meat Chopper ($12) quickly breaks up hamburger meat when making tacos or pasta sauce. Just chop away with the three fins until the ground beef is the way you like it. — MF

Perfect pie crusts

This wooden rolling pin ($20) comes with four pairs of discs that attach to either end, ensuring uniformly thick dough. We've used them for pizza, quiches, pies, and cookies and love the results. — MF

Favorite kitchen dishtowels

I love these white, blue-striped kitchen dishtowels. They're $18 for a set of 13. They are 100% cotton, thick and absorbent. I just retired my

former, coffee-stained set to the garage, and bought a new set. — MF

Stiff nonstick pan turner

I got rid of all of our flimsy floppy pan turners. They were useless. Why does anyone even make them? We have two of these $19 nylon turners and use them daily for everything we cook in a pan. The nylon won't scratch the pan, and the stainless steel handle looks nice. — MF

OXO Good Grips silicone pot holder

This pot holder ($10) is a padded fabric envelope with a knobby silicone sheet on one side, Nothing can slip from its grip. I even use it to open stubborn jar lids. – MF

Keep produce fresh longer

Buying in bulk does save, but when we buy the large plastic container of mixed greens from Costco, it usually gets slimy after 4-5 days. I tried the paper towel hack and placed one sheet in the middle and one on top and it extended its shelf-life by one week! — CD

Extend the life of your produce

My husband bought these Rubbermaid FreshWorks Containers ($27, set of 3), which prevent produce from spoiling by keeping excess moisture away. For the first time ever, I was able to finish a bag of spinach without it going bad. Usually I have to throw out my spinach after a week or less, but this container kept it fresh for more than two weeks. It's amazing! — CD

Ultimate refrigerator containers

My second favorite activity in the kitchen (after eating good food) is to stow leftovers in our trove of Snapware Glasslock containers with

snap-on lids. Glass makes the leftovers clearly visible and re-heatable in their container, and the snap lids with gaskets create a nearly vacuum seal, and their sturdy flat tops can be securely stacked in the refrigerator. They will never spill, and are superior to all the other systems we've tried in the past. Snapping them shut on all four sides makes me really happy. By now there are 10 different brands of glass with snap lids (including Amazon Basics), all with the same design, though they are not interchangeable. I have not tried other brands; we are still using the original Snapware/Glasslock ones from a decade ago and they seem to last forever. — KK

Soft butter anytime

Hands-down my favorite purchase this year was this $19 butter crock. It feels like a luxury

to always have soft butter available. It works better in cooler climates. I keep mine on the kitchen island away from the stove area and add an ice cube to the water every few days. — CD

Space-saving microwave covers

I prefer these flat microwave covers ($7) to the larger lid-type ones. They block splatters just as effectively, but take up less space and are easier to wash. — CD

Clean sink pipes

We bought an OXO Good Grips Silicone Sink Strainer ($8) last year and it does a good job of keeping the kitchen plumbing clog free. It's easy to clean too. Just hold it over the trash can and pop the rubber filter inside out. — MF

BARISTA ACCESSORIES

My favorite coffee maker

I drink coffee every day, and I use the Bialetti 6-Cup Espresso Coffee Maker ($40) more often than any of my other coffee-making machines (I have a few). I fill the lower chamber with water, add ground coffee in the funnel, screw on the top, and put it on the stovetop. In about three minutes I pour a cup of strong, delicious coffee. — MF

Fantastic frother

Lately, I've been drinking a lot of cold matcha lattes, and I'm using a terrific milk frother to make them: the Nespresso Aeroccino ($71). I pour in about 4 ounces of cold unsweetened almond milk and add a teaspoon of matcha powder, then press the button for 2 seconds (a quick press will automatically heat the milk, which my wife does for cappuccinos). In about 20 seconds, I have a delicious frothy latte. The frother is nearly silent and very easy to clean, because the stirrer is magnetic and pops right off the stem. — MF

Easiest way to make coffee

I've tried a great many different coffee makers, from a stovetop espresso machine to the Aeropress. But when I visited my parents last weekend and used their 12 oz Bodum Brazil French Press Coffee and Tea Maker ($15), I decided it was my favorite because it was so easy to use and clean, and it makes delicious coffee. I bought one for myself, and now everyone else in the family is using it to make coffee (and tea). — MF

Small reusable coffee cup

I wanted to be able to take my cappuccino to go on mornings I drive to work, but my travel mug is too big and mixes my drink when I pour it in. This 8oz reusable coffee cup by KeepCup ($15) fits under the portafilter spouts and fits in my car cup holder. It serves only one purpose, but it does it perfectly. — CD

Fast water kettle

To heat the water, I'm using a Cosori Electric Kettle ($30). It's made from borosilicate glass and has a stainless steel bottom. No plastic touches the water. A half liter of room-temperature water starts to simmer in a minute, and comes to a full boil in under two minutes. It shuts off automatically. — MF

Amazon grocery delivery

Amazon Fresh is Amazon's grocery shopping and delivery service. They sell everything a large supermarket sells, often at better prices. You can sometimes get same day delivery, but it usually takes 24 hours. This is a huge time saver for our family. You must be an Amazon Prime member. — MF

Meal kit delivery

I heard Kevin mention a meal delivery service called Sun Basket, so I checked it out and signed up. Once a week our family gets a box filled with fresh, organic, fruits, vegetables, and meats that have been washed and portioned (the ingredients are kept cool with recyclable ice packs). The box also includes a very nice, full-color recipe booklet for the ingredients. (We are on the Paleo plan — there are multiple styles to choose from). Next week we'll make Thai turkey salad with cabbage, basil, and mint; Italian sausage with spring vegetables; and Burmese salmon salad with lemongrass

CUTTING TOOLS

Kitchen knife gift

Everyone can use a perfectly balanced, lifelong kitchen knife. It's an ideal gift. One I like to gift is the Kuma Chef Knife which gets rave reviews from kitchen knife aficionados who normally review two-hundred dollar knives, yet the Kuma only costs $25. It's ergonomically optimized for your hand, easy to keep razor sharp, and will last generations. When I lift mine, I smile. — KK

Cheap but good kitchen knife

This $18 8-inch Winco knife is the first knife I reach for when preparing food. It sharpens well, holds an edge, and is heavy. Read the Amazon reviews to learn how many people swear by this workhorse kitchen tool. — MF

Large non-skid cutting mats

This four-pack of colorful, Bellemain 15" x 11" cutting mats is only $11. The bottom is textured so the mat doesn't slip when you use it. I've run them through the bottom rack of the dishwasher several times with no noticeable effect. — MF

and bell pepper. Our at-home meals are now exciting and fun to make. We get three meals a week for our family of four for about $150. Use this link and we will both get $40 off of our order. — MF

Good grilling

During the summer, we barbecue a couple of times a week. I have the classic Weber charcoal grill. I grill beef and chicken directly over the coals, but I've been using these grill mats to cook vegetables and fish. They are so thin that they look like they would incinerate in a second, but they are impervious to high heat. They are easy to clean, too. Nothing sticks to them. — MF

Strawberry huller

Gimmicky kitchen tools are usually worse than the knives, graters, and other kitchen tools you already own. This little strawberry huller is an exception. The spring-loaded jaws make it a breeze to remove stems, making short work of baskets of berries. I've used this $7 tool dozens of times since I bought it in 2015. — MF

Seed starting kit

This set of three plastic trays comes with 30 soil pods for foolproof

germinating of vegetable seeds. I used it to start bean, basil, tomato, and catnip plants in my kitchen windowsill. Transplanting is easy — just place the pod with the sprout into your garden soil or planting container. — MF

Peanut butter mixer

I recently opened a jar of natural peanut butter in which the oil and solids had separated so much that I couldn't mix it with a spoon. I had to use a drill and a stirrer I made from a bent metal barbecue skewer to mix the peanut butter. It was messy and the skewer bent, so I went to Amazon to look for a better solution. I found it: the EZPB Natural Nut Butter Stirrer. It's a zig-zag metal rod that fits most jars and requires patience, but will get the job done far better than a spoon

and without splashing peanut oil. Watch the video on the Amazon product page to see how well it works. — MF

The best can opener

I bought the Kuhn Rikon can opener ($20) in 2011 and I still get excited every time I use it. It opens cans without leaving sharp edges. After opening hundreds of cans with it, it still never ceases to amaze me. — MF

Two-sided magnetic measuring spoons

These magnetic measuring spoons are handy because they have two sides for each measurement. The oval side fits into smaller jars, and I can alternate between wet and dry ingredients without having to wash a spoon. Also, the magnets keep them together so I never have to search for the one I need. — CD

13

Silicone basting brush

Sometimes a recipe will call for me to "drizzle" olive oil on chicken or a vegetable before putting it in the oven or on the grill. I've been drizzling for years, and got resigned to the fact that most of the olive oil would end up on the bottom of the pan and not on the food. Recently I found a silicone basting brush in a kitchen drawer, which my wife bought a couple of years ago when she made a pastry, and it has turned out to be a game-changer. Now I just pour a little olive oil, or other sauce, into a small bowl and use the brush to paint it on the meat or vegetable before cooking. This brush gives me much more control, and there's less waste. My drizzling days are over. — MF

Cheapest soda hack

My beverage of choice is sparkling water. To eliminate single-use bottles in our household, we have a Sodastream machine to make our own fizzy water. But Sodastream has stopped

making the large 32 ounce CO_2 canister and has upped the refill price on the smaller ones, making it expensive. The solution is a hack: We now refill our own large 24 ounce canister for $5 at a sporting goods store using a paintball canister. (The squeamish can use a SodaMod food-grade canister.) All you need is a $19 brass adapter (mine is Protek) to fit the canister into the proprietary threads a Sodastream needs. — KK

How to load a dishwasher properly

Finally, a definitive "How-to" on how to load the dishwasher. Consumer Reports shared an interactive graphic and a video on the best method for most machines. I was surprised to find that dishes and pots with baked-on food CAN be placed faced down toward the spray arm. I was always told to not block it. — CD

Drying rack replacement

We replaced our old, space-consuming dish rack for this $7 Norpro Microfiber Drying

Mat. It's extremely absorbent and dries super fast. When I'm done with it, I just fold it up and put it in a drawer. It's also machine washable. I love it. — CD

Visual guide to portion sizes

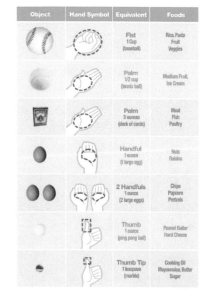

Object	Hand Symbol	Equivalent	Foods
		Fist 1 Cup (baseball)	Rice, Pasta Fruit Veggies
		Palm 1/2 cup (tennis ball)	Medium Fruit, Ice Cream
		Palm 3 ounces (deck of cards)	Meat Fish Poultry
		Handful 1 ounce (1 large egg)	Nuts Raisins
		2 Handfuls 1 ounce (2 large eggs)	Chips Popcorn Pretzels
		Thumb 1 ounce (ping pong ball)	Peanut Butter Hard Cheese
		Thumb Tip 1 teaspoon (marble)	Cooking Oil Mayonnaise, Butter Sugar

In all the time spent in the kitchen with my mother or grandmother I never once saw them measuring anything, and maybe it's a Hispanic culture thing, but I learned even less about appropriate food portions. So now I'm working on getting better at eyeballing portion sizes so that I don't overserve myself. This chart helps. — CD

HOME BAR

Keep track of whose glass is whose

My mother-in-law had these metallic markers ($10) on hand during the holidays to keep track of whose glass is whose. We had a full house of more than 10 people staying overnight, so this was perfect for keeping track of our wine and water glasses, and coffee mugs. — CD

Keep champagne fresh longer

I love drinking sparkling wine, but unless I have guests over it takes me 4-5 days to get through a bottle. I've tried a few different champagne stoppers, and this Fantes Champagne Stopper is the best designed. Others have broken or don't seal as tight. Even on the fifth day, my champagne will still be bubbly. — CD

Chill champagne faster

One of my favorite hacks helps to quickly chill a bottle of bubbly — very useful when you are a dinner guest. Fully wet a paper towel, wrap it around the bottle, then place it in the freezer. In about 10-15 minutes, the paper towel should be hardened and the wine will be chilled. — CD

Precision shots

This little stainless steel jigger from OXO ($7) is angled and has markings that make it easy to pour a precise amount of liquor or other liquid. The markings go from a quarter ounce up to two ounces. — MF

Best wine opener

I've had the same lever-style bottle opener — like this one — for years now, and compared to the classic corkscrew or electric openers it's definitely the easiest to use. I'm always surprised when I find that my friends and family don't own one yet, so I've decided it's what I'm gifting from now on. — CD

Whimsical wine pourers

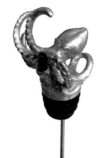

I came across Menagerie wine pourers/aerators at a winery and wish I would have bought more. They're made from stainless steel and they definitely feel heavy and high-quality, but mostly they're just really cute. They have almost 100 different creatures to choose from — animals and make-believe — I chose an octopus. – CD

EDIBLE

Longer-lasting herbs

If you are lucky enough to stumble across these lightly dried herbs by Gourmet Garden in your grocery store, give them your money. I always buy up basil, cilantro and parsley. They last more than a month longer than fresh herbs and taste just as good. — CD

My favorite mayonnaise

I've been spoiled by Kewpie mayonnaise, made in Japan. No other mayo comes close. The secret is extra egg yolk and MSG. My kids and I squeeze it on everything (especially sweet potato chunks roasted in coconut oil). Kewpie also has a U.S.-made version, but Amazon

sells the real Japanese version. — MF

Better butter

One of the disadvantages of never having TV is that I miss ads for things everyone else may already know about. For instance I recently discovered spreadable butter.

This is real butter that has been blended with a small amount of oil (olive or canola, your choice) to keep it super easy to spread straight out of the fridge. It comes in many styles at any supermarket; Land O'Lakes Spreadable Butter is a national brand. It's the best thing since sliced bread. — KK

Edible sweet flowers

These Wild Hibiscus Flowers in Syrup have become essential in my life. They can make any cheap champagne taste like liquid gold. The flowers themselves taste like a sweet fruit and they look so pretty sitting at the bottom of a flute. — CD

TEAS

Big bag of nettles

When I ordered this $18 bag of dried nettles leaves from Amazon, I didn't expect to get such a giant-sized bag. Even at the rapid rate my family drinks nettles tea, this bag will last at least a year. We've used nettles for years as a very effective treatment for seasonal pollen allergies. Even if it's just a placebo effect, the herbal tea is delicious. (I haven't experienced side effects, but WebMD lists them here.) — MF

Cool drink for a hot summer

It's been hot for the last couple of months here in Los Angeles and my family is guzzling the iced hibiscus flower tea I've been making. We go through a half gallon

a day, and each glass costs about a penny. I make it with this one-pound bag of Feel Good organic dried hibiscus flowers I bought for $15. I make it by putting two tablespoons of flowers into a half-gallon mason jar and fill it with boiling water. When it is cool enough I put the jar in the refrigerator. The ruby red liquid is pleasingly tart and satisfying. — MF

Golden monkey tea for less

Ever since I tried Teavana's Golden Monkey Tea a few years ago, no other tea can compare to its bold flavor. The problem is that 2 ounces cost $22. I've tried other, less expensive brands of golden monkey

tea to no avail, but finally found one that is as good as Teavana. It's called Yunnan Golden Special by Tealyra and 4 ounces cost $15. — MF

Flavorful dark tea

I'm on my second one-pound bag of this flavorful Assam black tea. It's dark and malty and my wife and I drink at least two cups each per day. At $24, it's a great deal. — MF

Darjeeling tea

I like my black tea to have a robust flavor, so I use a lot of it in each cup I make. This organic Darjeeling tea from Vahdam fits the bill. It smells wonderful and is very tasty. A 9-ounce bag costs $18. They say one bag makes 150+ cups, but I probably only get 100 cups out of it. Still a good deal! — MF

Favorite plane snack

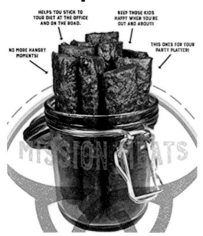

When it comes to airplane food, I agree with Anthony Bourdain: it's better to go hungry. But I don't like going hungry so I pack snacks with me. One of my favorites is the Graze Bar. It's a tasty, chewy stick of grass-fed beef containing no sugar, gluten, or MSG. — MF

Inexpensive bulk granola

We eat enough granola that we can't keep up making our own. But most store-bought granola is way too sweet with sugar. And it's expensive. For the past many years I've been gobbling up Bob's Red Mill Honey Granola. It is only mildly sweetened using honey, and not expensive. Amazon sells it in 18-ounce packages. We add our own nuts, raisins, etc. — KK

Big bag of cashews

I snack on nuts all day long. A couple of months ago I discovered Happy Belly nuts on Amazon. The price is good (a 44-ounce bag of cashews costs $23) and the nuts are fresh and tasty. — MF

Low-sugar gluten-free snack

Before I take a flight, I toss a few Dark Chocolate Nuts & Sea Salt Kind bars into my travel bag. The crunchy bars are

gluten free and have just 5g of sugar. The perfect snack for a plane or hotel room. — MF

Travel size coconut oil pouches

When I travel I take snacks with me: macadamia nuts, Starbucks Via instant coffee pouches, and Graze Bars. I recently added a new item: 0.5 ounce coconut oil pouches. They go great with my low-carb diet. I can spread it on chicken and vegetables to increase the calories without adding carbs. I love the taste of coconut oil on almost anything. — MF

Genetically modified dried apple

I welcome genetically modified foods (GMOs). A GMO that I currently enjoy is Arctic ApBitz dried apple crisps. Regular dried apples are soft and pliable. Arctic crisps have been bred to dry naturally without browning and to retain their crispness and crunchiness. They are french-fry shaped and textured. The dry snack is extremely lightweight (great for hiking), satisfyingly crunchy and flavor intense, and comes in 3 apple varieties: Delicious, Granny Smith, and Golden (the variety in the link). I really enjoy them, and I am told that kids prefer these crunchy apple sticks over traditional apple leathers. — KK

Dark chocolate bars with cashew butter and vanilla bean

I bought these dark chocolate bars for my wife as a

Christmas present, and now we're hopelessly hooked. They're a bit like peanut butter cups, but in bar form, and less sweet. A 4-pack runs $25, but if you order them via Amazon Subscribe & Save, it'll cost you $21.25. — MF

Awesome unsweetened chocolate bar

I've long been a fan of Montezuma's Absolute Black chocolate bars, which are made from 100% chocolate and cocoa nibs and no sweeteners of any kind. (The best way to

enjoy unsweetened chocolate is not by chewing them, but by letting a square melt in your mouth.) Recently, Montezuma's introduced a version with sea salt and almonds and it is even better. I buy mine at Trader Joe's for $3 a bar. — MF

Digest lactose

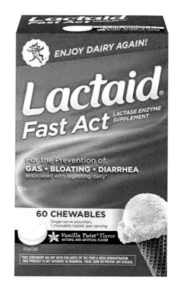

My wife is lactose intolerant and gets a stomach ache when she eats dairy, unless she chews a Lactaid tablet beforehand. It contains lactase enzyme, which breaks down lactose. It really works. She keeps them in her purse. — MF

Electrolyte tabs

I drop one Nuun tablet into my glass of water in the morning and another before I go to bed. Nuun tablets contain sodium, potassium, magnesium, and calcium. It's

very likely a placebo effect, but I feel better and more replenished from drinking water with a Nuun tablet in it. In any case, it's a fizzy, citrusy treat that I look forward to. — MF

Bargain Beans

My family is drinking a lot more coffee than we used to. We go through about a pound of whole espresso beans per week. On a whim, I bought Amazon's brand, Go for the Bold, which comes in 2 lb bags. It's better tasting than Starbucks, about the same as Pete's, and costs quite a bit less. — MF

Best box wine

Box wine is under-appreciated. I can get decent red wine in a collapsible bag/box so that I can drink just one glass daily (for medicinal purposes!) and have the full 3 liters never expire. Trader Joe's has a good Cabernet Sauvignon in a box. — KK

Half-size spaghetti

Why don't they just make spaghetti noodles half as long so you don't have to messily break them to fit into the pot? Well, they do! Half-sized, or what they call "pot size" noodles, are available from brands such as Mueller's and Barilla, and from big box stores and on Instacart. As far as I am concerned, this size should be the standard. — KK

How to roast any vegetable

Almost any vegetable you can think of tastes better roasted, and this article by Emma Christensen, shows you how to do it. The key is cutting the vegetable into bite-size pieces to increase the surface-area-to-volume ratio, using enough oil, and spacing out the pieces in the roasting pan. — MF

Plant-based burgers

I don't eat beef, pork or lamb, but I still miss a good burger. I'm a big fan of veggie Impossible Burgers, but I like Beyond Meat's burgers,

RECIPES

Savory meat marinade

My favorite marinade for meat is easy to make and savory. The original recipe is from America's Test Kitchen and exists behind a paywall so I can't share it, but the Southwestern Marinade ingredient list here is the exact same. I keep a printed copy in my kitchen. — CD

Juicy chicken recipe

This simple French Chicken in a Pot recipe made the juiciest, most

flavorful chicken I've ever cooked. It took me less than 2 hours to prep and make. I also had most of the ingredients on hand so all I had to buy was the chicken and some of the veggies which totaled around $10. As someone in the comments said, "It's idiot-proof." — CD

Chicken kebab recipe

My wife is Armenian, and we have eaten a lot of Middle Eastern food over the years.

We also like to cook Middle Eastern food. Here's my go-to chicken kebab recipe. My mouth is watering as I type, remembering how great this is. I cook it over a charcoal grill. — MF

Faster way to make yogurt

If you don't boil milk before using it to make yogurt, it will end up runny. But it takes time to boil the milk, then let it cool down before adding the starter. I recently learned that when using ultrapasteurized (or ultra high temperature) milk instead of pasteurized milk, you don't need to boil the milk first. I've been using my Instant Pot lately to make yogurt. I just pour in a half-gallon of ultrapasteurized milk, stir in a tablespoon of starter, secure the lid, and press the "yogurt" button. Eight hours later, it's ready! — MF

cooked at home, even more. They are really delicious in flavor and texture. You can get patties of Beyond Burgers at Target, Walmart, and Costco, among other retailers. The rest of my family, who do eat beef, love these plant-based burgers too. — KK

Good veggie burger

The plant-based vegetarian Impossible Whopper at Burger King is pretty good for fast-food. It tastes comparable to a beef Whopper, according to my memory. (I last ate mammals 15 years ago.) Now available in most BK outlets in the US, Impossible burgers can also

be found at other burger joints like White Castle. — KK

BACKYARD EGGS

Backyard eggs really do taste better than farm-raised ones. At least ours do. It may be because they get a more varied diet: we include our kitchen scraps, which they devour. Chickens will eat anything. I had always resisted raising chickens because of what I imagined would be a daily chore. But they are really very low maintenance. We've had half a dozen chickens for 6 years now. Their feed trough can hold a week's worth of feed, and an automatic water feeder keeps them watered indefinitely, so we can leave them alone for days at a time if we need to. We can always find someone willing to pick up some free, yummy backyard eggs. You can buy chicks from a mail order like McMurray Hatchery, but most feed stores, even urban ones, will sell chicks one by one. The best intro book is Raising Chickens for Dummies. — KK

Learn how to reduce food waste

There's really no excuse for food waste. On Save the Food you can find recipes to cook with your leftover scraps and food that's "past its prime." You can build a meal prep plan and create a shopping list based on the people in your household and how many days you are cooking for. They even have a storage guide with all the tips and tricks you need to keep your food fresh. — CD

Find your taste charts

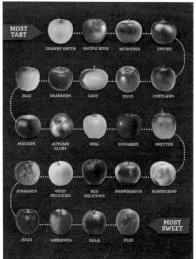

Two images I find myself pulling up from time to time are 1) this chart of apple varieties lined up from most tart to most sweet, and 2) a visual guide to major types of wine grouped by flavor characteristics. I may never be able to articulate tasting aromas or textures, but at least I'll be able to pick a delicious wine I'll enjoy. — CD

HOUSEHOLD

Home safety

I just purchased our fourth Nest smoke and carbon monoxide alarm for our home. As our old Home Depot smoke alarms go kaput one by one, I have replaced them with the more expensive, but superior, Nest. They seem to last longer, are smarter, less annoying, and are networked via wifi. In theory (no actual disasters yet), each Nest will broadcast a concern it detects to all the others, so a fire in my downstairs home office would be announced in a message by the Nest in our living room. It also sends alerts to my phone if I am away. — KK

Mesh Wifi to the rescue

We live in a house with walls that have chicken wire behind the plaster. They do a great job of blocking Wifi. To get around it, I installed a Frankensteinian hodgepodge of cables, powerline adapters, and wireless access points all around the house. They all had different SSIDs and the coverage was still spotty. It was frustrating. A decade later, I broke down and bought a Google Nest router and four wireless hubs. It set me back $500 but now we have great coverage throughout the house with no need to change SSIDs on our devices as we move from one room to the next. I expected my family to be grateful and instead they are mad at me, "Why didn't you get this sooner!?" — MF

Talk to your appliances

I bought this 2-pack of GoldenDot WiFi smart plugs for $17 on Amazon. I used one on our bedroom's air filter and the other on our garage door (to turn off the power so no one can open it with a remote). It was easy to link the plugs to Alexa and Google Assistant. I now control these appliances with my voice. I also put the air filter on a schedule, so it turns on at night and off in the morning. — MF

LIGHTS

Motion sensing light bulbs

Motion sensing lights are a rapidly evolving product. Nowadays the motion sensors are built right into the LED light bulb itself; no clunky hardware or switches. The same sensors in the bulb detect night, so the bulbs only turn on in the dark with motion from a body. They can be used in any socket, and can be placed outside with a little protection. I've been trying out the various Chinese-made versions. This one by Luxon costs about $9 and works well enough in our garage, hallway and porch. — KK

Battery powered security light

The Lumenology Portable LED Motion Sensor Light

($30) is powered by three AA batteries. It has a light detector and motion detector, so it shines only when it detects motion at night (saving the battery charge). It comes with two different mounts: one is magnetic and the other is a flexible tripod that can work as a regular tripod or be wrapped around a pole or a branch. I used the magnetic mount on my front gate and it shines a bright, wide spot of light for 30 seconds when anyone comes to the gate. — MF

Cozy outdoor lights

We tried out several outdoor string lights for our patio area. Most were too bright, but these LED, white globe myCozyLites ($23) were our favorite. They are so warm and inviting, we've set them on a timer so they are on every night. — CD

Safe alternative to candles

These Luminara battery-operated taper candles really do look real. I love having them on every night on the dining room table and watching the flame flicker. It makes the room look so elegant. There's even a timer setting to turn off automatically after 5 hours. — CD

Drawing lamp

My daughter needed a lamp to light up her drawing board, so I bought this $15

CeSunlight LED clip-on lamp with a flexible neck. She can adjust the brightness and color temperature to provide the ideal illumination for her work. — MF

Sunrise/sunset smart switch

I App Remote Control

Control your light from anywhere anytime

My outdoor lights were controlled by an indoor switch with a programmable timer. The tiny buttons made it very difficult to program and the tiny LCD display was nearly illegible. I gave up and bought this Meross Smart WiFi Switch. Installation was easy (make sure you have a neutral wire, not just a ground wire, or it won't work). My phone's GPS told the switch where it is and it now turns the lights on at sunset and off at sunrise, adjusting automatically throughout the year. Brilliant. And I enjoyed forcefully throwing the old switch into the trash can. — MF

VACUUMS

This vacuum cleaner really sucks

The Bissell Zing Canister (model 2156A) was only $50 and it exceeded my expectations. It is bagless, quieter than any other vacuum cleaner I've owned, and has powerful suction. It's great for hardwood floors (I don't know how well it works on carpeting since we don't have any). — MF

Hand Vacuum with batteries that hold a charge

I've owned ten or more portable hand vacs in my life. The batteries in all of them did

not stand the test of time. After six months or so, they couldn't hold a charge. But I bought the Black and Decker Cordless Lithium Hand Vacuum in 2015 and the battery seems to be as powerful now as the day I bought it. It's also the priciest, at $55. In the long run, it's also the cheapest, since I have not had to replace it. — MF

Easily remove hair out of vacuum brush

This LPT was a housekeeping game changer: Use a seam ripper to easily clean out hair tangled in a vacuum brush. My hair is long and everywhere and before I used to struggle with scissors to cut it out of the vacuum, but it turns out a seam ripper is the perfect tool for the job. — CD

Absorbent stone coasters

My wife bought this set of 6 cool-looking large white stone coasters with cork backings ($19). They have attractive black patterns that appear to be hand-painted. The stone is absorbent, so they soak up condensation. — MF

Smudge-free surfaces

I bought a bunch of these extra large microfiber cloths ($10) and now I keep them everywhere — home drawers, office, car, purse. I spend at least 10 hours a day staring at a screen and/or wearing glasses. I never knew I needed something so much in my life. — CD

Stiff-bristled scrubbing brush

The Bürstenhaus Redecker ($6) is made from beechwood and has incredibly stiff palm leaf fiber bristles. It removes things like burnt eggs from cast-iron pans with ease. I was a die-hard fan of the OXO scrubbing brush, but this is better. — MF

Heavy duty paper towels

These Scott Shop blue towels may look like ordinary paper towels but are much thicker, absorbent, and durable.

When one of our cats decides to barf on the floor (which is often) I reach for these towels, knowing my hand will stay dry when I clean up the mess. — MF

Fingerprint-free appliances

After our recent kitchen remodel, every appliance in our kitchen is now stainless steel and of course, easily smudged. My husband then added the Weiman Stainless Steel Cleaner to our cleaning supplies and honestly, I was surprised at how flawless it left every surface. Every home should have this. — CD

Sticky remover

I reuse jars from the kitchen for storage and for display items. Getting the jar labels off was a chore until I started using Goo Gone (which we've mentioned before but never explicitly recommended). It's an odorless penetrating oil

that unsticks adhesives from anywhere people stick stuff. Spray on, let soak and peel off. Leaves a temporary oil film that evaporates. — KK

DIY cleaner spray

We've been making our own cleaner spray for years. It's mainly water with rubbing alcohol, vinegar, and corn starch. It cuts right through grease, smells much better than commercial cleaners, and costs less than 50 cents a gallon. The recipe is called the "Alvin Corn Homemade Glass Cleaner" and is posted here. — MF

Best stain remover

Tipped off by the comprehensive research at America's Test Kitchen, I've found that the best — really the only — stain remover for laundry that really works is sodium percarbonate, which is a powder you need to mix in water before each use. (No liquid spray works nearly as

well.) You then soak garments for 6 hours and wash. It completely removes just about any food stain, even stale ones. There are generic versions available but a proven brand of percarbonate is OxiClean Versatile Stain Remover. — KK

Unclog sewer drains

We live in an old house and the sewer pipes get clogged a lot. I got tired of paying a plumber $150 to clear the pipe every time it clogged, so I bought this $22 hose attachment, called a Drain King. It's a rubber bladder that you insert into the sewer line opening. When you turn the hose on, the bladder expands, forcing the water to push the clog out. It has never failed me. Read the glowing testimonials on Amazon for this thing. — MF

Better toilet plunger

Plunging a clogged toilet is hard work, but it's a lot easier when you have a horizontal

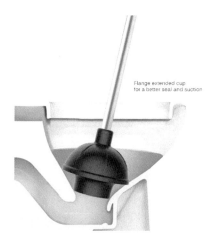

Flange extended cup for a better seal and suction

grip. The Mr. Siga plunger ($15) has a grip that allows me to push down with a lot more force than a simple pole handle. — MF

Bathroom phone shelf

You are sitting on the toilet but there is no place to park your phone safely. This is an everywhere-in-the-world problem, with a first-world solution: this hefty, heavy solid metal, toilet roll shelf. The shelf is flat, dry, and stable. The roll holder underneath is easy to use. It can also store books, wet wipes, etc. As a courtesy I replaced our guest bathroom roll holder with this, and I like it so much I may do the rest of the bathrooms. — KK

GARAGE

Pro-quality tire plug kit

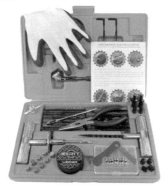

My car tire had a dry-wall screw in it. I bought a cheap tire plug repair kit at the local Pep Boys for about $12. It was hard to use because I had to apply a lot of force to the plastic handle and it hurt my hand. A month later I found another screw in my tire. I left the screw in until I ordered this heavy duty $27 tire plug repair kit. The all metal handles were a pleasure to use. The kit comes with a lot of useful extra tools and parts. Buy one today and you'll be happy you did when you need it. — MF

Fabulous electric car

I really love my all-electric Chevy Bolt which gets 240 miles from an overnight charge in our garage. Its immense power and acceleration is intoxicating. Unexpected bonus: silence inside. Also the car is basically an iPhone accessory. There are a few downsides: it has a boring generic style and the 4-door, 5-passenger hatchback has only a tiny trunk. Otherwise, functionally I get 95% of a Tesla at about half the price. — KK

Cheaper car charging

Setting up a charger in your garage to charge an electric car is currently more complicated than it should be. This primer in Forbes by Brad Templeton is a good rundown on what to expect and how to do it the cheapest. — KK

Waterless car wash

One of our Cool Tools readers, Jon Bonesteel, recommended Rain-X Waterless car wash. He wrote, "This stuff is magic! It saves a LOT of water and washes a car better than soap and water. The resulting finish beads water like wax and it's so easy. I was skeptical, but I will never wash a car with water again." I decided to try it myself and I agree with him. It's easy to use and my car is shinier than it's ever been. — MF

Concentrated windshield washer solvent

Instead of buying windshield washer solvent in gallon plastic jugs (and paying about $5) I bought this box of 24 6-ounce bottles of concentrated solvent ($34). One bottle makes 1.5 gallons of solvent. Easier to store, too. — MF

Garage parking aid

There's probably a simple DIY substitute for the AccuPark Vehicle Parking Aid, but I was happy to pay $11 for it. I adhered this yellow plastic mini speed bump to the garage floor using the attached double-side tape. We can now drive our electric car right up to the optimum spot to plug in to the charger port. — MF

Smart Wi-Fi Garage Door Opener

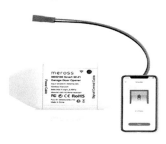

I wanted a way to open my garage door remotely, so I bought the Meross Smart Wi-Fi Garage Door Opener Remote ($30). It took just a few minutes to install and configure. Now I can open and close the door with my phone, and get an alert when someone else opens it. It also works with voice assistants. — MF

Best Christmas trees

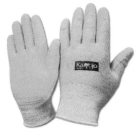

For the past decade I've found the place to get least expensive decent-sized real Christmas trees is at the local Home Depot. The trees are wrapped up commodities. I don't even bother unwrapping them to inspect them before I toss one into the car; they are all extremely uniform. I haven't been disappointed. — KK

Bamboo gardening gloves

I bought these $8 gardening gloves for pulling up roots in my yard. They have a textured, latex grip that kept the roots from sliding out of my hand. They've held up well after many hours of hard work. — MF

Ultralight kneeling cushion

This cushion ($8) protects my knees anytime I have to work

on anything close to the floor or the ground. I've had it since 2011 and am grateful to have it every time I use it. — MF

Push reel lawnmower

I have always used gasoline lawn mowers. I recently got a 5-blade push mower and am amazed at how smoothly it operates. It's very easy to push, and the blades whir like a fan, neatly cutting the grass. It's a pleasure to use. — MF

Outdoor furniture protection

These Adirondack chair covers ($22) by Classic Accessories look really good and are made of heavyweight water-repellant material. The fabric has handles sewn on so they're really easy to pull off and put on furniture, which otherwise would be a big deterrent for me. They have a variety of covers to fit all kinds of outdoor furniture. — CD

HOME OFFICE

Under desk foot rest

I have a height-adjustable chair and a sit/stand desk, but my work area was not complete until I bought this AmazonBasics Under Desk Foot Rest ($17). It helps me be mindful of my sitting posture, and I like that it swivels back and forth because I can stretch out my legs and calves. — CD

Best lap desk

One thing that has been making my workday easy and versatile is this very comfortable, useful lap desk by LapGear ($35). On it, I can fit my 15" Macbook, my mouse, and my phone. Which means I can easily switch up my workspace by moving it to my comfy chair or couch and still be productive. I am loving it and should have bought one sooner. — CD

Really big mouse pad

On a recent episode of the Cool Tools podcast, our guest Jane Metcalfe recommended the BUBM Office Desk Pad, a 31-inch x 17-inch mouse mat ($12). I have a desk with a glass top and didn't like how the cool glass sucked heat from my arms and wrists, so I bought the mat and it turned out to be a great purchase. It feels like textured leather and looks nice. Best of all, it provides excellent insulation between my wrists and the glass. — MF

Personal mini-heater

I work best if my office room temperature is at least 74 degrees Fahrenheit or more. The days of arguing with my husband over the thermostat are over, because I bought myself this AmazonBasics mini heater ($20), and now this

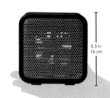

perfect-sized, 500-watt heater sits on top of my desk and keeps me warm while I work, and this is my favorite thing right now. — CD

Good postal scale

My daughter is funding her next trip to Japan by selling a wide variety of stuff on eBay. She's been doing well and is committed to the project, so I did my part by getting her this $20 digital postal scale. It weighs packages up to 11lbs. — MF

3M Scotch Tear By Hand Packaging Tape

3M Scotch Tear By Hand Packaging Tape looks like ordinary packaging tape. The difference is that you can tear off pieces by hand, instead of having to use scissors or the serrated edge on a dispenser. I started using it years ago and it's worth the extra price for the safety (no more ripped finger skin) and convenience I gain. — MF

Wrist relief

I've been using the 18" version of this gel-filled wrist pad for five years (I'm on my second one — they last a few years). It goes behind my keyboard, giving me a soft-but-firm place to rest my wrists. This is essential equipment for me. — MF

Favorite stapler

After watching 1999's Office Space (directed by *Silicon Valley* creator Mike Judge), I wanted the red stapler belonging to the hapless cubicle worker. Soon after, Swingline started making a red model. I've had mine since 2008, use it daily, and it still looks new. Amazon sells them for $11 . — MF

Low maintenance label maker

I bought this DYMO Portable Label Maker ($23) because it was an Amazon best seller and I didn't want to put that much research into it, but now it's been almost a year that I've owned it and it's still incredibly useful and has not let me down. It's so intuitive that months have gone by between use and I don't have to remind myself how to work it. I love that it's so light. I can walk around with it, type on it, print and cut my label and put it back in one fell swoop. — CD

Virtual background for Zoom meetings

I recently conducted a Zoom interview with over 200 people in the audience, and a colleague who watched later told me I should not be Zooming to a large audience with my bedroom in the background. But instead of moving my computer set up, I bought this Webaround Portable Greenscreen. It's a 56-inch circular chair-mounted background and it

works perfectly with Zoom's Virtual Background setting. You can use any photo as your background. — MF

Cable management

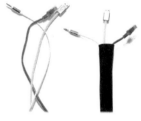

Before...   *After...*

It didn't take long for my new kitten to discover all the fun cables dangling behind my desk, so I bought these black sleeves to keep them tied together and concealed. Now it looks neat and sleek. I also bought this 50-piece set of velcro cable ties to tidy up all the other cords around our house. It's practically a lifetime supply for only $7. — CD

Laser printer toner

I gave up on color inkjet printers because they are slow and finicky. Years ago I bought a cheap Brother laser printer and am very happy with it. I get third-party toner cartridges in bulk, which are about $8 each when purchased as a 4-pack. — MF

Best seat

I was having some back pain and pinched nerves, so I got this Steelcase Gesture Chair for my work desk. Those issues are non-existent now. So many different ways to position and sit in it. It's so comfortable I have to set reminders throughout the day to get up or else I never would. — CD

Cheap business cards

In most parts of the world business cards are still a cultural norm. I designed my business card in Photoshop, and every few years I update the info and send the file to PS Print online and they mail back a small box of 250 for $18. Easy, quick, and cheap. — KK

Instructions on how to clean your laptop

After ruining a keyboard years ago, I took a long break from cleaning my laptop. Turns out I just needed someone to instruct me, like this article does, on "How to Properly Clean Your Gross Laptop." I had all the supplies at home: microfiber wipes, compressed air, cotton swabs and 90%-100% isopropyl alcohol. — CD

Silverfish solution

For years we've had silverfish darting around our guest bathroom. I bought some silverfish traps (little cardboard boxes with sticky goo to ensnare them) and those helped, but didn't stop them. A few weeks ago I read that lavender oil is a good silverfish repellent. It's only $8 for a small bottle on Amazon, so I decided to give it a try. I wetted the end of a Q-Tip with the oil and ran it around the perimeter of the bathroom floor, adding a little extra to the seam between the floor and the wall. It smelled nice and we did not see a single silverfish for two weeks. When I finally saw one, I reapplied lavender oil on the perimeter of the floor and haven't seen any since. — MF

Moth catcher

We have pantry moths in our kitchen cupboards, and can't get rid of them. But we

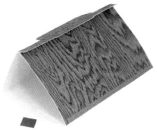

can greatly reduce how many there are with these moth traps. They look like little scout tents but the inner walls are coated with a sticky substance. Once every 9 months we replace the trap, which by then is covered with the creatures. — MF

Effective no-kill rat trap

I bought this small rodent trap ($17) a couple of years ago and have caught several mice and rats with it. It doesn't kill the animal, it just traps them in the cage when they touch the lever with the bait. (I use a bit of peanut butter for the bait, and put a little bowl of water in the cage so they don't get thirsty before I check the trap.) With this kind of trap you still have to deal with the problem of what to do with a live rodent, of course. — MF

CLOCKS

Eternal clocks

The strange American habit of switching hours twice a year for Daylight Saving is a real bummer if you have wall clocks. Glancing at a clock, BTW, is a lot more handy than pulling out a phone. The solution to Daylight Savings hassle is to get an "atomic radio" wall clock which uses radio signals from government atomic clocks to keep perfect time and update themselves during seasonal changes. They come in analog or digital varieties. For several decades we've used La Crosse analog atomic clocks (about $22) in our kitchen and office for constant precise time and never need to think about them. — KK

Cheap bedside alarm

I bought this small $10 clock so I could avoid looking at my phone in the morning. The alarm is

progressive and the ticking is as close to silent as possible. There's a button to illuminate the time in the dark that also doubles as a snooze button. Perfectly simple and useful. — CD

Wake up earlier, naturally

I wasn't sure if I would like the Philips Wake-Up Light Alarm Clock, but in one month it's trained me to wake up earlier, naturally. I set the alarm for the time I want to wake up and the light gradually increases beginning about 20 minutes before the alarm is set to go off. During that time is when I usually wake up. When the wake-up light doesn't work, I get woken up by the sounds of birds chirping. Either way, I'm never startled or grumpy. — CD

PET STUFF

LITTER BOXES

A self-cleaning litter box that works

The Litter-Robot is what it sounds like – a cat litter box that performs a self clean every time one of my three cats uses it. The manufacturer sent me one to try out, and it's changed an unpleasant twice-a-day cleaning routine into an easy once-every-two-days task of dumping a tray of litter clumps into the trash. It's basically a rotating barrel with a screen. Your cat hops in and does her business, and a few minutes after she hops out the barrel slowly rotates, depositing the clumps into a tray, and returning the clean litter to the barrel. It comes with a smartphone app, which I initially thought was ridiculous, but turned out to be useful in alerting me when it's time to empty the tray. This thing costs $500, which is a crazy amount of money for a litter box. But think of it on a two-year timeframe: is it worth a dollar a day to eliminate an unpleasant chore? — MF

Easy-clean litter box

One of our cats is getting too old to comfortably hop into our Clevercat litter box, so I needed to get a litterbox with a low profile that she could easily get in and out of. I ended up buying this one (Pet Mate 42036 Arm & Hammer Large Sifting Litter Pan) that has a plastic screen so you can clean the litter without a scoop. It works surprisingly well! – MF

Best litter box for side-peeing cats

My cat is a side pee-er so the best litter box for her is the Modkat Litter Box with top entry. There's less litter on the floor, it's easier to clean and it looks great. — CD

CAT OWNER STARTER KIT

Our cats use the Ultimate Scratching Post about 50 times a day. They no longer scratch upholstery, as they find the scratching post more satisfying.

Claudia is getting a kitten, and knowing that I have three cats, she asked me for recommendations on things to buy. Here they are: Boxiecat Premium Clumping Clay Cat Litter is nearly dustless and not perfumed. I've tried many different kinds of cat litter and this is the best. PetLovers Extra Sticky Lint Rollers are a necessity.

Cosmic Catnip Cat Toys come in a variety of shapes. They play with them, bliss out, and roll around on the floor for about ten minutes. They will lose interest if you leave the toys out, so it's better to hide them and give them to your cats as an infrequent treat.

Cats never seem to get frustrated about not being able to catch a laser pointer dot. My cats get really excited when they hear me open the drawer where we store our laser pointer and they will run into the room and start meowing and looking around wildly for the red dot.

The DuraScoop Jumbo Cat Litter Scoop is made from cast aluminum and looks like an Art Deco collectible. It's very sturdy and makes cleaning the cat litter much less unpleasant. — MF

TV for cats

My daughter likes having our cats hang out in her room with her when she does her homework, but when they start to bother her by rubbing against her or standing on her papers, she told me she shows them YouTube videos made for cats. I didn't believe they worked, but I tried one (it shows mice and birds eating seeds) and my cat was engrossed for the entire 14-minute video. – MF

A view for your cat

The best gift you can give your indoor cat is a great view and a comfy place to nap. I've owned both the original Kitty Cot ($50) and the

less expensive version by Oster ($20), and they're both great. The Kitty Cot offers more size options and the Oster Sunny Seat has a machine-washable cover and can hold up to 50 pounds. Every time I witness my little furry Frida sleeping or lounging in her perch enjoying her view, I think about what a smart purchase this was.
— CD

Find the perfect pet bird

I've owned birds in the past, and I'm not in the market for one now, but my daughter showed me this fun quiz that matches you up with the perfect type of pet bird and points you to rescue centers near you so you can adopt one. The quiz result said my kind of bird is the lineolated parakeet, and I agree. — MF

Potty training app for puppies

I was immediately overwhelmed when we brought our new puppy home two weeks ago. Puddle & Pile was a mind

saver. I log when my pup eats, drinks, pees and poops and the app will predict when he'll need to potty next and alert me. The more I log the more it learns about his habits and becomes more accurate. It's not perfect, but it's prevented a lot of accidents and I can't find a better app for the job.
— CD

Fastest way to remove pet hair

We have a chocolate lab and a long-haired cat and their dark hairs can be found on every surface of our house. This $25 reusable roller (ChomChom Roller) is the fastest and easiest way to clean our couch and comforter. You just roll back and forth over flat surfaces and the roller catches all the hair in a dust receptacle that you empty out. Much more efficient than sticky lint rollers. — CD

CLOSET

Laundry organizer

My husband and I bought these mesh bags to organize our laundry. We use black sharpie to write washing instructions on them like "no fabric softener, dryer ok" or "cold wash, hang dry." This has cleared up a lot of confusion. — CD

Shorten your drying time

We have yet to upgrade our old washer and dryer, but my husband upped our laundry game by buying these Wool Dryer Balls ($7, 6pk). They accelerate drying time by absorbing moisture and help prevent static cling. — CD

Erase wrinkles

My mother has a garment steamer (The PurSteam Elite, $70) and everyone in my family used it to get rid of the wrinkles in the clothes we packed into suitcases for my nephew's wedding. The steam from the handheld wand made the wrinkles melt away. We immediately bought one for our house. — MF

Ironing hack

I rarely iron anymore. I just throw a wet hand towel and whatever wrinkled top I want to wear into the dryer. Then I run it on high heat for a little less than 10 minutes, and go about my morning routine. Some people use ice cubes. — CD

Happy hangers

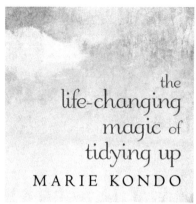

Following the advice of Japanese decluttering expert Marie Kondo, I've gone through my closet and kept only those clothes that "bring me joy." The second step was to extend the joy by arranging the dress clothes on uniform, decent wooden hangers, and recycling the mess of wire misfits I had accumulated. I got 20 wooden hangers for cheap from Amazon for $24. Happy clothes! — KK

Keep purses organized

I keep my makeup, charger, and other loose belongings in zippered pouches because it makes it easier to move from purse to purse without misplacing or leaving something behind. These mesh bags work well, because you can see what's inside. — CD

Sturdy bag hooks

These sleek, spring closing rings are great for when you're at a bar or restaurant and have nowhere to hang your bag. I bought a few to keep on different purses so I'm never without one. They can hold up to 30 pounds which is better for backpacks. — CD

Ten dollar watch

I wear a watch, not as expensive jewelry, but as a clock I find easier to inspect than a phone. I have four requirements for a watch: 1) Bold, easy to read numbers on an analog face. 2) Easy band. 3) Long battery. 4) Dirt cheap. The cheapest analog-faced wrist watch I've found is the Casio MQ24. It costs $10. I've worn most of the cheap ones (Swatch, Timex) and this one lasts the longest. (What usually gives out first on these cheapies is the winding stem for changing the time.) — KK

Authentic bling

My wife picked a small cubic zirconia synthetic diamond for her engagement ring. Because it is just one carat it looks like a diamond. Nobody can tell it is synthetic. Really. It cost $24. Real diamonds are a ripoff. — KK

Silicone ring

I bought my husband a QALO ring to wear while he's cycling/ working out and he loves how it's so well-made and comfortable. It's made out of medical-grade silicone and it doesn't look like a cheap rubber ring. I like how it looks on him so much I want to start wearing one. — CD

Most comfortable robe

My husband bought me an UGG robe for Christmas and it is so soft and

comfortable that I actually sleep in it from time to time. It's lined with lightweight fleece, so it's very warm but not bulky. — CD

Kimono-style pajamas

I just got back from JoCo Cruise 2018, a week-long cruise around Baja Mexico. This was JoCo's eighth annual cruise. It was started by musician Jonathan Coulton, who has a delightfully nerdy fan base of board-game loving, scifi reading, cosplaying, ukulele strumming folks of all ages. Over 1,600 "SeaMonkeys" took over Holland America's ms Oosterdam and we had a terrific time playing games and music, and attending panels, workshops, concerts, readings, and performances. I bought a pair of kimono pajamas ($24) for the cruise (one day was pajama day, where everyone was encouraged to wear pajamas all day) and I got a lot of compliments on them. I like them enough that I'm going to start wearing them at home, too. — MF

Bra alternative

Over the years, I've had to buy a variety of bras for different types of dresses and tops (racerback, backless, strapless, etc.), but the most useful purchase I've made has been Nippies. I've had these for a couple years now. They are washable, reusable and so comfortable I forget I have them on. — CD

Double-sided tape for your clothes

- Secure plunging necklines
- Hold up strapless gowns and halter styles
- Keep accessories in place

If I'm wearing a low-cut dress or a finicky blouse, this little tin of double-sided apparel tape (Hollywood Fashion Secrets Fashion Tape Tin, $8) always saves the day. I make sure I pack this in my luggage when I travel and in my purse if I dress up or go to weddings. — CD

Best belts

I no longer use leather belts. I only use nylon web belts, sometimes called tactical or military belts, even for dressing up. They look like a belt but since they don't have holes, they are infinitely adjustable. And they use hard plastic for the buckle so I don't have to remove it in airports. There are many styles and colors, and all can be trimmed for length. The one I use is this generic model. — KK

Plastic buckle no-hole belt

I'm always looking for ways to reduce the hassle of going through airport security. A couple of months ago I bought this $10 belt with a plastic buckle. It won't trigger the metal detector, which means I can keep it on. — MF

SHOES

Foam clogs

After reading Barbara Dace's recommendation for Amoji Foam Clogs ($20) I ordered a pair on Amazon. They are indeed as comfortable as she said, and they are easy to slip on and off. Even without a heel they stay secure on my feet as I walk around the house. They come in a variety of colors. I bought red, the most obnoxious color available. — MF

Super comfortable slippers I can wear outside

I rarely drive anywhere these days, and aside from taking walks a couple of times a day in the neighborhood, I'm sheltering in place. I decided to give my feet a break and I'm wearing slippers instead of shoes around the house. These $15 memory foam slippers from RockDove have an open back that makes them easy to slip on and kick off, and the memory foam insoles are incredibly comfortable. Most importantly they have a thick waterproof sole, so I can wear them in the backyard. — MF

Comfortable closed-toe sandals

I work from home 80% of the time and was in need of comfy footwear more substantial than flip flops but not as relaxed as slippers, in case I need to run outside. These Sanuk Yoga Sling Cruz Sandals were exactly what I wanted. They are cushiony and comfortable for standing at my desk, they keep my feet warm, and in my opinion, look good with jeans, plus I don't feel like a slacker when I'm working without real shoes on. — CD

Most comfortable flip-flops

Sanuk Yoga Slings are made from recycled yoga mats and are unbelievably comfortable to walk around in. The thong sandals have stretchy fabric straps that you

can pull around your ankle so that they never fall off. I gave a pair to my mother-in-law, who was born and raised in Hawaii and may be the ultimate authority on flip-flops, and she loves them. — CD

Slip-on sneakers

My friend Cory Doctorow gave me a pair of Native Jefferson Slip-On Sneakers about 4 years ago, and I haven't worn any other kind of shoe since. They are made from the same rubber as Crocs, but they look better. I don't wear socks with them. They are very easy to slip on and off at airport security, too. — MF

No show, no slip socks

I've tried a few different brands of low-cut "no show" socks and these are the lowest

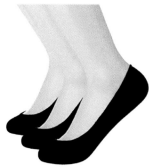

and best. They are super stretchy and they don't slip off. Seven pairs cost $15. — MF

Foot petals

One of my favorite pairs of sandals recently cut my heel open. These foot petals now prevent that from happening. They also keep my shoes in place and make them much more comfortable to wear. — CD

Shoe cleaning kit

My favorite sneakers are both Vans and have white soles that get really dirty. I want them to last a long time, so once a month I clean them using this ShoeAnew Shoe Cleaner Kit ($17). It comes with

a brush and a microfiber cloth and it only takes a few minutes to spray and scrub all the dirt off. — CD

Better laces

I have replaced all my regular shoelaces with these no-tie elastic laces. Ultra thin bungee cords snap the shoe closed without having to tie or untie. Instant on and off. Easy to slip your foot out, yet snug when needed. Not too dorky even for dress shoes; in fact, they look cool. — KK

Easy shoe lacing

Put the lace tip into the eyelet.   Gently push the lace tip inside.

These elastic silicone shoelaces look like regular shoelaces and eliminate the tucked-in hidden knot, which is always uncomfortable. It turns my Keds into slip-ons. — CD

Non-iron shirts

All my dress shirts are now "Non-Iron" cotton material. I don't know how this stuff works, but the ones I clumsily fold into my luggage will unwrinkle shortly after I put them on. I use Non-Iron Oxford shirts from Land's End and L.L. Bean, but most clothing brands seem to carry them. Eagle brand Non-Iron shirts are popular on Amazon. — KK

Long-sleeved T-shirts

I'm my own boss, so I set the work dress code and it is: t-shirts. But I live on the Pacific coast in the fog where it is cool year round, so I only wear long-sleeved t-shirts. And I don't wear logos. For many years long-sleeved t-shirts in color without logos were hard to find, but I recently got my newest batch from Amazon of all places. The Amazon Essentials long-sleeved t-shirt is heavy duty, inexpensive, and Prime delivery. Perfect for my office. — KK

Logo-free baseball cap

In my never-ending quest to wear clothes without logos, I found a great source of logo-less baseball caps (better than the discontinued Daiso hats). These hefty Falari caps are $9 and come in a refreshing variety of 34 solid colors. Mine are canary yellow. — KK

Different ways to tie a scarf

Every Fall, I end up googling all the different ways I can tie a scarf. I finally found a YouTube video I can save and go back to when needed. Warning: it's kind of hypnotic. — CD

Expert ways to tell if clothes are well-made

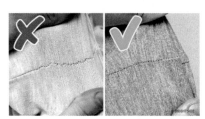

Ever since I took a sewing class I'm obsessed with how clothes are made, and now avoid buying "fast fashion" if I can. This article by BuzzFeed shows you 14 easy ways to figure out if clothing is made cheaply or not. It's illuminating. — CD

Organize your deep drawers

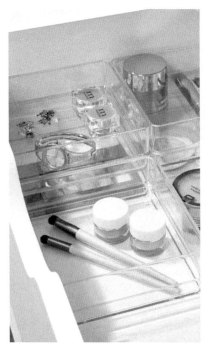

I bought multiple sets of these STORi Clear Plastic Drawer Organizers to organize my makeup drawer. They come in different sizes and can be arranged in multiple configurations to fit any drawer. They are completely transparent so even though they are stacked on top of each other, I know where everything is. There is no wasted space. — CD

Easier to find

If you are looking for something in your house, and you finally find it, when you're done with it, don't put it back where you found it. Put it back where you first looked for it. — KK

WORKSHOP

Best work surface

I have a large self-healing mat on my workbench, and I have smaller cutting mats I lay on a table if I am working. The non-skid surface keeps parts and pieces stationary, while the cushion prevents dings in the table top beneath. And of course, the self-healing mat is ideal for cutting fabrics, paper, etc. with razors and blades. It also protects from spills better than cardboard. It is easy to clean up: just tilt and wipe. It's become my default surface for any work. Get the largest size you can. At the minimum, an 18 x 24 inch mat covers well and yet is portable and easy to store. — KK

Hand protection

I have a supply of nitrile gloves on hand. I wear them to prevent my hands from getting dirty, like when handling rat traps or greasing the wheels on my garage door. I also use them to keep my hands from smearing nice things, like high-quality art paper for my wide-format printer. Two hundred ambidextrous gloves cost $13.50 on Amazon. (Tip: some tasks require just one glove.) — MF

Powerful tube squeezer

The Big Squeeze Tube Squeezer ($35)  forces every last drop of goop out of a tube. It can handle tubes up to 3.375" wide. To use it, insert the end of the tube between the two rollers, squeeze the handle and turn the key. The tube is completely flattened, and because of the serrated design of the rollers, the tube is crimped so it stays flat. I've used it on tubes of toothpaste, acrylic paint, and lithium grease. It's all metal and heavy duty. — MF

Telescoping aluminum ladder

Like magic, my 12-foot ladder will telescope down to less than 3 feet. I can throw  this Telescoping Aluminum Ladder in the trunk of my car, but more importantly, I can effortlessly move it through our house under my arm when I need to reach high ceiling bulbs or skylights, etc. It collapses instantly when done and stores in a closet. It's what a home ladder should be. There are a bunch of no-brand models, almost identical, for about $100. — KK

MAKERS TO WATCH

Cheap mobile home

For generations hipsters have been retro-fitting vans into mobile homes. Once they were VW vans; today they are Dodge Sprinter vans. The best source I've come across for tutorials on how to remodel a used cargo van into a roaming house is a YouTube channel by Dylan Magaster. Magaster collects diverse videos of hundreds of regular folks building their vans and tiny homes in great and satisfying detail. — KK

Watch this guy put things back together

My sister texted me and told me to watch the YouTube series called The Reassembler.
I was 7 minutes into an episode when I texted her back: "This is the greatest thing I've ever seen on YouTube." I don't even think I was exaggerating. Each episode starts off with host James May in a workshop, standing over components of something that has been taken apart (like a lawnmower, an electric guitar, or a model train set). He then puts it back together, narrating as he does so. As he says in the introduction, "it is only when these objects are laid out in hundreds of bits and then slowly reassembled that you can truly understand and appreciate how they work and just how ingenious they are." — MF

Maker videos

Maker Update is a YouTube show where host Donald Bell presents his favorite maker projects, kits, and tools. Episodes are less than 10 minutes and are well-produced. — MF

Woodworking DIY channel

April Wilkerson is a woodworker and her YouTube channel is filled with her projects, like a chicken coop, a multipurpose garage storage station, a cedar fence, a

walking cane, and more. She's great at showing and explaining her work, and letting you see her mistakes and workarounds, which is very valuable. — MF

Maker extreme

I enjoy the way Adam Savage, formerly Mythbuster co-host, builds complicated things. He has a new show, Savage Builds, running on Discovery Channel. In the first episode he made a "real" bullet-proof, flying Ironman suit, which is inspiring. For the next 7 days only, that episode is streaming for free on the internet. — KK

One-minute tool reviews

Recomendo is produced by a tiny team of people who are passionate about tools. In addition to this newsletter,

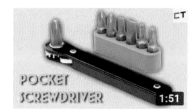

Screwdriver for tight spots

we have a website called Cool Tools with thousands of reviews of useful tools, and a new YouTube channel with brief hands-on video reviews every other week. If you like Recomendo, it's worth your time to check them out. — MF

Bootstrap workshop

Homemade Table Saw & Setting up Shop for $50.00!

I like this guy's YouTube channel, the $50 Workshop. He's bootstrapping a woodworking workshop starting with $50 worth of store-bought tools, and then using them to build his own table saw, drill press, etc. He makes things from scrap wood with his current tools to buy parts to make better tools. It's encouraged me to make my own tools. — KK

Hot glue tips

I derive great enjoyment and instruction from watching YouTube videos of Jimmy DiResta making stuff. All kinds of things from knives, to tables, to weird art. He is a master general-purpose craftsman, and with few words, he lets his actions speak. When he gives tips, he is awesome. For a great example, witness his Hot Glue Tips. – KK

Best Maker YouTube Channels

Most of my discretionary media time is spent watching YouTube. I derive immense pleasure in finding out how things work and how to make and repair things. Over several years of watching all kinds of video, lousy and great, I've collected a bunch of channels for dependable high-quality content. In a long post on our blog Cool Tools, I review the top 30 YouTube informational channels that I subscribe to. (#1 on my list is Cody's Lab.) — KK

King of Random

I'm a big fan of YouTube tutorials by folks who make things. One of the best YouTube channels for cool and unusual doable (by an average person) projects is King of Random. This channel was started by Grant Thompson, who died recently in a hang-gliding accident. While his associates continue his channel, Grant's earlier "maker" videos are worth seeking out. His detailed instructions are impeccably researched, his building details are clever yet totally reliable, and his project designs are extremely fun and even "dangerous" in a good way. — KK

Reviving spray cans

Don't toss a can of spray paint out — or any spray can — because it's clogged. I keep a bunch of inexpensive replacement caps (mostly sold to graffiti artists) on hand to fix this problem. Swap a new cap in and the can is like new. I've mentioned this hack before but this sample bag from The Yard Art Supply ($14) has a better variety of 50 male and female caps to fit any can. — KK

Super easy paint touchup

After you finish painting a room, pour a little of the left-over paint into one of these small BIBR touch up bottles. One for

each color. The plastic bottles contain a small applicator brush inside (plus a marble to shake/stir the paint) which makes it super easy to break it out to touch up as things happen. Gareth Branwyn suggests keeping the touchup bottle in a drawer in the room itself, making it a no-brainer to grab when needed. Touch ups will never happen when the paint is at the bottom of a can in the basement. — KK

Workshop tip

When mixing epoxies, resins, goops, paints, and glues, I always need to dispose of the gunked-up mixing container afterwards. I try to hoard used take-out containers and paper cups yet run out. By far the best solution is to use flexible silicone mixing bowls. Nothing sticks. Turn them inside out to clean, and use again and again. They come in all sizes. You need only one of each size. Since I mostly use small amounts of epoxy, I use the smallest silicone cup I could find, the Norpro Mini Pinch Cups. — KK

Goo Gone to go

If you have an Amazon Prime account, you can buy a plastic dispenser bottle of 24 Goo Gone wipes for $9. It has a pleasant citrus smell and works like a charm to remove chewing gum, jar labels, tree sap, sticker adhesive and more from most any surface. — MF

Label lifter

I use Goo Gone to remove stickers from glass and plastic, but when I need to remove a label from a book cover or cardboard, the Scotty Peeler Label and Sticker Remover does the trick. The flat tapered edge fits between a label and the surface and, if you work slowly and carefully, will remove the label without marring the surface of your book or other item. — MF

Instant bond

I never had much luck using superglue. It really wasn't instant, it didn't seem to bond tightly, and I'd get it all over my fingers. The trade secret to using superglue (which all serious model-makers seem to know) is to use an accelerator with it. You spray the glued joint with this catalyst solvent and it cures the glue instantly. Or you can spray one half of the joint with the accelerator and when it touches the other half with the glue it bonds instantly. Yes! I got a small spray bottle of accelerator (the brand name doesn't matter much) but it is so useful I now get the combination of glue+accelerator in larger quantities. — KK

Moldable Glue

Sugru is a moldable rubber material you can use to repair things. When you open a pouch, it has the consistency of Silly Putty. You have about 5-10 minutes to work with it, then it begins to cure. After 24 hours it's like hard rubber.

It sticks to almost anything, including plastic and glass. I've used Sugru over the years to fix and modify dozens of things, from worn cables to a broken icemaker. An 8-pack is currently on sale for $12. — MF

Superglue and baking soda for fixing broken plastic parts

My friend Bob sent me this video about using super glue and baking soda to fix broken plastic parts. When it cures it is rock hard. I used this material to repair a broken dimmer switch knob and it didn't break when I intentionally tried to snap it between my hands. — MF

Plastic restoring gel

Old yellowed plastic looks unrecoverable but it can be magically brought back to its original whiteness or bright color using hydrogen peroxide gel from a hair salon. The gel prevents the concentrated hydrogen peroxide from slipping off; you also wrap it in cling plastic to keep it moist.

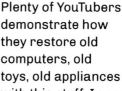

Plenty of YouTubers demonstrate how they restore old computers, old toys, old appliances with this stuff. I used Super Star Cream Peroxide to bring back white plastic parts in our bathroom. (Also good for whitening old bones.) — KK

Freeze dried taxidermy

Occasionally a small bird strikes one of our windows and dies. Rather than bury it, I freeze dry it. I insert the whole bird into a baggie with a pack of desiccant to keep it dry. The desiccant gel slowly absorbs the moisture in the bird even after it freezes. After a year it is fully dried, and can be kept on a shelf or display indefinitely with all its feathers. This works on birds the size of a sparrow or smaller. — KK

Bleaching bones

Any bones or skulls you collect can be whitened up without using chlorine bleach, which can weaken the bone. Use concentrated hydrogen peroxide, which will fizz and brighten bone to a brilliant white very quickly. You need stronger stuff than the dilute peroxide found in drug stores. Head to the hair care aisle or hair product stores, and look for bottles of concentrated H2O2 in bottles labeled as Clairoxide or the like. — KK

Most handy

A true miracle device in my workshop is a right-angle attachment to my power drill that lets me drill or screw in tight places. This small geared unit allows me to fit the drill or screw tip into narrow spaces I can't get the length of the drill into. Just imagine being able to twist the tip of your driver 90 degrees to the side. Now that I have one, I use it all the time. There are several makes. I use a Dewalt right angle ($21), because I have Dewalt tools, but it'll work on any brand driver. — KK

Good cordless driver

I finally upgraded my one-speed cordless driver with a variable-speed drill driver ($35). Made by Tacklife it has adjustable torque, and speed is controlled by how much you pull the trigger. A built-in light turns on when you use it. I wish I would have bought this a long time ago. — MF

Long-nosed precision marker

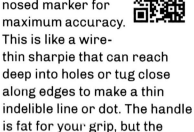

In my workshop I use a Dixon needle-nosed marker for maximum accuracy. This is like a wire-thin sharpie that can reach deep into holes or tug close along edges to make a thin indelible line or dot. The handle is fat for your grip, but the business end is only 2mm wide and several inches long (like a hummingbird beak) making it perfect for precision marks on fabric, plastics, metals and wood. This Dixon is a slightly cheaper version of a similar Pica brand marker recommended by Adam Savage. — KK

Needle-nose marker

I am a convert to a needle-nosed marker. It's a sharpie pen with its inky tip at the end of a long thin stalk, thin as a bamboo skewer. I am amazed how often I need to mark something through a hole, in a slot, or in a tight corner, or trace a pattern — situations the usual fat pen or pencil tip won't fit in. Its body is as thin as its tip, except at the end where it's fat enough to hold. This makes it easier to mark anything. A number of different but similar brands make these; I use the FastCap Long Nosed Pattern Marker

($7), which also has a chisel tip marker on its opposite end. — KK

Better than sandpaper

I've started whittling spoons again and I recently discovered flexible sanding sheets made by 3M. I'll never use sandpaper again. These sheets are made from some kind of semi-stretchy plastic that makes it very easy to get the grit into tight spots (like the hollow of a spoon). They last much longer than sandpaper, too. — MF

IKEA as platform

People have been hacking Ikea furniture forever, customizing and upgrading its modular units. Now Ikea has become a platform that high-end designers create skins for. You buy the economical guts of an Ikea kitchen, shelving, or a sofa, and then apply new doors, handles, countertops, or fabrics created by legendary designers. This is a great New York Times summary article describing the ecosystem with links to the many companies that offer refined design layers for the Ikea platform. — KK

STORAGE & ORGANIZATION

Maker space storage

My daughter and I have converted part of the family room into a maker space. We needed something to hold and organize lots of small parts, and that didn't eat up a lot of tabletop space. This $28 cabinet with 44 drawers was just what we wanted. It's tall, but some double-sided tape on the bottom has anchored it to the table to prevent tipping over. — MF

Small parts storage

My preferred system for storing lots of small parts (screws, Legos) in my workshop or studio is a multi-bin

case. Many brands (Sortimo, Stanley, Amazon) made these at different price points but the form is similar. The clear lid of the flat case opens to a grid of different sized bins, which can be moved around to suit the contents. The cheapest ones, good enough for me, are 20-bin Storage Cases from Harbor Freight for $9. I have 20 of these trays stacked in a rack. — KK

Damage-free hanging

I use these neat hooks from 3M when I want to hang something on a surface I don't want to damage, either a stucco wall, or a hotel room, or for a temporary hanging on a wood surface. Command Hangers employ an innovative glue strip to hold and release. The strip will securely hold the hanger for as long as you like (difficult to pull off), but will remove itself entirely, and easily, without marks or damage to paint at the end, using an ingenious particular physical pull. Hard to explain but it really works. I find they hold more than they specify. Command hooks come in all kinds of sizes, many styles, and are reusable, too. — KK

Garage and workshop storage shelves

About 8 years ago I hired someone to help me organize my stuff. After we met at my house, she told me to order some Gorilla Racks for our garage. They turned out to be a good purchase. They're easy to assemble and sturdy. — MF

Advice on building a home

Over many decades, homesteader Lloyd Kahn has built his three beautiful homes by hand, and is the author and publisher of books about building personal homes. Lloyd lives in a fire-prone part of California. He compiled a useful list of hints for people rebuilding homes after fires. The tips are so helpful they would be useful to anyone building a home anywhere. — KK

CUTTING TOOLS

Micro flush cutters

If you do soldering work, I recommend getting a pair of these Hakko micro cutters. They'll cut copper wires flush with the blob of solder, making your work look tidy. And they cost just $7.60 on Amazon. — MF

Best paper cutter

For fast, clean, straight paper cuts, I pull out my Fiskars SureCut Deluxe Craft Paper Trimmer ($21). It's foolproof and kids can use it without supervision because there's no exposed blade. — MF

Tools for cutting stone

I needed to find a cheap and easy way to cut some fossils out of some rocks. Turns out you can buy a cheap $10 diamond cutting blade for a generic $22 electric angle grinder. It eats stone and spits out dust, so wear a mask, but otherwise it works. — KK

Plastic razor blades

These look like old fashioned safety razor blades, but they're made of plastic and you can't shave with them. You can't cut paper with them, either. But they excel as scrapers. Put one into the included handle and you can cleanly remove labels and stickers stuck to almost any surface (add a bit of Goo Gone to speed up the process, if you wish). I used one to clean the labels off a cigar box for a project I recently made. — MF

Tool I use the most

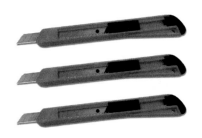

Everyday, multiple times a day, I use my handy snap-blade utility box-cutter knife. It costs 2 dollars. It's made of day-glo orange plastic. I use it like a pocket knife for opening and liberating all kinds of things, but it weighs almost nothing (no pocket wear), is easy to re-sharpen (snap off the end), instant to engage, and quick to put back. They are so cheap and featherweight I keep one in all my pants, coats, and bags. If I lose it I don't care. I really miss having them when I travel by air (although I know from unintentional experience they are usually undetectable by the machines.) — KK

Cheap new tools

It is easy to mock the importer Harbor Freight for their insanely cheap Chinese-made tools, but in fact I've had great success with the tools I've bought from them. I may only use them a few times a year, and for that frequency their quality is more than sufficient, and their self-proclaimed "ridiculously low prices" are in fact a tremendous bargain. Over the years I've bought a welder, a larger sanding wheel, a buffer, and recently a new compound miter saw for less than $100. – KK

Best wirestripper

The Vise-Grip self-adjusting wirestripper is the best wirestripper, period. It perfectly strips the insulation off of small wires for electronic projects, or large wires for running power. No muss, no fuss; it just works automatically. This hand tool fits kids and pros. It's the one I grab. — KK

Get PDF first

Owner manuals and installation guides contain far more information about a product than either the sales brochure, the online descriptions, or even Amazon reviews. The manual will have exact dimensions, all the parts, and caveats about what it can't do. So my rule of thumb these days is to always download the product's manual before I purchase the item. Impossible in the old pre-internet days, it's a no-brainer today. It has saved me many times. Regrettably, not 100% of products have PDFs that are findable, but the better products do. — KK

Free magazine for Raspberry Pi projects

The Raspberry Pi is a $35 Linux computer the size of a credit card. Add a keyboard, mouse, microSD card, and a TV or computer display and you have a perfectly usable computer. You can learn about hundreds, if not thousands, of cool projects you can build with a Pi by downloading free PDF copies of MagPi magazine. — MF

Renting Tools

Reminder: Your local Home Depot or other big box building store rents an amazing array of tools. Not just carpet shampooers, but carpet dryers, concrete cutting saws, pipe locators, ditch diggers, stump grinders, wallpaper removers, cherry pickers — all kinds of tools you will use only once in your life. Check out their selection. It's a great way to try out a tool. My rule is if I want to rent a tool a second time, it's worth buying. Last year I rented an electric power-washer. This year, I bought one. — KK

Easy 3D design application

I got a great new 3D printer (the award-winning Original Prusa i3) and I've been using it to print useful things for around the house. The 3D design program I use is the free, web-based Tinkercad. It's easy to get up-to-speed by watching a couple of brief introductory videos. I'm going to design a plastic ukulele with it. — MF

Emergency key

Although it is less common to lock yourself out of your car with electronic locks and ignition these days, it happens often enough that I keep a spare key hidden in our vehicles. Grant Thompson (King of Random) has a great YouTube tutorial on how to make a key-hold big enough for modern fob keys — the kind that contain a transponder that works at a distance. This is the crazy-strong magnet I used for our hidden key-holds. It is cheap insurance compared to a locksmith visit. — KK

Handy key chain

I use a non-locking carabiner, kind of like this one, to hold all my key rings. I can quickly and easily unclip my excess keys while I'm driving to keep them from jangling. — CD

Switchable magnets

I've recently discovered magswitches. These are magnets you can turn off and on. I use them in my workshop to hold down fences, stops, and featherboards. When they are turned on, you can't move them. When off, they lift off instantly. They are non-electronic; the switch is an ingenious mechanical contraption hidden inside a very tiny case. You can buy fixtures with magswitches built in, or you can buy the switches to make your own devices. I found that even a single magswitch alone, such as the small MagJig 95 ($26), is a useful stop in the workshop because you can position it anywhere quickly on a metal surface and have it instantly hold. — KK

Best tape measure

I've used many different tape measures over my four decades of making things. My go-to measurer for the past 5 years has been a 25-foot Stanley Fatmax. It is comfy to hold, and not too big for my small hands. 25 feet is plenty for most jobs in the home or workshop, and best of all, because of its wide curved width, it will extend 10 feet straight out on its own. Reasonably priced. – KK

Dual scale tape measures

In my ongoing campaign to make myself literate in metric (used everywhere in the world except the US), as much as possible I try to measure only in metric. I got a Komelon dual scale measuring tape (both metric and inches on one side) and after a month or so, I can think in metric. I really like Komelon measuring tapes because they are inexpensive but high quality. They have four in different sizes in dual scale, from 3.5m/12ft for only $5, to a 9m/30ft for $8.50. The 9-meter one is big in the hand but an incredible bargain; however their 5 meter is probably a good size for general use. — KK

Dirt cheap magnification

I've sung the praises of this 40x lighted hand held magnifier many times before. It's $2 on Amazon. I splurged and bought three. I can now read the numbers on tiny capacitors, inspect splinters in great detail, and check my kid's head for louse nits. Uses 3AAA batteries (not included) — MF

Head-mounted magnifier

I use this $10 head-mounted magnifier at least once a week. It has two levels of magnification and LED illumination. It's great for soldering or most other kinds of detail work. — MF

LIGHTS

Smallest, cheapest flashlight

This ThorFire is the brightest, cheapest ($15), smallest, lightest LED flashlight that runs on a single AA (rechargeable) battery. Rugged, made of metal, it will stand up on its end. I have them everywhere. — KK

Best small flashlight

My friend Rob gave me the ThruNite Archer LED Flashlight ($30) and it is the best small flashlight I've ever owned. It throws a bright beam, and because it's made from aluminum, it feels solid. Importantly, it uses AA batteries instead of less-common batteries often required in bright flashlights. I bought one for my father for Father's Day because I knew he'd appreciate it. — MF

Wide-angle LED headlamp

This battery-powered headlamp ($15) has a bunch of LEDs spread across the front so it throws a very wide beam. I used it recently to bring trash cans in at night and it was much better than a flashlight or traditional headlamp because I could see everything in front of me without having to turn my head. — MF

Toolshop tips

I'm enjoying Gareth Branwyn's new email newsletter, Gareth's Tips, Tools, and Shop Tales. Each weekly issue has several handy tidbits about interesting tools, novel ways to use tools, and how to maintain your workshop. The latest issue has a tip from Adam Savage on where to store infrequently used tools: "'If I didn't have it right now, where would I look for it?' And that's where he stashes it. He tries to not get clever, not overthink it, but rather, he goes with the first place that pops to mind." – MF

Workshop tips for everyone

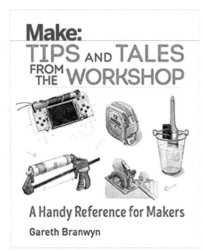

Make:
TIPS AND TALES
FROM THE WORKSHOP

A Handy Reference for Makers

Gareth Branwyn

Our friend Gareth Branwyn has a new book out, called Tips and Tales from the Workshop. It's loaded with very useful tips, not only for makers, but for everyone, really. The majority of the tips are new to me (like using hot glue as an electronics insulator). I know what I'm giving friends for Christmas this year. – MF

Super plywood

Plywood is an underrated material. But the really good stuff can be hard to find. Baltic Birch plywood is a super-duper version of plywood with many thin layers without voids that is as sturdy as metal, but lighter and much easier to use. You can fabricate things from it that you otherwise might use

Ultimate Guide to Baltic Birch Plywood: Why It's Better, When to Use It
From laser cutting to furniture building, here's what you need to know

ULTIMATE GUIDE TO BALTIC BIRCH

metal or plastic. But real Baltic plywood is hard to find. Big box stores like Home Depot and Lowes often carry Birch plywood that is hard wood only on the outside layers; inside is softwood, which is okay but not great. I found I could get real, dense, all hardwood Baltic Birch plywood online in smaller sheets. For the kind of projects you'd want to use super plywood for (jigs, boxes, toys, prototypes), you don't need, or want, large sheets. These 20x30 inch x ¾ inch thick sheets ($16) from Woodworker Source are perfect for me. — KK

The joy of pressure washing

I borrowed a friend's gasoline-powered pressure washer to clean the mossy-covered

bricks in my back yard. The machine was noisy and smelly and I had to keep refilling the tank, but I loved the results, so I bought an electric pressure washer (the Sun Joe SPX3200 for $168). It's superior in every way to the gasoline-powered washer. It's quiet and goes into idle mode when you release the trigger. It has five different nozzles, including one to spray soap. If you have never seen what a pressure washer can do, this subreddit will make you a true believer. — MF

Save your knees

I bought this 11 x 18 inch Fiskars Ultralight Kneeling Cushion in 2011 for $8 and have used it hundreds of times since then. It has come in handy when repairing appliances, working on and washing cars, weeding, and any other activity that requires getting on my knees. More recently I bought these $7 Fiskars Ultralight Knee Pads, which let me crawl around the backyard or garage without pain. —MF

Open clogged drains

Our 50-year-old grease-encrusted drain pipes kept getting clogged, and lye-based drain openers weren't helping. Even frequent plumber visits weren't fixing the problem. In desperation, I bought this 25-pound pail of powder called Green Gobbler. I poured a few cups down a clean-out drain with a bit of hot water. It started bubbling and our house soon smelled like rotten eggs (this is apparently normal when using this stuff). It worked — no more slow draining sinks. Much cheaper and more effective than a plumber! — MF

Custom coiled cables

I've been making my own coiled cables thanks to a tip I learned from Gareth Branwyn's Tips newsletter (which we co-publish). Gareth pointed me to a John Park's YouTube tutorial on heat treating ordinary USB cables into expandable coiled cables, like the ones on old telephone handsets, or headphones. (Jump to the 23-minute mark.) The hack really works and results in much more manageable cables for audio, photography, and desktop gear. — KK

How to wrap cables

I made a 30-second video that shows how to wrap cables so that they stay wrapped, don't get tangled, and are very easy to unwrap. — MF

Untangling knots

The best way to untangle a knotty tangle is not to "untie" the knots, but to keep pulling the loops apart wider and wider. Just make the mess as big, loose and open as possible. As you open up the knots they will unravel themselves. Works on cords, strings, hoses, yarns, or electronic cables. — KK

Unlocking battery brands

Because the batteries of cordless power tools cost almost as much as the tools themselves, I, like everyone else, tended to lock into one tool brand to make the most of shared batteries. But new inexpensive adapters allow me to use my existing set of batteries for any brand of tool. I can now get the best bargain tool no matter the brand of battery. This guy (Sixtyfiveford) on YouTube has compiled a fantastic list of cordless battery adapters for any of the 60 different possible tool/battery brand combinations. Check his shownotes for the purchase links. — KK

Rechargeable 9-volts

I feel kinda dumb I had not figured this out earlier. We've managed to replace all the batteries in our household with rechargeable batteries, except for those 9-volt batteries. The ones with the two nipples on top that are in things like smoke alarms. But you can get rechargeable 9 volt batteries! Duh. As the current 9-volts die off, I'm swapping them out with these AmazonBasics 9-volt Rechargeables. I use this HTRC all-battery charger to charge them. — KK

GADGETS

Good cheap tablet stand

The $9 AmazonBasics Adjustable Tablet Stand was just what I was looking for in a kitchen countertop iPad stand. It's made of sturdy plastic, adjusts quickly, and doesn't skid or wobble. It can hold any size tablet — even smartphones. — MF

Echo dot

We installed AI into our kitchen to get a glimpse of the future. Now we talk to Alexa, and ask it to do all kinds of things. "Alexa, what is on my calendar today?" "Alexa, add granola to my

shopping list." The cheapest way to do this is not with an Echo (size of wine bottle), if you already have speakers, but with the Echo Dot. The size of a large hockey puck, it's always on, waiting for your command. And it will get upgraded over time. — KK

Wake command

You can wake up Alexa by using the wake command "Computer" as in Star Trek. Go to the Alexa app on your phone. Right-swipe to open a panel with settings choices. Pick your device and scroll down to wake commands. You have a limited choice of four words, including *computer*. There is a movement to make that command a common voice interface among all devices. Are you listening, Siri, Cortana and Google? — KK

Alexa houseguest guide

You can program your Alexa with new skills. I just trained our Alexa to serve as a home guide for houseguests, babysitters, and petsitters. I used an Alexa Blueprint to create an audible guide for finding things, or giving instructions like "where are the bath towels?,"where does the trash go?" or "how to turn off the porch light?" Visitors just ask Alexa, after saying, "Alexa open the home guide." — KK

Fire TV Stick 4K

I bought the original Fire TV stick when it first came out a few years ago. When the HD version

with a voice-activated remote control came out a couple of years later, I bought that and I appreciated the extra speak and talk-to-search feature. Amazon recently released the Fire TV Stick 4K. The remote comes with volume controls and an on-off button for the TV so I don't need to use the TV remote anymore. It's also much faster than the previous versions of the Fire TV stick. It's a worthy upgrade. — MF

Cheap DVD Reader

No one in my family of four has a CD or DVD drive in their computer. That's a good thing, because we rarely need one. When we do (usually to rip a movie or copy photos or music), I pull out this $15 USB CD/DVD drive and plug it into a laptop. — MF

Multiple power lines

I use a squid outlet when I travel. In cheap lodging there is often barely one accessible power outlet on the wall and I have lots of things to charge, from camera batteries, to a laptop, to more than one

phone. That's just me. With a travel companion there'll be even more items to charge. A squid splits the power to four flexible outlets. The flexibility gives more room for devices than a simple power strip. This 2-pack Squid is the cheapest, lightest, smallest one I've found. — KK

Best USB-C cables

Cables matter. Despite the name Universal in USB, USB cables are not universal, especially the emerging new USB-C style. Ones with the same plug can charge at different rates, and transfer data (or not) differently. Cheap generic ones are not always compatible, which I

have learned the hard way. Wirecutter has researched recommended USB-C cables with clarity. — KK

No-Look USB

These reversible micro USB cables are a miracle. Both the USB male and the micro plug can be plugged into a port without worrying which side is up. A 3-pack is $9. — MF

Correct USB plug orientation

You try to insert a USB plug and it doesn't fit. You flip it over and it still doesn't fit, so you flip it back to the original side and now it fits. Ugh! How many thousands of times has that happened? Just remember this: the topside of any USB plug will be smooth metal and the underside will have a groove down the center. Keep the smooth side up. — KK

HEADPHONES

Fall asleep listening to podcasts

I like to listen to podcasts in bed. I also sleep on my side, so earbuds and headphones hurt my ears if I use them. I bought the CozyPhones Sleep Headphones ($18), which is a headband with 1/8" thick cushioned headphones inside. They are comfortable and they roll up for travel. — MF

Don't mute, get a good headset

We are all Zooming, Skyping, Webexing, and Google hanging. Nothing will increase the quality of a video conference better than having a good mic pointed at everyone's mouth. The least expensive way to get a good mic is with a headset. Lightweight ones don't have to look dorky. It's what I use. Which headset should you get today? Matt Mullenweg, founder of Wordpress, whose entire 900-person company has worked remotely for a decade, outdid Wirecutter in trying out and testing all USB headsets. He posted his work and recommendations here on his blog post, Don't Mute. — KK

Earphone adapters

For a reason that no longer makes sense, airlines use a headphone jack that has two prongs, one for each ear channel, instead of the standard single 1/8" plug used everywhere else. That means you need a small 1-to-2 adapter if you travel with your own earphones/earbuds. These adapters are tiny, easily lost or left behind. I wanted to replace the several units (extra for companions) that I carry and lost, and could not figure out what they are called to order them. No specification I could think of worked. Eventually I discovered they are called Airline Headphone Adapters. You are welcome. — KK

Best noise cancelling earbuds

I don't get on a plane unless I am wearing Bose QuiteComfort 20 Noise Cancelling earbuds. These squeeze into a tiny super-lightweight pocket when off (unlike the headphone variety), and are simply the best noise cancelling apparatus, period. I routinely wear them the entire duration of a 13-hour flight. I arrive far more refreshed. — KK

Powerful tiny amp

"Class-T amplifiers" have been around for over 20 years. They are tiny, cheap, and look like toys. But they sound amazing. I bought a Bluetooth model for $40 (Nobsound G3 5.0 Amplifier) and hooked it up to a pair of old speakers. The sound is very clean with zero buzz or distortion. Anyone in my family can play music through the amp right from their mobile phones. — MF

Heavy duty power brick

The myCharge RazorXtreme ($100) is a portable charger with two

USB A ports and a USB C port that charge small devices as well as laptops (20V, 45W). It's bigger and heavier than typical portable chargers (almost 9-inches long and 1.3 lbs) but it keeps my family's numerous electronics juiced all weekend when we are away from an AC power source. — MF

Affordable teleprompter

When I make videos where I need to talk to the camera (the audience) I can't remember what I need to say, so I use this affordable teleprompter. Teleprompters project my visible text on an angled glass that the camera is shooting through. Normally this is a very expensive, very cumbersome rig, but the Parrot Teleprompter uses a cheap plastic case, glass mirror, and a selection of lens rings to fit on to many digital cameras. It cleverly uses your smart phone as the screen. For about $100 I got a perfectly useful compact teleprompter mounted on my tripod that worked exactly as I needed. I can deliver my lines

easily while directly gazing at the viewers and it looks very natural. — KK

USB chargeable lighter

Forget butane-lighters or matches. This $13 gooseneck electric arc lighter has a lithium-ion battery that can light hundreds of candles and barbecue fires on a single USB charge. — MF

Cute, handy printer

I love my Mini Magic Wireless Thermal Printer. I don't have a regular printer in my home office, and don't really need one, but I've been using this

GADGETS

tiny, handy machine to print out lists, pictures of my pets, and poems that I want to save. I am growing a collection of whimsical receipts! Because there is no ink required and because it came with six rolls, I constantly feel inspired to print something. — CD

Aluminum mousepad

Those neoprene mousepads make my skin crawl for some reason. I found this one, which is made from aluminum, and it's a joy to use with my optical mouse. I even like the sound my mouse makes as I run it over the lightly textured surface. — MF

Ergonomic wireless mouse

My Magic Mouse was giving me claw hand from the way I had to grip it and I needed to a find an alternative mouse, so I immediately googled Wirecutter's tested picks and bought their upgrade pick of the Logitech MX Master Mouse ($70). Full disclosure: I thought I had purchased this from a list of the best vertical mouses. Even after it arrived

and I began using it, I still mistakenly thought I was using a vertical mouse and that I had quickly overcome the steep learning curve that everyone talks about. By the time I realized that it was not a vertical mouse — just a very good ergonomic one — my claw hand was gone and I was happy with it, so I just kept it! My favorite thing about this mouse is I was able to customize the buttons and scroll wheels to do everything my Magic Mouse used to do. — CD

Ultra-thin wireless keyboard

I took the Logitech Keys-to-Go Ultra Portable Wireless Keyboard ($50) to use with my iPhone on a recent overnight trip, leaving my laptop at home. It

worked beautifully. I was able to easily write email, Google docs, and text messages with the keyboard. — MF

Tiny bluetooth speaker

This itty-bitty wireless speaker ($11) is a lot louder than I expected, and the sound is very clear. It's perfect for listening to music and podcasts in a hotel room, because it takes up almost no room in my luggage. — MF

Find misplaced items

I put a Tile bluetooth tracker in my wallet and forgot about it. Last week, my wallet fell out of my pocket when I was at the movies, and I didn't realize it until I was in the car. I went back to the theater, opened the Tile app on my phone and pressed the "Wallet" button. The tile in my wallet chirped loudly and I found it wedged between two seats. A useful little gadget! — MF

PHONE

Block telemarketer calls on your phone

Truecaller is a free, ad-supported smartphone app that blocks telemarketers' calls. When a call from a spammer comes in, your phone will display a red screen that says "Identified as Spam." And if a telemarketer slips through, you can easily add the number to Truecaller's database. — MF

Prank spam callers

When I get a call from a fraudster (like a "Microsoft tech support" scammer or an IRS impersonator), I merge their call with the Jolly Roger bot ($12/yr). This is software that has canned voice responses

designed to confuse and waste the time of the criminal who calls you. The Jolly Roger website has recordings of some entertaining conversations. — MF

Stopping phone spam

For the past 2 years I've been using the free Nomorobo service to stop spam calls on my landlines, and it works fantastically. A few months

ago I started using the paid Nomorobo app on my phone, and suddenly all those dumb spam calls have ceased. There are a number of phone spam eliminator apps, but Nomorobo is one that does not scarf up your friends' phone numbers in order to make its white list. — KK

Avoid the port-out scam on your mobile phone

If you use 2-factor authentication that sends a text message to your phone to get a code, beware of the port-out scam. This happens when a bad person impersonates you and tricks your phone company into issuing them your phone number. You can prevent this by calling your carrier (dial 611) from your phone and telling them to add a security PIN to your account. Anyone who tries to access your account will be asked for the PIN. Read more about port-out scamming here. — MF

Better phone calls

Our house phone sounds awful and we get poor cell phone connectivity at home. But we have wifi and I've started using FaceTime Audio as much as possible to make phone calls. It works on any Apple hardware and the sound quality is crystal clear, even when using cellular data. — MF

Favorite phone service

T-Mobile
4 lines
$160/mo

AT&T
4 lines
$275/mo

For many years, I paid $275 a month for an AT&T mobile phone plan (for a family of four iPhone users). Then I switched to T-Mobile. It's $175 a month,

we get unlimited data, and best of all, international data is free. It's great to travel to another country and freely use the internet (for maps, reviews, texts, Instagram, etc). Phone calls are also free in Mexico and Canada, and other international calls are usually $0.20 a minute. — MF

Two SIMS

I'm still waiting for the ideal phone carrier who will let me use my phone anywhere in the world without thinking. True global coverage at reasonable rates. In the meantime I buy sim cards when I am outside of North America. They are cheap and useful. Downside is my phone has a new number. My solution: I put the foreign SIM in a second phone, an older phone I no longer use. (We all seem to have one of those. If you don't a friend will.) That way, my primary phone number still works on wifi in hotels and cafes, but I get full roaming capabilities such as Google maps, web searches, or texting locally on the other phone as I need them. — KK

Bulk delete contacts

Somehow I merged Google contacts from both my work and my personal email with my iPhone contacts and I couldn't figure out an easy way to bulk delete. This article outlines how to delete multiple contacts at one time using Groups. The app is a little clunky, but it was

free, and an added bonus was I was able to also merge duplicates pretty easily. — CD

Smartphone shortcuts

The ever-helpful David Pogue has a fantastic list of smartphone shortcuts I had no idea were possible. They save lots of taps. I programmed my phone to set up macros (a series of steps into one step) initiated by a voice command, like "Hush Now" which silences your phone until you leave your current location. — KK

Texting tip

When texting, at the end of a sentence hit the space bar twice and it will easily put a period in the right place. — KK

ACCESSORIES

Useful protective case

I've been dropping my iPhone a lot lately — enough to make me really grateful for my Spigen protective case. It's slim enough to not feel bulky, and the lip on the front of the case has protected my screen from cracking on 30+ clumsy occasions. The kickstand feature is my favorite. — CD

Selfie helper

We got our teenage daughter a LuMee iPhone case. It has LEDs embedded in the perimeter to illuminate your face when you take a selfie. She loves it and the photos really are a lot better looking. — MF

Magnetic phone mount for cars

I've tried many different phone mounts, and this magnetic one ($7) is the best. It's a rubberized magnet that attaches to a car vent. It comes with a metallic sticker to attach to the back of your phone. When I get in my car, I just hold the phone against the magnetic surface and the phone snaps against it. It is much more convenient than other phone mounts that use spring-loaded clips. — MF

Gooseneck phone holder

I bought this gooseneck phone holder (Lamicall, $27) on Amazon not knowing what I would use it for exactly, but in what I can only call a "spark of genius," I attached it to my stationary rower so I can watch streamable TV while I row. It has a rubber clamp stand that opens up 2.75 inches, so I can secure it to most furniture in my house. I am working out more and craning my neck less. — CD

Clean the earwax out of AirPods

It's really hard to clean earwax from the speaker meshes in Apple AirPods and EarPods. I've assembled a kit of 3 tools to make the job easier. 1) OXO Good Grips Deep Clean Brush Set ($6) — use the smaller of the two brushes and the silicone wiper to loosen up and wipe out as much wax 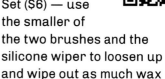 as you can; 2) Poster Putty ($3) — press this into the opening and it will pull out a surprising amount of residual gunk. Resist the temptation to press the putty too hard, or you'll push the earwax through the mesh; 3) Handheld Illuminated Magnifier ($7) — this will help you make sure you've thoroughly cleaned the mesh openings. My AirPods now look great, not grungy. — MF

Self-ID for iPhone

If you find an iPhone and want to know whose it is, who lost it, use that phone to ask Siri: "Siri, who's phone is this?" and it will tell you. — KK

Dictation transcription

Notes is the default built-in note taking app that syncs between Mac OS and iOS. The new thing for me is using it as a dictation device on my iPhone, since I am a lousy thumb typer. When I want to make a note, I depress the microphone icon near the space bar on the virtual keyboard in Notes and talk. My voice is transcribed into text with remarkable accuracy, even in noisy environments. Notes then syncs these written notes onto my laptop. — KK

One-finger zoom

Here's a tip for zooming on smartphone maps. Instead of pinching to zoom, tap the screen twice, but leave your finger on the screen on the second tap. Then slide your finger up or down to zoom in or out. — MF

Control your iPhone cursor

To activate the trackpad, press firmly on any part of the keyboard. When the keyboard becomes grayed out, like this, the trackpad is active.

My recent discovery is that I can use my iPhone keyboard as a mouse to scroll through text and place my cursor exactly where I want it. All you have to do is hard press the keyboard. This makes editing text on an iPhone a million times less frustrating. — CD

Android/iPhone note sharing

Google Keep on iPhone (Free) makes it painless for me and my Android partner to stay

synced-up on shopping lists and reminders. — CD

Better than Snapchat

I use the Marco Polo Video Walkie Talkie app (iOS, Android) to keep in touch with my family who all live far away. I'm in a "group" with my mom, 2 siblings, and 2 nieces. Even though we live in different time zones we can all carry on a coherent conversation and be more connected. I like that I don't have to worry about videos expiring, and when I check in at night the videos I missed load automatically so it plays like a mini-movie of what my family did throughout the day. I also think it's much easier for kids to use than Snapchat. My 6-year-old niece is a pro at using filters to make creative video messages that always crack me up. — CD

View animals in 3D

Tiger

Something cool I just learned is if you have a supported smartphone, you can search for an animal on Google and view it in 3D! Here's instructions on how to do it and a list of all the animals currently available at this time. — CD

Print from your iPhone or iPad

Modern printers are made to allow you to print from your iOS device. But we have an old wireless laser printer and I couldn't get it to play nice with my iPhone. Then I found a $20 Mac app called Printopia. It was surprisingly easy to set up. Now everyone in my family can print from their mobile devices. — MF

Pop-up emoji keyboard (Mac)

Here's a tip for Mac users: Control + Command + Space reveals an emoji keyboard. My friend Glenn Fleishman added an extra tip: "If you type text in the little field, it shows both the literal characters in the

preview, but also any matching text among Unicode, etc. And you can select a character, and it shows alternates that live among the Unicode jungle. 👍— MF

Free app finder

Daily App Advice shows you which paid apps are currently being given away for free in the iTunes App Store. I've found many useful free utilities and games here that usually cost between $1 and $10. — MF

How-to fix your phone

My two-year-old iPhone 6 Plus wasn't holding a charge as well as it used to. I ordered the iFixIt battery replacement kit for $25, which includes necessary tools, and excellent step-by-step instructions (video and PDF). It took less than 30 minutes, and I enjoyed looking at the inside of my iPhone. — MF

PHOTO

Best way to find photos

I use Google's AI to find particular photos out of the 200,000 photos I have taken. First I uploaded all my 200K photos to Google Photos using their app so the upload runs in the background; new photos will automatically be uploaded in the future as well. Then I search through the photos using keywords. I have not labeled, categorized, or captioned any of the images. I type in basic terms, like "barn", or "procession" or "sailboat," and Google will find and display all the pertinent images. It can do simple compound queries like "barn + snow" or "procession + umbrella" that are more selective. It is free. — KK

Legal images

I use Google Images Search anytime I need pictures for a talk, website, presentation, or idea scrapbook. It's not obvious, but you can filter the search results for those images that let you legally reuse them. Click the Tools button (to the right of Settings) beneath the Google search box, select "Usage Rights" and then choose your filter. (You can also filter by color, size, type, etc., in addition to license directly from Advanced Image Search page.) The results will be a pile of select images that have Creative Commons or other fair use status. — KK

Truly free photos

Collection #177 – Unsplash
10 photos · Curated by Unsplash

Unsplash is an online collection of high-quality photos that are free to use for any reason, even commercial purposes. You aren't required to credit the author, but you can if you wish. A good resource for bloggers and designers. — MF

Best free stock photos

AARON'S TOP 5
FREE STOCK SITES

Using an image or photo on a website or social media without permission of the copyright holder could turn out to be an expensive mistake. This YouTube video covers best practices for using other people's images. The best part of the video is the list of excellent free stock websites. Many of the images on these websites are in the public domain, which means you can use them even without crediting the creator. Here are the sites: https://unsplash.com, https://pexels.com, https://pixabay.com, https://barnimages.com. — MF

Free stock images and photos

AllTheFreeStock gives you easy access to a bunch of different sites offering free photos, illustrations, stock videos, sound effects, fonts, and icons. A lot of the stuff is

of surprisingly high quality.
— MF

Download all images from a website

I have a massive "swipe file" of illustrations from online portfolios. I use them for inspiration when I design or draw something. Owidig is a website that can suck every image file from a website and save it to your computer. It's easy to use once you get the hang of it, but here's a good video to get you familiar with it. — MF

Easiest way to make a transparent png

png transparency creator options

I have Photoshop and I've taught myself multiple times how to make a transparent png, but then in a pinch I always forget. So now I just go to this website (Online PNG tools) to quickly convert images into transparent pngs. It's so simple and fast and I don't have to use any brain power. — CD

Easy background removal

Remove.bg became an instant hit, and for good reason. Just upload any photo of a

person, animal, or thing, and it will erase everything in the background, replacing them with transparent pixels. It even works well when the person in the foreground has wispy or curly hair. — MF

Easy image vectorizing

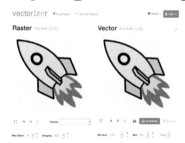

I frequently need to convert a photo or scan into vector art. I typically use Adobe Illustrator's Trace function, but it's finicky. Illustrator is also very expensive. Recently I discovered this $19 app called Super Vectorizer 2 that does just one thing – converts raster images into vector images. I'm impressed with the results. — MF

Fast photo resizing

Upload any image to Web Resizer and shrink it to a manageable size. You can also round the corners, tint or

	Optimized Image	Original Image
size	14.42KB (62% smaller)	38.75KB
width	200 pixels	200 pixels
height	210 pixels	210 pixels

sharpen the image, or apply other filters. It's faster than Photoshop, and free. — MF

Unique photo filters

I needed to make a cartoon thumbnail portrait of myself so I used a free app for iOS and Android to render my photo into artwork. Prisma uses artificial intelligence to "redraw" any photo on your phone into a painting done in 20 different artistic styles, including cartoony ones. (It's similar to a previous app Prizmo, but renders the art almost instantly.) — KK

Pixel art utility

Piskel is a web-based utility for drawing "pixel art" in the vein of retro video games. You can create static or animated images, and download them as animated GIFs. The interface is intuitive. It's surprisingly powerful and fun to use. — MF

Photoshop tutorials

My favorite way to learn new Photoshop techniques is by watching the Phlearn YouTube channel. I've learned how to remove objects, remove backgrounds, touch up skin, remove glare from eyeglasses, and my favorite: how to use the clone stamp tool. — MF

Lightroom tips

These amazingly great tips for using Lightroom are each presented in 1 minute or less. I've been using Lightroom to edit my photos (better than Photoshop) for years and didn't know any of these. — KK

Web-based photoshop clone

I recently discovered Photopea, a free web-based image editor that closely mimics the look and feel of Photoshop. It even imports and exports .PSD files. — MF

Fun and powerful photo editing app

It's incredibly fun to use the Luminar photo editing application to bring my photos to life. It has tons of adjustable preset filters and a lot of specialized tools such as portrait enhancement, where you can make the subject's eyes larger and face thinner. You can also easily add in new skies and even a sun with rays. I typically use the "AI" set of adjustment tools to change the brightness and contrast because it does a great job without a lot of fussing on my part. The developer also has

lots of excellent videos that show you how to use all the features in Luminar. — MF

Photography lessons

I've done a lot of photography but I am still learning. A favorite teacher is Peter McKinnon's YouTube channel. He is the usual hyperactive YouTuber (thus his millions of followers) but he does convey very useful info by showing how he works. For instance his lesson on product photography was neat and satisfying. — KK

Best photography blog

The best photographer blog and/or photo magazine for both pros and newbies, and for all photographers in between, is on the web as PetaPixel. Sure, they have the latest nerdy camera gossip, but they also have plenty of features about the million different ways people actually capture and use images. Every day I am amazed and informed. Add it to your RSS feed. — KK

Best cheap prints

I use my local Costco to get good photo-quality prints from my photo files. They are usually ready to be picked up overnight once uploaded to their website. An 8 x 10 costs $1.79. A huge 20 x 30 inch poster is just $10. The quality is surprisingly decent. — KK

Metal prints from Costco

Everyone is now a photographer and our audience is on the small screen. But there's a real joy in seeing a large image on a wall. The best way to do that is via the Metal Print from Costco Photo. You send a digital file to Costco online and then you pick up the piece at your local store. Your image is printed in gorgeous quality on a thick piece of aluminum sheet so that it is 100% flat and glossy – much flatter than can be done by framing. No glass or plastic cover required, which makes this style very light weight even for big pieces. And since it is frameless, and hung with an internal French cleat, it is cheap. A huge 24 x 36 inch picture, printed and ready to hang in your room or gallery, is $120. A large 11 x 14 is only $34. These show pieces really wow. Even a decent shot from a new phone will work. — KK

Digitizing old photos

A friend who took a mountain of photos in the last century (1950s-90s) recently asked me how to get all his old analog

photos digitized, cataloged, online, and printed. Here is what I told him: I get all my old stuff (slides, negatives, prints) scanned at ScanCafe because the price is right. They have the cheapest yet most reliable scanning service. I box them up quickly and sort them after they are scanned. The files are returned on a DVD or a thumb drive. But you need time, several months, since they send them overseas (with incredible care and safety). — KK

Photo canvases on demand

I've used Canvas on Demand twice now and I am very satisfied with the quality of their premium thick wrap canvases. Sign up for the newsletter and wait for their 50-70% off promos, which happen about once a month. — CD

Best photobooks

Every year for the past decade I've made 2 or 3 commemorative photo books to mark an anniversary, or document a vacation. I've tried just about all the different brands and modes of making photobooks and keep coming back to Blurb. It's not the cheapest, or most expensive; but it's the highest quality and very versatile. You can make a Blurb photo book three ways: 1) Use a layout program like InDesign to custom design your book, exported as a PDF; 2) use the Blurb function built into Lightroom to handily use photos in your LR library; or 3) use Blurb's own fancy app, Bookwright, which will let you grab off-the-shelf templates, or completely customize your own templates. This year so far, I've made a small 20-page book, a huge 400-page book, and am working on another one. — KK

Pretty framing

Framebridge has the best looking selection of affordable frames that I have seen online. I ordered a digital print framed in gold bamboo

because I wanted to break up all the wooden frames we have hanging, and it looks fantastic! The print quality was great and it was delivered within 7 days. — CD

Instant photo prints

I will never go back to analog film, no matter how retro hip it becomes. Digital photography is just better in all respects — except for one special case. When I shoot in exotic localities I carry a Fuji Instax Mini which produces small — quite small — instant prints, similar to Polaroids. Portraits done with these and instantly handed out are wonderful icebreakers. Popular at parties as a mini photo-booth, too. — KK

Compact photo printer

My favorite use for the Fujifilm Instax printer is for printing out small photo gifts. It's portable, so you can take it to parties, and it only takes a few minutes to wirelessly connect and print out photos straight from your phone. — CD

Backpackable photo drone

I wanted a tiny starter drone for taking mostly still photos from on high. The DJI Spark (about $350) fits the bill. It's so small and lightweight it fits easily in my daybag. About the size of my open hand, I operate it from an app on my phone. Its range (via the phone) is about 100 meters, which is all I need. Lasts 15 minutes per charge. Despite its smallness, it does pretty well in a stiff wind. — KK

Ultimate portable tripod

I believe in "earning" any best-in-class tools; start out cheap and move up through use. Over my 50 years in photography I've used and owned many tripods, so I was ready — and willing to pay for — a world-class state-of-the art tripod. Last year on Kickstarter I sprung for what I consider the best portable travel tripod ever. It's a carbon-fiber Peak Design Tripod. It's ingeniously compact (full size folds into the diameter of a water bottle), feather lightweight, opens and closes rapidly easily, and is remarkably ridgid, even at 6 feet. Its head mount is fast, fluid, and agile. It fits into a daypack or carry-on luggage, and is optimized for a tripod you have to carry a lot, but of course works in a studio as well. The Peak Tripod is a masterpiece of design and fabrication. I love using it. The aluminum version is $350, while the ultimate carbon-fiber model is $600. — KK

BROWSER

Organize multiple window screens

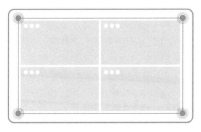

Magnet is a window manager for Mac that lets me quickly resize and organize up to 4 windows per screen using keyboard shortcuts. It is a must-have productivity tool and it's only 99 cents. — CD

Website status checker

If you're getting a 404 error while trying to view a website, it's not always clear where the problem is coming from. If you enter the URL at Down For Everyone Or Just Me you'll find out if the website is actually down for everyone or the problem is somewhere else. — MF

Go dark

I recently upgraded my Macbook to Mojave and I'm loving the new Dark Mode. Then I discovered Dark Reader, the Chrome extension that makes every website dark and now everything is easy on the eyes. You can toggle the extension on and off so you don't have to commit to one mode. I find that it's hard for me to free write on a dark screen, so I keep my Gmail and Evernote in light mode. — CD

Find similar websites

The Google Similar Pages Chrome extension helps you quickly find websites similar to the page you are currently browsing. — CD

Website not loading? Get the Google Cache

Sometimes a website is temporarily offline. It could be that the server is down, or the site is experiencing unusually high traffic. If that's the case, enter the URL at the Cached Views website to see what the page looked like when Google's indexing spider last scanned it. — MF

Block specific sites from Google search results

I use a Google Chrome extension called uBlacklist to stop Pinterest results from showing up in Google searches. You can create a list of other sites you don't want to show up in search results, too. uBlacklist replaced Google's Personal Blocklist extension, which it got rid of a while ago. — MF

BOOKMARKS

Organize bookmarks bar

I'm a **vertical** separator. Drag **me** to your bookmarks *toolbar*.

I used a link from this page and dragged vertical lines into my bookmarks bar to separate and group related links. This works best if you've created an icon-only bookmarks bar and move all your folders off to the side.
— CD

Every bookmark manager ever made

My bookmarks are getting out of hand, so I knew I had to devote some time to finding a manageable solution. This is a great list of "Every bookmark manager ever made" (last updated November 2019). Thanks to that list, I went with the app that I found most visually-appealing, called Raindrop. io ($28 yearly), which lets me do a full-text search of every webpage I've ever saved.
— CD

Get reminded of links at your convenience

Never lose another link.

Save interesting links and Link Drop will send them straight to your inbox whenever you want.

I've been using my Pocket extension less and this Link Drop Chrome extension more. If there is an article or webpage that I want to check out, this bookmark tool helps to ensure I get to it before the end of the day. Every link I save gets emailed back to me at 3PM that same day as a reminder. You can change the "drop time" to whatever works for you.
— CD

Rediscover things you saved

I uploaded a copy of my Chrome bookmarks to Mailist, and now once a week I get an email newsletter with 10 random links to pages and sites I have saved. It has reunited me with travel ideas, things I want to buy, and useful online tools. I also use it as a way to clean house and delete bookmarks I no longer have use for.
— CD

Clean up bookmarks bar

I was excited to find out that I could create more room on my Chrome bookmarks bar just by right clicking edit and deleting the text. Now all I have are favicons to click on and my browser looks much neater and organized. Works on Firefox too, just right-click properties. — CD

Quickest way to start a new Google Doc

If you use Google Docs, Sheets, Forms, Slides, or Sites, here's a tip. Just enter doc. new, sheet.new, etc. into your browser and it will instantly create a new, blank version.
— MF

Google search tips

Type "movies" and your zip code to see what's playing in theaters near you. Enter a flight number to see the status of the plane. Enter any shipper's tracking number to see where your package is.
— MF

Chrome tips

Title of this article says it all: 27 useful things you didn't know the Chrome browser could do. Pretty neat. — KK

Read only what you want

The Just Read Chrome extension blocks pop-ups and makes ad-smothered webpages easy on the eyes. You can select and isolate the text you want to read, delete elements, customize styling, and print. I've been using it daily. – CD

Easier website reading

I use Chrome, and when I want to read an article, I click the Reader View extension icon in my tool bar. It makes the text larger and gets rid of ads and clutter. (Safari has this feature built-in.) It also tells you how long it will take to read the article. — MF

Download an entire archive.org collection

Lately, I've been listening to cassette tapes from the 1980s and 1990s on archive.org. I was able to download the entire collection of tapes by using a Google Chrome extension called Archive Downloader. Once it was installed, I went to the page at archive.org and clicked the Archive Downloader extension icon on my browser. Then I selected the mp3 files from a pop-up list and downloaded them. — MF

Wayback chrome extension

The Internet Archive has a chrome extension for their Wayback Machine that has become essential to my browsing. I can search through previous versions, lookup domain info and traffic statistics, and I can even look at public tweets linking back to the website. — CD

Extract images from Google docs

Why can't I just right-click on a Google Docs image to download it to my computer? Until Google allows that, I'll use

this free add-on called Image Extractor. To install it, scroll down to Method 3 here. — MF

Quick definitions

You can easily look up the meaning of words by entering define:word in your browser's search bar, like this define:doryphore. — MF

Open last browser tab

Reopen the last browser tab you closed by pressing ctrl + shift + t (Windows) or cmd + shift + t (Mac) — MF

Browser trick

If you type something in the URL bar and then press control + enter, whatever you type will be surrounded by www. and .com. — MF

LinkedIn email finder

I use LinkedIn to get in touch with people for stories and interviews, but I don't like using the built-in messaging service (InMail). I'd rather email the person, but LinkedIn doesn't provide email addresses (they want you to do everything in the confines of their walled garden). I use a Chrome extension called ContactOut which provides a pop-up with the person's email address. It hasn't failed me yet. — MF

Website email finder

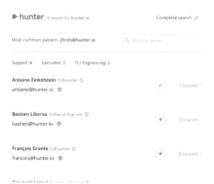

Hunter lets you quickly find personal and support email addresses from any company website. I have the chrome extension and it's great for when I have a customer service or billing issue and want a response as soon as possible. I cc: all the relevant generic email addresses for the company and so far have gotten a response and issue resolved within hours. — CD

.new shortcuts

Google's .new domains are exclusively reserved for action-based shortcuts, like doc.new for creating a new Google Doc. And now there's a growing list of companies who have created easy-to-remember shortcuts for things you might already do. Like "story.new" to create a new post on Medium or "sell.new" to create a new listing on eBay. For the up-to-date list check out this page. — CD

Change the color of hyperlinks

When I look at Google search results in the Chrome browser, I have difficulty telling the difference between the default colors of the links for previously visited and unvisited sites. One is blue and the other is blue-purple. I found a Chrome extension that solves my problem. It's called Color Links. It does just one thing - lets me choose a custom color for visited links. There's no mistaking one type of link for the other now. — MF

Open all links at once

With the Linkclump extension I can drag and select all the links on one page and open them up all at once. It's a real timesaver when I'm proofreading and need to make sure all the embedded links redirect to the right places. — CD

Force a public Wi-Fi login page to open

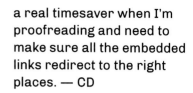

Here's a problem I frequently encounter when I'm trying to use public Wi-Fi at the airport — the login page won't load on my browser. This troubleshooting cheat sheet lists the different things you can try to get a Wi-Fi login page to open. In short, they are: 1) Turn off alternative DNS servers; 2) Try to open the router's default page; 3) Open a non-HTTPS site in incognito; 4) Restart your device; 5) Create a new network location. One or more of these actions usually does the trick. — MF

A better way to connect to stubborn airport WiFi

A while back I recommended some troubleshooting tips for forcing a public Wi-Fi login page to open. A Recomendo reader ("J.C.") sent me a superior tip: just enter "http://neverssl.com" and the access point's login page will load. On my last trip I used it at the airport and on the plane and it worked like a charm. — MF

UTILITIES

Mac OS installer on a flash drive

I had a spare MacBook Air that was running the Linux OS. My daughter suddenly needed a laptop to replace her recently broken one, and so I had to reinstall the Mac OS on the Air. I had difficulty figuring out how to do it until I came across this Apple website that explained how to create a bootable installer for MacOS on a flash drive. Now I have an emergency USB drive and I'm sure it will come in handy again. — MF

Use cloud storage like a local drive

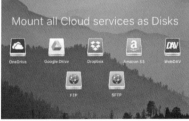

Mount all Cloud services as Disks

I use several cloud storage services. The easiest way to access them is with CloudMounter, a $49 Mac utility that mounts OneDrive, Google Drive, Amazon S3, Dropbox, and others as local hard drives on my desktop. Setup

was painless and it works flawlessly. — MF

Over 180 useful Mac apps for $10 a month

Setapp is a subscription service for Mac applications. I pay $10 a month for over 180 useful applications. I don't use all of them, but the ones I use are indispensable throughout my day. I use Meeter to quickly enter scheduled Zoom meetings. I use Mosaic to move and place windows on my desktop. CleanMyMac X has a bunch of useful utilities to free up disk space and delete apps and large files. IM+ puts my Google chats and Slack groups into one convenient place. Downie makes it easy to download YouTube videos. Forecast bar is a great menu bar weather application. I could go on and on, but you get the idea. Setapp also adds new applications into their offerings frequently, and I'm always eager to check them out. If you have a Mac

and are interested in design, productivity, and utilities, this is a no-brainer. (I've mentioned Setapp on Recomendo before but they've added so many useful apps to their collection that it was time for an update.) — MF

Keep your Mac clean

I've been using a utility called CleanMyMac X for a number of years. I use it to completely delete applications (and all their associated files), locate and delete space-wasting unneeded files, and scan for malware. It has a lot of other features, all of which are presented in a simple interface. — MF

Speed for slow typists

I've been using TextExpander for at least 10 years and it has saved me hundreds of hours of typing. It's a global utility that converts short snippets of text into canned text. For instance, when I type "mf" it changes it to "Mark Frauenfelder." When I type "adr" it changes it to my home address. "Bio" spits out my biography and a link to my headshot photos. I have a lot of canned boilerplates for email responses that save me a ton of time. It can also add anything that's saved in my clipboard to a chunk of boilerplate. It also corrects frequently misspelled words. The Mac OS has snippet expansion but lacks many of the features and the snap of TextExpander. I can't stand using other people's computers to write or do email because not having TextExpander slows me way down. — MF

Easy file format conversion

Permute is a Macintosh desktop app that converts video, audio, and image files from one format to another. It's versatile and has not failed me yet. I was able to use it to convert a video that was terribly jittery that no other application could fix, but Permute converted it to an mp4 and it came out perfect. It costs $15 from the developer and it also comes with Setapp's large library of applications available by subscription for $10 a month, which is how I found it. — MF

Easy unlimited backups

You can't have too many backups. You need at least one off-site online backup of your work. I previously recommended Crashplan but they have fallen behind in user interface, speed, and price. I am now a happy user of Backblaze, which has an unlimited plan for $60 a year. I back up 5 Terabytes (!!) of photos and videos (from more than one disk), and Backblaze was quick uploading and is super easy to manage. — KK

Better Dictation

Over the last couple of years, I've been teaching myself to touch-type, but my progress has been slow and frustrating. I tried Apple's built-in speech-to-text feature, but it has a bad habit of shutting off while I'm speaking. I recently discovered Dictanote (which runs in Google Chrome), and I really like its accuracy and the way it doesn't shut off while

I'm using it. It has a number of other features too, such as custom voice commands, which will paste text snippets triggered by a spoken phrase. I use it to write blog posts, reports, a novel I'm working on, and this newsletter. I now consider it to be a mission-critical tool. A lifetime subscription to Dictanote is $19. — MF

Improved Dictanote

I recommended Dictanote a few weeks ago. It's a Chrome-based application that converts speech to text. It's faster and less buggy than my Mac's built-in dictation. Recently, Dictanote released a Google Chrome extension that lets you use Dictanote within almost any website. Now I'm using it to answer emails in Gmail, which has been a big timesaver. It doesn't work with Google Docs, which is unfortunate, but for longer form speech-to-text writing I use Dictanote's notebook and copy and paste the text (in fact, I'm using the notebook to write this recommendation). It's $19, and because I'm such a terrible typist, it paid for itself within the first day or two. — MF

High-quality computer transcripts

I've been using Rev.com for transcripts of audio conversations. It's $1 a minute. But I recently tried Trint.com, which uses software instead of humans to turn recordings into text, and it was as good as Rev.com. It's 25 cents a minute. Worth a try! — MF

Dirt cheap transcription

VoiceBase takes audio recordings and turns them into text. It also analyzes the text to identify subjects and keywords, and can play back the audio as it highlights the text. It's not as good as a human transcriber, but it does a decent job and is much cheaper (2 cents a minute compared to $1 a minute for a human) .You get $60 in free credit to try it out, too. — MF

VIDEO

Cheap stock images and videos

Jumpstory is a royalty-free stock image and video service with millions of photos, videos, and illustrations that you can use for websites, books, presentations, and more. The images have been curated from public domain sources, and they've done a great job of tagging and organizing everything. I use Jumpstory images on my website, Boing Boing. A lifetime subscription is $99. — MF

Live streaming broadcast studio

I've been a guest on a number of live streams that use StreamYard. StreamYard is the emerging tool that enables you to broadcast live streaming video. The host invites up to 10 different guests to join via their incoming video connections. The guests meet off camera in a "green room." Then like a studio producer, the host can mix which guests appear in the stream, which remain on deck in the green room, which other visuals to show, and have overall control of what is streamed out live to YouTube, Facebook, etc., or your own website. Works pretty well. Conceptually this is a mini-broadcasting studio. It costs $25 per month to host, with a free trial option. Guests only require a web browser. — KK

Using your phone as webcam

Your phone is probably a better camera for streaming than your laptop or third-party webcam you are now using. To see how you can use your phone as a webcam, check out this technical video from Norm Chan at Tested. You'll need two free open-source apps on your computer, and an inexpensive app on your phone. Following the instructions I got very high-quality streams from my iPhone 8. This is good for YouTube, Facebook, and Twitch streams but not for Zoom, Meet and other video conferencing yet. — KK

AUDIO

Audio utility

The free NaturalReader smartphone app (iOS and Android) converts text to speech. To use it, open the app, select a document from DropBox, Google Reader, or a website. NaturalReader will upload it and read it in a voice of your choosing. — MF

Best song identifier

I've been using the SoundHound smartphone app for years to identify songs, but my 15-year-old told me to switch to Shazam. She's right, it's much easier to use the features that I need. My favorite way to use: If I'm in a store or a coffee shop that's playing unfamiliar music that sounds great, I just press the large button on the screen and it will grab the title and artist of every song and save it for later. I can then easily add the songs to Apple Music (you can also save to Spotify) and save them to my library. — MF

What song is that?

Maybe everyone already knows this, but I just figured out you can ask Siri on your phone to identify music playing in the background. No need to load an app; similar function is built in to Android, too. But further coolness: if you go into the iPhone's iTunes Store app, tap Menu upper left, then tap Siri, you get a list of all your queries so that, of course, if you want to buy the music, there it is. At least it's a way to record/remember the new tunes. — KK

Figure out what song was playing

Whenever I'm watching TV and a song catches my ear, I often don't have the chance to ask Siri what it is. Tunefind is great for that, because the next day I can just look up whatever show I was watching and listen to clips of all the songs that were played during that episode. Once I find the song, I can be redirected to listen on Spotify or search for the song on YouTube. — CD

Measuring noise with your phone

Decibel X is an app for the iPhone ($3.99 per month, also available on Android) that is a noise meter. It pretty accurately measures noise on a decibel scale. I use it to monitor the noise levels in restaurants and workplaces in an effort to increase quiet. When I am recording podcasts I use it to ensure there's little background noise. It's also entertaining and instructive to measure sound levels outside in nature and urban areas. — KK

Better volume control

If you have a Mac, holding option(alt) + shift while pressing the volume up/down buttons adjusts the volume in quarters. Before I discovered this, I was always toggling between my Mac and media player buttons to find the perfect volume. — CD

Best portable audio capture

I upgraded my audio capture for video. For the past year when I make videos I have been using a Rode Wireless Go microphone and receiver. The system is two small squares each about the size of an Apple watch. One slips onto the hotshoe of a camera, and plugs into the Mic jack, the other rides in the pocket of the subject speaking (or clips onto their clothing) and connects to a small lapel mic. From up to 100 meters away, your camera will record sound/voice in excellent fidelity, even if the subject is moving. No wires, no sound boom. It's tiny and featherlight, and works instantly with plug and play. Best of all its cheap audio — $200 for the set. I highly recommend. — KK

Learn what synthesizers do

I spent 45 minutes interacting with the sliders and buttons at Learning Synths and now I understand concepts like envelope, attack, decay, sustain, and release. I was having so much fun I didn't realize I was being taught a lesson, either. — MF

Inexpensive MIDI keyboard

My 16-year-old daughter and I like listening to lo-fi electronic music in the car, and we got interested in making some lo-fi music of our own. Instead of buying a synthesizer, we just bought this cheap 32-key MIDI keyboard (Model AKM320). We are using it with Apple's Garageband app, which has built-in software synths. It was literally plug-and-play, because it required no software drivers. It comes with a USB cable. — MF

Free music soundtracks for video

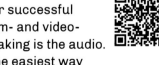

The secret sauce for successful film- and video-making is the audio. The easiest way to add a musical score and sound effects to home-made video, particularly if you will be uploading it to YouTube, is to use the large collection of license-free music and effects in the YouTube Audio library. It's free. Many tracks are pretty good. And the music is guaranteed to be "clear" and not cause copyright or monetization issues on YouTube. I've been using them on my videos. — KK

Free music for videos and other projects

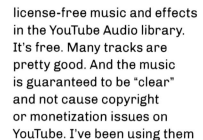

Dig CC Mixter is a library of music you can use for free in videos, performances, podcasts, video games, or other projects. It's well organized and it's easy to listen to samples of the music. — MF

Free sound effects

Get free, high-quality sound effects of almost anything you can think of for your podcasts, apps, or movies at Freesound. — MF

Movie scores

Some of the best music being written these days is for movie soundtracks. Because they usually lack dialogue and lyrics, I find movie scores easy to listen to while working. If you want some suggestions to start with, this is a decent list of the best scores since the start of this century. Quite a few of them are available on Spotify. — KK

DESIGN

Typeset in the Future

I'm spending hours studying this coffee-table book celebrating the typography and design used in science fiction movies. What do we see on screens "in the future"? More broadly, this dense picture book, Typeset in the Future, is a roundabout way to examine where the interface design of technology is headed. — KK

Early Bird Fonts

Future Fonts is a website where type designers offer early versions of beautiful typefaces at low prices ($5 and up). Some are not 100 percent finished but work for many applications. If you buy a typeface, you are guaranteed to get free updates. — MF

Classy free fonts

There are about 1,000 very classy fonts available for free on Google Fonts. These are fonts you would actually want to use in your book or on your website. Some are commissioned by Google and designed by world-class typographers, such as the font Roboto used in Google Maps. Many of these fonts come as families with different weights, italic, bold, extra glyphs, etc. This set of open fonts is also offered by Adobe and Monotype; what Google Fonts offers is a very nifty web interface for navigating through the collection, including good search and filtering. I particularly like their font "pairing" function, which suggests good combinations of fonts (like text and captions pairings). All the fonts are license-free. — KK

Downloadable fonts

AaBbCcDdEeFfGg

Fontsquirrel.com has tons of free fonts, classified by type (e.g., pixel, grunge, retro, etc). They also have very nice "almost free" fonts, usually costing less than $10. — MF

Quick formatting tools

UPPER CASE   Capitalized Case   aLtErNaTiNg cAsE

Two of my favorite bookmarked sites for quick formatting fixes are StripHTML and Convert Case. StripHTML strips all formatting from text, and Convert Case transforms text to lower case, all caps, sentence case, title case, etc. — CD

Digitize printed text

When I need to quote a passage from a paper book or a Kindle, I take

a photo of the page with the TextGrabber app (free for Android/iOS). It scans it and turns it into ASCII text, which can be emailed, texted, or saved. It's very accurate and has saved me a lot of time. — MF

Web graphic tool

I wish I'd found Snappa sooner. It's an online tool for creating web and social media graphic tiles from photos or art. You can upload your own images, or use their images. You can go as simple or as wild as you want with the modification options. A basic account is free. — MF

Graphic inspiration

I collect visual reference books to provoke me when I make things. I recently discovered the work of the prolific illustrator Charley

Harper, who in part created the graphic look of the 1950s and 60s. His illustrations are witty, spiffy, and timeless. Many hundreds of his designs have been gathered into a nifty book called Charley Harper: An Illustrated Life. It's not nostalgia: I get at least 10 new ideas each time I open it. — KK

Design inspiration

If you are looking for an illustrator or looking for inspiration for your own design, Dribbble is a fine place to

start. Enter a search term and you'll be presented with a grid display of work by dozens or hundreds of contemporary designers. You can save your favorite images to any number of "buckets" for later perusal. — MF

Email design database

If you're in the newsletter business, Really Good Emails has a huge database of marketing emails and newsletters that you can search for inspiration. You can "collect" designs that you like, view code, and see examples of how it looks across different email clients and devices. — CD

The best of design thinking

I loved the first season of Abstract on Netflix. Each episode playfully explores a field of design by closely following the work of a key designer in that field. Toys, cars, costumes. To investigate typography, they follow the efforts of a type designer as he tries to design a new specialty font, explaining how all fonts work. That goodness was exceeded by the new Season 2, which has even more brilliant expositions. Since each episode is crafted by a different director, the format of the show is itself innovative and creative. Every minute is a joy. — KK

DESIGN

Logo inspiration

I have started dozens of projects and ventures that require logos. Logobook is an online library of thousands of logos, organized in categories. It's fun to browse if you're logo-curious like me. They are all black and white, which I like. (All logos should have black and white versions.) — MF

Characters that aren't on your keyboard

A lot of characters aren't on your keyboard, but you might find them useful. An easy way to browse and use these hidden characters is by visiting Symbololology, a one-page site with about 500 non-keyboard characters. Symbololology, where have you been all my life? — MF

Emoji to go

Microsoft

Samsung

WhatsApp

I found a good searchable emoji database. You can search for emoji by subject, and when you find one you like, just copy and paste it as you would with any text-based character. — MF

Icons for everything

Icons for everything

The Noun Project is a huge searchable database of icons you can use in PowerPoint slides, websites, signs, or for any project requiring symbols. As a test, I searched on the word "chicken" and got hundreds and hundreds of chicken-related icons. Most of the icons are free under a Creative Commons license, and if you pay a small fee, you don't have to credit the creator. — MF

3D design skill tutorial

SketchUp is a general-purpose 3D design software for makers that is free in its basic version, and is very popular. There are dozens of other programs for precision parts, or organic shapes, but SketchUp scales nicely between 3D printing to woodworking to architecture, and is super easy to learn. By far the best tutorial on how to learn SketchUp (a skill transferable to most other 3D apps) is this free YouTube series, SketchUp Tutorial by April Wilkerson. She is an ace teacher, with the kind of practical hints I needed. — KK

Online figure drawing

I live close to the Art Director's Guild headquarters in Los Angeles, which has weekly evening figure drawing classes. My daughter and I go there occasionally, but I recently discovered a site called Line of Action that has a useful figure drawing practice system. It shows you a series of figure models posing for specified periods of time, just like a real figure drawing session. The hands-and-feet tool is especially useful (and challenging) for me. — MF

Geological modern art

Some of the best modern art on my walls are geological maps. These graphics are bright and cheerful while boasting scientific integrity. Geology from around the world can be used, but I favor geologically extreme places like this sample from Utah. For

a maximum of both art and science I highly recommend the Geologic Atlas of the Moon maps. Last printed in 1977, these Pop Art gems are now available as downloadable PDFs. (Crop and save as a jpeg.) I print mine on a 20 x 30 inch Costco poster board for $25. — KK

Huge gallery of high-res retro art

Believe it or not, Flickr is still around, and I hope it stays because it's a great place to store and share images. One of my favorite Flickr folks is designer James Vaughan, who has amassed a gallery of over 20,000 images from decades past, including advertising illustrations, paperback book covers, movie posters, LP covers, and more. I frequently get lost here. — MF

Generating art

I've waited all my life for a tool that would create art for me. It's here. Artbreeder

is a website that breeds new visual images from existing images. Using deep learning (AI) algorithms it generates multiple photo-realistic "children" mutations of one image. You — the gardener — select one mutant you like and then breed further generations from its descendants. You can also crossbreed two different images. Very quickly, you can create infinite numbers of highly detailed album covers, logos, game characters, and exotic landscapes. I find it fiendishly addictive. — KK

The exciting world of procedural generation

I recently came across a subreddit called r/proceduralgeneration. Here, you'll see examples of amazing artwork, animated lifeforms, game environments, fantasy maps, and more, all created from algorithms (as opposed to being created directly by a human). If you doubt that software can produce beautiful and original art that surprises even the people who write the programs, this subreddit might change your mind. — MF

Design your own shirt

I've ordered a few custom t-shirts from Uber Prints, and I am very happy with their customer service and product. They have recently widened their selection of styles, and for most there is no minimum order requirement. — CD

Vintage sewing patterns

Vintage Patterns Wikia is a collaborative website where you can search through pages and pages of sewing patterns from the past. A lot of the patterns are available and for sale on eBay or Etsy, and if they're not, you can add your contact information to the wiki page in case it becomes available in the future. I found a $2 robe pattern in great condition through the site. — CD

MONEY

Money management

I'm liking the new Mint much more than before. Now that it's merged with Mint Bills, I can manage both bills and accounts in one place, and it was a lot easier to connect to all my accounts than before. Also, being able to view all my transactions in one place and categorize them permanently makes budgeting painless.
— CD

Online piggy bank

I've been using Smarty Pig for years. It's a website where you create a savings goal by specifying a date and an amount of money that you want to have saved by that time. Smarty Pig will transfer funds from your bank each month so that you meet your savings goal. I've used it for vacations, computers, insurance premiums, and holiday shopping. — MF

A home budget that makes sense to me

For years I've tried to keep a home budget, but it never seems to work. I end up spending more than I budgeted in some categories, less in others, and I don't keep good track of what I've spent. When our Cool Tools podcast guest Lillian Karabaic recommended something called You Need a Budget (YNAB) a couple of months ago, I decided to give it a try. I'm glad I did. YNAB's websites and mobile apps are excellent, as are the podcasts, videos, blog posts, and mailing lists they produce. It took me a while to wrap my head around the YNAB method, but now that I get it, I'm a true believer. For the first time in my adult life, I feel in control of my finances.
— MF

Hire a negotiator to lower your bills

Trim is an online service that negotiates with your phone, cable TV, and Internet providers to reduce your monthly bill by asking for a discount. Sure, I could do this myself, but I'm happy to pay someone else a 33% commission on the money they save me. So far they've successfully reduced my annual bills by $543.24.
— MF

Grocery shopping tips

Living in SF and lack of parking makes me avoid grocery shopping. I buy in bulk and use grocery delivery services when I can, but there are minimum purchases for free delivery and sometimes the prices are marked up. Greatist has research-backed tips for more efficient in-store shopping. Planning the week's dinners and committing to a list has helped me minimize unnecessary trips. Listening to music and avoiding all other aisles are helpful too. — CD

Budgeting tip

I appreciate this r/personalfinance tip to control impulse purchases by adding things to a wishlist first. I sort of already

do this by "saving for later" a lot items on Amazon, but I will definitely practice this more intently and wait a week before I buy anything that is not necessary. — CD

Personal finance advice

This interview of Ramit Sethi by Tim Ferris gives an alternative view of personal finances, which I thought was refreshing and worth listening to. Sethi advocates selective thrift in order to permit passion spending in one area, the value of access over ownership, and other heresies. He also discusses pre-nups, which he rightly claims, is discussed nowhere else. — KK

Best credit card for Amazon

I'm a very happy Amazon Prime customer. The free shipping and other benefits make the $119 annual fee well worth it. I also have the Amazon Prime Rewards Visa Signature Card, which I use to make all my purchases on Amazon, because you get 5% on every purchase you make on the site. Amazon is offering a $100 Amazon.com Gift Card instantly upon credit card approval when you apply for a card. — MF

CRYPTOCURRENCY

Bitcoin for the Befuddled

I've taken a deep dive into Bitcoin and blockchains for the last couple of years and have read about a dozen books on the subject. Bitcoin for the Befuddled is the book I recommend to anyone who asks me where to start. It does a great job of explaining how Bitcoin works, going into detail without being overly complex. — MF

Interested in Bitcoin? You need a hardware wallet

I wrote a story for Wired about forgetting my password on a small USB device that stored my bitcoin keys and how I hired a hacker to help me unlock it. Despite my experience, I'm still using the same hardware wallet (the manufacturer updated the firmware to address the exploit) because it's still the best way to keep hackers away from your cryptocurrency. It's called a Trezor and it costs about $85. If you have more the $1000 in bitcoin, ether, bitcoin cash, or other cryptocurrency, I recommend getting one. — MF

Free Princeton video series on cryptocurrencies

The Bitcoin and Cryptocurrency Technologies Online Course is a 13-hour video series from Princeton. After a very brief introductory video, they get right down to business with a video about hash functions that's easy to understand. You can also download a companion textbook. — MF

Shop with Bitcoin on Amazon

I have a small amount of money in the form of bitcoin. I discovered Purse, which lets me buy things on Amazon using bitcoin at a 15% discount. So far I've purchased two items over $100 each, and it has worked without a hitch. — MF

Personal charitable foundation

If you were lucky to acquire some wealth — and let's be honest, this is mostly luck — a sensible way to pay it forward is by funding some needed non-profits. Let's say you scored a bonus, an IPO, a bitcoin sale, early tech stock, or an inheritance. A donor-advised fund (DAF) is an easy way to gain the advantages of a personal foundation, without the hassles or expense of a personal foundation. A DAF is basically a mutual fund investment that you contribute to with cash or by transferring existing stock, with immediate tax benefits, and all the financial growth over time from that investment is completely tax free. But everything in the account, including gains, must be given to certified non-profits of your choice. You can start small. Fund aggregators like Fidelity, Schwab and Vanguard offer them. I recommend the Fidelity Charitable DAF which I have been using for several decades. Very clean, quick online interface. — KK

High-leverage philanthropy

I've been making micro-loans to entrepreneurs in the developing world via Kiva for 10 years. I loan small amounts (less than $100) to say, women in Africa hoping to buy a sewing machine to start their own sewing business, or herders in Bolivia needing some equipment to make cheese, and soon enough they will repay the loan, so I can re-loan the money again to someone else. I've gone through 4 cycles of loans for my first money, and there is less than 0.1% delinquency — a rate any bank would die for. 100% of my money goes to helping the individuals I select; Kiva's operating costs are funded separately. The money keeps going around. It's one of the best bargains in the world. — KK

Equipping students

Few things in life are as satisfying as getting handwritten thank-you notes from school kids for helping them learn. DonorsChoose is a non-profit that features thousands of public school teachers seeking basic school supplies, or extra gear for special projects (rocket kits for science!). The teachers post their pitch. You choose a project. When it gets fully funded they post verification pictures of the kids using the resource which your funds provided, and later they'll send you a fistful of amazingly detailed (and endearing) letters from the students themselves. You'll want to do this. — KK

Free US tax software

You can access federal tax filing software for free from the IRS. The IRS Free File webpage is hard to find because paid tax software vendors like Intuit's TurboTax overwhelm Google with ads for pseudo-free software. Intuit successfully lobbied the US government to prevent the feds from making free tax software widely available, and in a compromise, Intuit offers IRS Free File by Turbotax, free tax prep software for anyone earning less than $36,000 per year. — KK

US and World debt clocks

This website is a dashboard view of national debt, student loan debt, budget items, tax revenue, jobs, and dozens of other rapidly rising numbers. It also has a page of debt numbers for other countries. It's alarming to watch the numbers rise before your eyes. What can be done about it? — MF

SECURITY

Password manager

If you are not already using a password manager like 1Password, Dashlane, or LastPass you are inviting trouble. I am not a very security-minded person generally, but a password manager on your phone, tablets, laptops and desktops is outright essential today. Let it generate strong passwords for you, keep your credit card and bank info, and supply them wherever and whenever you need them. No regrets. — KK

Secure messaging

Edward Snowden recommends the free encrypted chat and call app Signal. It works on

Android, iOS and the desktop. Built by volunteer Open Source contributors and a group of grant-funded developers, Signal is slick and solid. I'm asking everyone I know to start using it. — MF

A beginner's guide to online security

APPS

 IVPN

 Encrypt.me

 ExpressVPN

Securitycheckli.st, is a clear guide for staying safe online. There's no fluff or marketing, just the straight dope on how to use a password manager,

create a strong device passcode, use two-factor authentication, set up a mobile carrier PIN, and much more. — MF

Virtual credit card

Privacy is a browser extension that generates a virtual credit card for each online purchase you make. It offers different options when you create a virtual card — you can make a one-time-use card, a card with a limit (so that it expires once a certain amount is spent), or other kinds of limits. This seems like a great way to protect yourself from getting scammed by one of those sites that trick you into unwittingly signing up for a nearly-impossible-to-cancel monthly fee for something. — MF

Downloading my Facebook data

I'm keeping my Facebook account, but for educational purposes I downloaded all the data Facebook has on me. I highly recommend you do the same, just so you know what the bargain is. Start with this link, and follow the directions. You'll get an email with a new link that will enable you to download a zip file. The folder with the most goodies is the Index page. Go back and adjust your privacy settings as desired. — KK

Mobile justice

If you spot police officers doing something wrong, you can record them with the free Mobile Justice app from the ACLU. It sends the video directly to an ACLU server so even if the police illegally confiscate your phone they won't be able to delete the incriminating video. — MF

See what other websites know about you

Visit Webkay to see what any website you visit knows about you, including your location, the device you are using, your IP address, social media accounts you are logged in to, and more. It also tells you how to plug these information leaks by using various services. — MF

Hacker checkup

As part of my regular digital hygiene I type my email into the website "Have I Been Pwned?" to see if my email/password has been leaked to hackers by a sloppy company. They will tell me if and when a breach occurred which yielded my email on a list for sale on the dark web. This is an indication to change my password for that login. The check site is free, instant, no signups, and specific in needed action. — KK

Have you been hacked?

8

TOTAL PERSONAL RECORDS EXPOSED

SpyCloud is a scary and useful website. Scary, because it showed me how many times my passwords have been hacked from website databases. Useful, because I quickly changed those passwords to protect myself. A personal account is free. Do this now. — MF

Keep tabs on neighborhood crime

If you don't have a Ring doorbell or security camera installed, you can still be alerted of nearby crimes and theft using the Neighbors by Ring app. Once you set up the parameters for your neighborhood you can watch video footage of suspicious activity posted by neighbors (up to 5 miles away). I already own Ring products, so I set up the free Neighbors app to alert me of crimes in my Dad's neighborhood that I can then forward on to him.— CD

Tip to keep your home address off the internet

This tip comes from my friend Cory Doctorow, my  co-editor at Boing Boing. Last year he posted a tip on how to keep your name and address off the internet. I've been using his tip and it works. He wrote,

"There are dozens of free "peoplefinder" sites that buy up commercial databases and combine them with other sources to make your home address searchable. You can find instances where this has happened to you by googling your name and home address, and then you can google the removal forms for each of the services and get yourself delisted. But your name will keep getting re-added: if you set a Google Alert for a search on your name and address, you'll get a message every time you get caught in these databases and you can remove your name again. This won't work on the for-pay background check sites that Google doesn't index, but it will keep your name and address clear of low-level scumbags who stick with free sites for their doxing activities." — MF

Advanced internet security

Some folks such as journalists, activists, tech executives, crypto fans, and politicians may need more online security beyond the already strong

2-factor authentication they should be using. Google offers an Advance Protection Program for the legitimately paranoid. — KK

Best Mac disk space management tool for non-techies

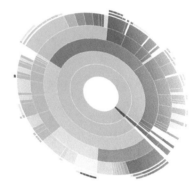

I use my DaisyDisk app ($10) at least once a month to keep on top of what's hogging up my disk space – usually it's Dropbox folders that are synced locally that don't need to be, or really large files I downloaded that I no longer need or apps I tried out that I don't want anymore. It's easy to use and understand, and it's perfect if you're like me and have a compulsive desire to organize and keep on top of what's on your computer. — CD

89

WORKFLOW

Application shortcut mapper

The Application Shortcut Mapper has visual keyboard shortcut guides for several popular applications, including most Adobe applications. Spending a few minutes with it could save you a lot of time down the road. I wish I'd learned about it years ago. — MF

400 free online tools

This list of 400 Awesome Free Resources You Can Use to Grow Your Business is useful for anyone. There are links to online image editors, extensions to enhance your email, design inspiration, and tools to help you focus — all free. — CD

Cheatsheets for everything

I found a useful Photoshop keyboard shortcut cheatsheet at Cheatography. It has hundreds of cheatsheets for programmers, designers, students, photographers and other kinds of newbies. — MF

HTML reference guide

If you maintain a website or blog, HTML Reference is a site that has examples of different HTML tags. Many of the tags are new to me, but look useful, such as the article tag. — MF

Pinterest scrapbooks

A lot of folks, especially guys, kind of sneer at Pinterest, but I use it all the time. I have the Pinterest plugin activated on my web browsers, so anytime I come across an image or visual idea on a webpage I want to save, I simply click on the little red Pinterest bug that appears in the left corner of that image, and it is saved to a "pin board" of my choosing. The advantage

of this method over say Evernote is that each image saved can unearth many more similar images from all the Pinterest boards. So, say I am researching how to make a lumber rack. I can collect a few examples from Google Images, or from some online forum, and then Pinterest will generate many more similar images that others have collected. I can then curate my own collection from those, which is better than just looking at pages of Google results. You can keep your collections private or make them public, as I do with some of mine. — KK

Easy brainstorming

I needed an easy way to organize categories in a hierarchical order. It would have been painful to use pen and paper, but thankfully Google led me to MindMeister. The free version was all I needed. There's a lot of free mind-mapping software out there, but they can be clunky, MindMeister is smooth and intuitive. — CD

Social publishing center

I publish the same material on different social media platforms from my computer using a web-based app called Hootsuite. With Hootsuite I can pre-schedule material ahead of time. I can post images from my camera on Instagram, which otherwise is hard to do. I get analytics, respond, and manage Twitter, Facebook, Instagram, Tumblr, Pinterest, etc., all from one dashboard. There is a limited free version but I pay for the basic $30/month small business version. — KK

Task management

I learned about the the task manager, WorkFlowy from a Cool Tools review. It's a hierarchical list maker with a couple of bells and whistles, but its power is in its simplicity and ease of use. I've tried more task managers than I'd care to admit, but this is the one I'm going to use from now on. I pay $5 a month just to support them, but the free version is all I really need. — MF

How to bullet journal

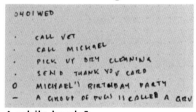

A while back I reverted to using an analog to-do list because it forces me to be accountable when I have to carry over my tasks to the next day. Then, this YouTube video on How to Bullet Journal entered my life and took my notebook skills to the next level. — CD

Virtual white board

I've been trying out Miro, a shared white board for video calls. This is a free web-based tool that allows all participants to draw, or post notes, on the same white page in real time. You open Miro in another browser tab while you zoom, so you and your collaborators can sketch, diagram, and write down formulas together. Like standing around a white board. You'll need a drawing tablet such as an iPad, Surface, or Wacom tablet on your end. — KK

No-frills to-do app

I like to blame my To-Do List apps if things don't get done. I get annoyed with reminders, then turn off notifications, and eventually delete. Daily Zen Planner's super simplistic design is non-threatening and easy to use. I type up tasks and move them to either the Today or Soon screen. — CD

To-do notebook

I picked up this surprisingly inexpensive ($5.50) to-do list notebook last month, and I love it. The Maruman Mnemosyne 197 has ruled, perforated pages with two columns of checkboxes. The 80 sheets are ring bound and the cover is stiff, textured black plastic. The paper holds ink very well. — MF

Organize your notebooks

I'm a notebook hoarder/collecter and regularly use 2-3 different notebooks a day for work, journaling, lists, brain dumps, etc. Sometimes I need to flag pages to revisit and instead of post-it notes, I've been using these Redi-Tag Divider Sticky Notes ($5). These are so useful for indexing your notebooks and annotating pages. I'm still spread out all over the place, but this helps me keep track of what's important. — CD

Conquering the to-do list

To keep my to-do list on track, I've been committing to the habit of asking myself the four questions from this Ted article. The most effectual being, "What's the most important thing I can do today that would make tomorrow better?" and "Should I do this task now or can I do it later?" — CD

Immediacy filter

One of the most useful bits of advice I ever got came from the writer Anne Herbert. She said that whenever she got an invitation to do something months away or even a week away, she asked herself whether she would accept the gig/meeting/task if it was tomorrow. The answer was often no. I use that immediacy trick all the time, and it has served me very well. — KK

Two favorite diagrams:

How to stop worrying, and Good, Fast, Cheap. — MF

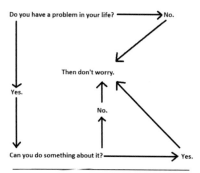

Make better decisions

Upgrade your pros and cons list by assigning additional value. Rate how important each list item is to you from 1 to 5, and when you're done add them up to find out which has more points. You might find that even if you listed more items in one column, the other might affect your life more. — CD

Outsourcing

I'm productive because I outsource my detail work to global freelancers. If I can specify a job, it can be assigned to one of a million expert freelancers working somewhere in the world. Often for cheap, always fast, and securely. I use Upwork (which used to be called Elance and oDesk). It's a reliable system. I can find programmers, web and graphic designers, artists, photoshop experts, transcribers, marketing mavens, and so on. Their work is a good as anyone you might hire. — KK

Solutions search

When troubleshooting anything my first step is Google/YouTube. But when an initial query does not yield much, I simply add the suffix "solutions" to the query. The terms "problem X + solutions" is more likely to yield sources that have answers, not just the same problem I have. — KK

Career advice

80,000 hours is the typical length of the average career. 80,000 Hours is a blog that dispenses free career advice based on science, rather than on hunches. As much as possible this non-profit (Cambridge University) gives advice based on the latest academic and scientific research into the nature and economics of work, careers, happiness, and the economy. When I am asked for career advice, I point candidates here to their Career Guide. — KK

One-stop career center

The Sokanu Career Test is like a supercharged version of the one I took in high school. A 20-minute test will give you your top matches out of 800+ careers based on your personal interests, personality characteristics, and ideal work environment. You also get info on degree paths, salary, and links to job listings. — CD

Work from home successfully

I work from home four days a week and what helps me be most productive is having a separate work space (not in a bedroom) with lots of natural light, getting dressed as if I'm going to the office, sticking to a 9-5 schedule, and giving myself short breaks every hour to walk around or cuddle with my dog. This article on How to Work From Home and Actually Get Stuff Done has a lot more suggestions for productivity. Eating lunch away from my desk is something I have to get better at, and one thing I hadn't considered is to do some work before breakfast: "The usual recommendation is to start with a healthy breakfast, to fuel you for your busy day ahead. However, when you're home all day, breakfast can be a drawn-out luxury, with reading, checking social media, and other distractions preventing you from getting started. Try diving into a quick work task, checking it off the list, and then sitting down to breakfast." — CD

Working from home tips

This may be a new thing for you. Working from Home Temporarily is a free 72-page ebook that offers extremely practical advice on how to set up this new lifestyle. Some of the stuff is obvious, but there's a lot of great tips such as how to upgrade to good connectivity, how to set office hours, how to share your home with others who are also working, etc. Available in 3 ebook formats, all free. — KK

You 2.0: Deep Work

This podcast episode of NPR's Hidden Brain with Cal Newport, author of "Deep Work: Rules For Focused Success In A Distracted World," reminded me how important it is to protect your brain from distractions and to create flows of deeply focused work. I find that on days when I schedule 4-5 hours of uninterrupted work,

WORKFLOW

I accomplish a lot more within a short time span, and can use the rest of the time to respond to emails and get ahead of the week's tasks. To combat interruptions, I find using a Pomodoro timer and turning off email notifications in 30-minute batches works for me. I used to feel guilty for scheduling out every hour of my work day, like a robot, but ultimately scheduling in both deep work and time for distractions allows me to feel "finished" at the end of the workday, and to quickly unwind right when 5 o'clock hits. Cal Newport suggests having a shut-down phrase for when you've completed your schedule, something he was previously embarrassed of, but now embraces, like "Schedule shut-down complete." I am totally stealing this and adding it to my workflow. — CD

Optimizing autonomy

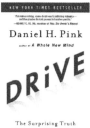

NEW YORK TIMES BESTSELLER

Daniel H. Pink
author of A Whole New Mind

DRiVE

The Surprising Truth
About What Motivates Us

One of the benefits of working from home is that you potentially have more autonomy in your work. As Dan Pink explains in this brief but densely animated talk entitled: "Drive: The surprising truth about what motivates us,"

autonomy is one of the three main drivers of getting stuff done (money is not). Use this reset time to optimize these three factors in what you do. — KK

Productivity tip

Lately, I've been marking each task on my to-do list as a high-attention task or a low-attention task, and throughout the day, I will alternate and work only on the things that match my energy level. I've noticed that these "energy audits" have enabled me to power through bunches of tasks that I tend to avoid because they seem tedious or time-consuming. (Source: 6 tools that are more powerful than to-do lists for productivity). — CD

Focus a wandering mind

This infographic has 9 suggestions for focusing your wandering mind. A couple of them I've never heard before, like taking 1 minute to doodle to help cognitive performance, and a yoga hand trick to reduce stress. — CD

Free focus timer

Tomato One is a free focus timer for iOS, based on the Pomodoro technique. I use it when I have trouble focusing. The timer goes off every

25 minutes for a 5 minute break. I make sure the sound is turned down so that the timer ding is discreet, and allow notifications on a locked screen in case I don't hear it. Most of the time, I end up working through the breaks and get more done. — CD

Less, More and None

Less, More, and None

− Less

- online shopping (Amazon, eBay)
- social media (Twitter, Instagram)
- browsing (malls, bookstores, online)
- reading product reviews
- talking about technology
- reading multiple books at the same time

+ More

- animal rights activism
- running races
- long bike rides
- whole, local foods
- hiking trails that I have never hiked
- revisiting trails with a book and my hammock
- learning Hawaiian history
- learning Hawaiian places
- eating local foods
- sitting zazen
- organized, clean, and clutter-free places
- picnics at parks
- swimming in the ocean
- spending time with animals
- calling old friends
- reading in completely distraction-free environments
- quiet mornings
- self-sufficiency
- playing of board games
- building with students
- real 100% ecovery from workouts

⊘ None

- reading the news
- political media
- reading about electronics/tech
- adding new debt

Jacoby Young, who works at an elementary school in Hawaii, created a list on his website called "Less, More, and None," which categorizes activities he wants to do less often, more often, or not at all. It's a great idea. I want to make a similar list for myself. I'm starting with less Twitter, more time outside, and no working on holidays. — MF

CALENDAR

Free calendar scheduling

Select a Day

Sat Apr 2 | Sat Apr 9 | Sat Apr 16

unavailable

I use Calendly to manage Kevin's calendar. Calendly connects to Google calendar, blocks off the times you are busy and creates a unique and permanent url to share so people can self-schedule. The scheduled event is then automatically added to your Google calendar. There is a basic, free plan that does this, and paid plans with more features. — CD

Other people's time zone

Like almost everyone else, I now need to interact with others working in different time zones. Determining their current time is the chore of this neat menu applet for the Mac called There. Unlike a world clock, the There applet tracks the time per person. I can instantly look up a friend/colleague and it gives me their current time; if they do travel and are a There user as well, I see their time at their new location. Ditto if I travel. You can import a whole Slack team and get their local times. It is currently free and will soon be available on Windows and phones. — KK

Best group scheduler

The best way to schedule a meeting for a bunch of busy people is via Doodle, a free easy website. No need to sign up. Just lay out all possible time slots and let everyone else go to the site, and click the times that work for them. The site sorts out the best time/date. No email tag. Quick. Painless. I've been using the site for years. — KK

Good Google Calendar tricks

I use Google Calendar to schedule everything. Some of the tips in this PC Mag article were unknown to me, but I'm glad I found out about them. Particularly useful: "Find a Time That Works for Everyone," and "Block Off Appointments." — MF

Time zone aid

I have difficulty with time zones. It's easy enough to use the world clock on my smartphone to find out what time it is in another country right now, but I don't trust myself to count forward or backward to figure out what time it will be in Edinburgh when it's 10am in Los Angeles, for example. I have 24 Meetings bookmarked to do the math for me. A simple slider lets me see what time it will be in different cities. — MF

Add Weather to your Google Calendar

I like using Google Calendar's "month view" to plan my life, and I realized it would be helpful if I could see a weather forecast while I'm scheduling hikes and social outings. The easiest way I found to add a weather calendar was here. Now I have a two-week forecast always visible. — CD

EMAIL

Use Dropbox within Gmail

If you use Dropbox, installing the Dropbox Chrome extension is a timesaver. I no longer have to search for files in subfolders to copy and paste share links. With the extension, I can access all my folders and recent files and attach them in a message without having to leave Gmail. If someone sends me a dropbox link, I can download it directly to my computer without being redirected to another window — all these saved clicks add up! — CD

Gmail tips

Gizmodo has a useful article on several ways to improve your Gmail experience. One example: my address is markfrauenfelder@ gmail.com. I can sign up for newsletters by using markfrauenfelder+lists@ gmail.com and then filter the email to a "newsletter" label. — MF

Quick unsubscribing

I get signed up for a lot of newsletters and PR lists without my consent. I used to take the time to scroll down to the bottom of each email newsletter and click the unsubscribe link (if there was one), but now I just use Gmail's "Block" to send them forevermore to my spam folder. — MF

Prewritten emails

Here is a helpful minimalist website with short and sweet canned emails for things like needing advice, asking to be paid back, rescheduling appointments, unsubscribing aggressively and more. — CD

Chrome extension for managing multiple Gmail accounts

I have multiple Gmail accounts that I use throughout the day and I developed a bad habit of keeping them open and constantly clicking through tabs to check the status of

my inbox even though I know nothing's changed. Checker Plus is a chrome extension that lets you preview, delete, star and archive email without opening up Gmail or leaving your current window, and it works with multiple accounts. Since I've been using it, I have definitely been more productive. — CD

Fast email unsubscribe

I get signed up to a lot of email lists without my knowledge. I started using a service called Leave Me Alone to quickly unsubscribe to hundreds of them. Unlike other unsubscribe services, this one makes money by charging a small fee instead of selling your data to advertisers. You can unsubscribe to 10 email lists for free to see how it works. — MF

Burner email addresses

I started using Burner Mail a couple of months ago and bought a premium subscription because I find it so useful. The basic concept is simple: it's a service that generates unique email addresses that get forwarded to your regular email inbox. You can use a burner email address to sign up for newsletters or register a new online account. If you decide you don't want email from a burner address (or if you start getting spam), it's a simple matter of flipping a switch and you will never get email from that address again. Best of all, it has a browser extension so you can generate a new burner from the dashboard with one click and it will appear in the email field of any web site form. You can also use Burner Mail to send email anonymously. — MF

Free encrypted email

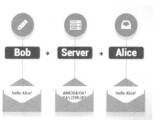

Proton Mail offers free end-to-end encrypted email in a clean and simple ad-free web interface (there's also a smartphone app). The company is based in Switzerland, a country that offers strong privacy protection. In addition, the company says it doesn't have access to the plaintext of your emails, so they couldn't give it to a third party even if they wanted to. — MF

Forward email to unsubscribe

My personal gmail is a mess of promotional emails and spam. I've tried to clean it up in the past using unsubscribe services and marking messages as spam, but it's a neverending struggle. Recently, I've started forwarding spam emails to unsubscribe.robot@gmail.com and that seems to work. There's no guarantee, but it's free, easy and they don't sell your data. I just checked my usage on the website and it reports that so far I've been definitely unsubscribed from 6 emails and probably unsubscribed from 7. — CD

Merge email threads

Currently there's no official way to merge gmail threads with different subject lines, so I just copy and paste the text I want to add to an existing conversation and send it to myself. Here are instructions. — CD

Streamlined Gmail

If you're a Gmail user, install this Chrome extension (Simplify Gmail) that strips out all the distracting stuff (like the large Google logo) and leaves you with a streamlined interface. It was created by Gmail's former lead designers. It's Gmail as it should be. — MF

Multiple inboxes

I use Gmail in my browser, and what I find most helpful is the Multiple Inboxes lab. When I'm working on a project, I create a label for all relevant email and that label becomes an additional inbox. That way, I don't lose sight of my to-dos by placing them in a folder, and it keeps my inbox from cluttering. Kind of hard to explain, but it simplifies your life once you do it. Here are instructions. — CD

Spam beater

10 Minute Mail is a disposable email address. Just go to the website, and you are presented with a newly-minted email address

that self-destructs after ten minutes. Here's a sample address: l544960@mvrht.com. Use it when a web form requires an email address and you don't want to end up on their list. From the FAQ: "If the website makes you verify the email address by sending you a link you have to click on, then you can read the email right here on www.10minutemail.com and click on the link." — MF

Undo email send

> Sending has been undone.

How to unsend sent email. There are many reasons you might want to undo (or redo) an email you sent. A common reason for me is that I just remembered something I wanted to add. Gmail has a little known "undo" feature that you have to enable. On the web, click on the gear icon in the upper right corner, select "Settings." About a third of the way down the list check "Enable Undo Send." Pick the 30-second

maximum grace period. Be sure to "save changes." Now when you send an email in Gmail you get a little box in the upper center just below the blue/white magnifying glass in the search box, that says "Your mail was sent." For 30 seconds you have the chance to click on "Undo." It reopens your message to give you the chance to edit or delete. — KK

Nifty email

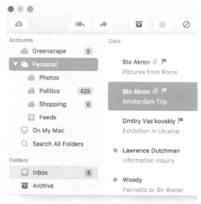

I'm old school. Email is my chief communication mode, and I primarily work on a laptop or desktop. While there are many things to recommend about Gmail on the web, it's interface is not one of them. I use Postbox as my desktop mail client to reach my Gmail (it runs on Mac or Windows). I've tried other clients now and then but keep coming back to Postbox for its intuitive (to me) design and interface. And I'm still uncovering new capabilities I didn't know it had. I use Spark on my phone. — KK

Google dead man switch

If you suddenly die, your Google data — email, docs, contacts, tasks, wallet, etc. — will be inaccessible to loved ones who might need it. To make it easy for trusted people to access your account, use Google's Inactive Account Manager. It will grant access to up to 10 trusted friends or family members after Google detects that you haven't signed-in to your account for a specified number of months. — MF

Gmail reverse conversation

This chrome extension does only one thing: reverses my Gmail thread views so that the newest message is always on top. Which is the way it should be. No more scrolling or collapsing old messages to get to the most recent. — CD

Free, printable motivational poster

This is not like those cheesy, motivational posters you've seen. This is a collection of effective action plans to defeat procrastination. Every tip feels new and helpful and mind-opening. You can download your own poster to print out here. — CD

Calculate your free time

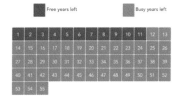

I like this free tool created by Erik Rood that calculates all the free time you have left in your life. Just input your age and the hours per week you spend on things like sleep, work, commuting, eating, etc. Apparently I have 34 free hours per week. It really makes me rethink what I want to do with it. — CD

Do nothing for 2 minutes

Expand this webpage to full-screen, turn up the sound and listen to ocean waves for two minutes. If you click on your mouse, or press the keyboard, the timer starts over. Just enjoy the break. — CD

Timer in your browser

In your browser search bar, enter "five minute timer" (or whatever time you need) and Google will display a timer that beeps when it runs out. — MF

Focused daydreaming

I am giving up social media and other distractions for the 2-hour rule, which encourages setting aside two hours each week for purposeful mind-wandering. The author of this article touts this method as used by Einstein and other geniuses. He says that while it helps to focus on specific questions, the biggest benefit comes from the time spent after you've run out of things to think about. — CD

Use your computer like a tool

This blog post served as a nudge to remind me that my computer is a tool, not a distraction device, and had some good strategies for making the most of my screen time. Like, "Full Screen is your Friend," and you don't need time-tracking software to help you focus on a task, just use a sticky note. Write down what you need to focus on and put it on your monitor where you can see it, and only use your computer with that specific purpose in mind. It's fool-proof. — CD

Screenshot tip

This tip comes from Andy Baio (@waxpancake). He tweeted: "Did you know that you can paste screenshots straight from your clipboard into Twitter or Slack? On macOS, capture any part of your screen to the clipboard with Shift-Ctrl-Cmd-4, then Cmd-V to paste it into your tweet or Slack message. I use this constantly." — MF

What's on that barcode?

If you're curious about the information on a barcode or QR code, take a photo or screengrab of it and upload it to this website. It will decode the contents and present it to you in human readable form. I used it recently to get a shipping tracking number I needed. — MF

Quickly scan pages using your phone

The FineScanner app ($9.99/ year) makes it so easy to scan and share documents  using only my phone. Batch mode auto-captures and crops pages in seconds, turning them into a readable, black & white PDF that I can immediately upload to my iCloud or Google Drive. There's a lot more features and more ways to share that I haven't explored yet. — CD

Free PDF editing

My Acrobat Pro maxed out on being able to reduce the size of a PDF. I used Smallpdf to finish the job and it reduced it by half. It's free to use twice per hour. There's a lot of other editing features you can you use too. — CD

Free file conversion

CloudConvert is a free conversion service that supports more than 200 file

formats and you don't have to download any software to use it. I mostly use it to convert Google WebP files into JPEGS so that the images are usable in WordPress and Adobe products. — CD

Quickly sort lists

This website is worth bookmarking if you ever need to sort a list of numbers or names. It's quicker than copy and pasting into a spreadsheet, which can be finicky sometimes. — CD

Clean copy and paste

Since the beginning of time the keyboard shortcut to paste something has been Command/Ctrl + V. Not as well known — but should be, for the raging headaches it can cure — is that if you add a third key — the Shift — what you paste will be plain text wiped clean of any formatting it might carry from its source. I call it a clean paste. — KK

End text formatting problems (OS X)

Here's a beautiful life-changing tip for Mac users. Once you set these preferences, pasted text will be formatted like the destination, not the source.

Why isn't this the default setting? — MF

Global Forever stamps

Occasionally I need to mail a letter in an envelope, with you  know, paper inside. I hate going to the post office, so I buy Forever stamps online. These US stamps are good for domestic mail forever (no matter how many price increases there are) so I buy a wad of them. Now the US Post Office has released a Global Forever stamp ($1.15) for mailing anywhere in the world. Since they are good forever, I got a bunch of them as well. They are distinctly circular, so they look cool too. — KK

Snail mail in your email

USPS's Informed Delivery is free and available almost everywhere in the US now. Every morning, I get an email with scanned images of my mail before it's delivered. Most of the time it's junk, and those days I don't even bother checking my mailbox, but this service is great if you're expecting something important. — CD

WRITING

The story of my life

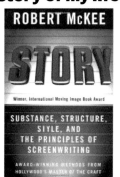

Story, by Robert McKee, is the best book written on how to construct a great story. McKee's masterclass on story writing is well known in Hollywood. It is condensed into a 4-hour audiobook (better than the written book), performed by McKee himself. It is not just a manual for screenwriters; these short 4-hours turned me into a super fan, able to appreciate stories on whole new levels. Indeed, I found this book profound and realized that it is a useful guide to constructing an interesting life, which in the end is also a story. — KK

How to make your point

These succinct tips for how to write an op-ed piece

15) I'd wish you luck, but good writing depends on conscious choices, not luck. Make good choices.

are clear, 100% correct, and useful for any kind of factual writing. Compresses a whole course, or book, to 15 bullet points. — KK

How to be a better writer

My friend Gareth Branwyn has been writing books and articles for top-tier publishers for decades. He recently wrote an article called "How to Be a Better Writer: Tips, tricks, and hard-won lessons: from creating drafts to working with editors," and it's a gold mine of treasure for anyone interested in improving their writing. — MF

Cut out everything that's not surprising

Derek Sivers was the founder of CD Baby and maintains an interesting essay blog. One of his recent posts offered good advice for writers and speakers: "People only really

learn when they're surprised. If they're not surprised, then what you told them just fits in with what they already know. No minds were changed. No new perspective. Just more information. So my main advice to anyone preparing to give a talk on stage is to cut out everything from your talk that's not surprising." — MF

Proofreading hack

Sometimes my eyes deceive me when proofreading. I came across this blog post and now I've been double-checking long paragraphs by right-clicking on them (using Chrome) and selecting Speech > Start Speaking. If it sounds off, it usually means I dropped a word. — CD

Search for example sentences

ludwig
Find your sentence

If I'm not confident with how I've used an expression, I will google the turn of phrase inside of quotation marks, and if I get Google Books results with similar examples then I know I've used it correctly. Lately, I've been using Ludwig for the same kind of phrase searches. I like that it gives me back example sentences from different sources like encyclopedias, news and science publications. — CD

Power thesaurus

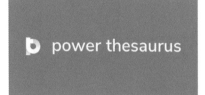

I keep this crowdsourced thesaurus bookmarked. It's easier to navigate than thesaurus.com and the fastest way to find the word I want to use. — CD

Q&A site for all your English questions

When I can't find the right word or phrasing using Power Thesaurus or Ludwig, I'm on the English StackExchange searching for answers or posting questions. You can ask anything relating to grammar or usage or word choice and English experts will start responding right away. You can also check the "reputation" of any user who responds to confirm they know what they're talking about. — CD

Effortless editing

Write   Edit

Hemingway *Editor*

Readability

Grade 6
Good

Words: **133**
Show More ▾

2 adverbs, meeting the goal of 2 or fewer.

1 use of passive voice, meeting the goal of 2 or fewer.

1 phrase has a simpler alternative.

1 of 11 sentences is hard to read.

1 of 11 sentences is very hard to read.

I tend to write like I think, run on and using a lot of commas. If I drop my text into the Hemingway Editor it will highlight unnecessary words and tell me what to fix to make my writing more concise. — CD

The 1913 dictionary is better

I found out about Webster's 1913 Dictionary from David Perell's excellent Friday

Finds newsletter. Perell uses this 107-year-old dictionary because he thinks "modern dictionaries have lazy definitions that focus too much on simplicity at the cost of precision." I also love the extreme simplicity of the interface. It's worth bookmarking. — MF

7 secrets of advanced writing

I like this graphic shared by DailyInfographic which lists seven tips for better writing. Some advice for mastering them is to just focus on one or two at a time until they become habits. I am working on parallel construction by taking out words I've listed and confirming the sentence still makes sense. — CD

Compose better emails

I've gotten too casual with my email correspondence, and this blog post on "How to write better emails" reminded me that I should strive to be more effective and efficient with my communication. All of the tips are useful but the ones I really need to work on are: 1) Use specific dates instead of "yesterday" or "tomorrow"; and 2) Be specific on what you request from whom by referring to each recipient explicitly using the @ symbol. — CD

Convert words to time

Wordstotime.com is a quick way to calculate how many minutes it would take to read a specific number of words out loud. I recently needed to fill up at least 8 minutes of talk time for an audio recording, so I started with this website and aimed for 1,250 words as I typed. — CD

AI writing prompts

Talk to Transformer

See how a modern neural network completes your text. Type a custom snippet or try one of the examples. Learn more below.

Follow @AdesDanielKing for updates and other demos like this one.

Custom prompt

Type something and a neural network will guess what comes next.

COMPLETE TEXT

After reading this post on How to begin a novel using AI, I've been having fun using this

neural network, Talk to Transformer, to come up with prompts for new poems. I'll just type in a few lines or start with an image that haunts me, and I'm always surprised by the seemingly original imagery that it gives back to me like this one (prompted by my aunt's back tattoo of a phoenix): "The days passed like smoke under my feet. That should be enough for now. She paused and sighed again. But still the phoenix kept going." — CD

Online typing tutor

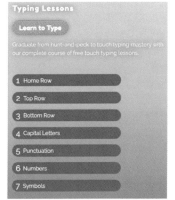

After decades of being a hunt-and-peck typist, I'm finally forcing myself to learn touch typing. After trying a bunch of different typing websites, I've settled on How To Type as my favorite. It's not fancy, but the drills have helped me to become more accurate. — MF

Cheap alternative to Freewrite

I've been coveting the Freewrite typewriter since

the Kickstarter launched a few years back, but I can't justify spending $500 on one. Thanks to this blog post I discovered that the now discontinued Alphasmart Neo2 is a cheap alternative. I found one used on Amazon for $35 from a reputable seller who listed it in working condition and included the USB cord. I wasn't sure if a distraction-free typewriter would actually help me write more, but the answer is yes, it does! — CD

A notepad that follows you

After my recent computer upgrade, I lost my Papier chrome extension that I previously recommended for taking notes in your browser. The website no longer works

and it doesn't exist in the Chrome store, and I was really bummed because it's so useful to just be able to open a tab and have a space to write out your to-do list, or do a brain dump, or collect quotes. Thankfully, I was able to find an alternative created by a Google AI designer called Mindful (Beta). What's better about Mindful is that it syncs with my Chrome account so I can access my notes on both my desktop and laptop. — CD

Pretty note app

I use Evernote for work and personal note keeping, but I have to admit that Bear, which is referred to as the "beautiful writing app," is more enjoyable to use on my phone. It's so clean and pretty and easy to format. I've been using it as a daily journal and for poem writing. — CD

Menu bar notepad

Tyke is a free, simple MacOS menubar app that opens a small text-only scratch pad. It

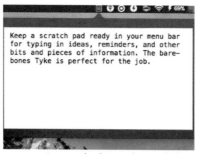

converts copied text into plain text, which I like. I've only had it for couple of days, but I'm already using it multiple times a day. — MF

Minimalism notebooks

I've long been a fan of blank (no-lines) Moleskine notebooks, large and small. I recently switched to Minimalism Art notebooks which are very similar, maybe better quality, and half the price. They also come in bright cover colors. — KK

Smallish green wirebound notebook

This 8¼" x 6" spiral bound notebook costs $3.50. It has light green paper and 30

college-spaced rules per page. I like the smaller-than-usual size because it takes up less room on my desk and in my backpack. — MF

A good 25-cent mechanical pencil

My wife ordered a 24-pack of these cheap Bic mechanical pencils. I tried one out and I actually like it a lot. The lead diameter is 0.9 mm and it has a number 2 lead inside. It also contains one extra lead in the barrel. A 24-pack sells for about $.25 a pencil. They are supposed to be disposable, but why not buy a bunch of 9mm lead for cheap and keep using the pencil? You can even get colored leads! — MF

Stay-sharp mechanical pencil

I like mechanical pencils, and my favorite is the Uni Kuru Toga with a lead-rotation mechanism (Model No. M54521P.24). Every time you touch the tip to the paper, the mechanism inside the pen ratchets the lead a few degrees. The result is the point stays rounded instead of taking on a chiseled profile as often happens with mechanical pencils. It's inexpensive but very well-made. Mine has lasted for years. — MF

New favorite pen

I met one of my favorite cartoonists this week, Tom Gauld (his new

book: Baking With Kafka). He draws all of his cartoons with a Pilot Precise V5 Roller Ball Stick Pen. He gave me one of his and I love it. They are $13 for a pack of 12. Tom said the ink does not fade, even after many years. — MF

Erasable Pens

Pilot Frixion pens and highlighters have hard plastic erasers. Rub them over the ink and

the writing vanishes. Unlike a pencil eraser that wears away the paper, a Frixion eraser creates heat, rendering the ink invisible. I use them for my paper to-do list, book highlighting, and tabletop gaming. — MF

Trusty pen

Every now and then I try out a new pen, but I keep returning to my trusty Pilot G2 Gel pens.

Smooth, fine, dark, cheap to lose, and pocketable. YMMV, but they are perfect for me. — KK

Pocket gel pens

A few years ago a reader turned me onto a nifty variation of my favorite Pilot G2 gel pen, which is a mini pocket version of the same pen. Same liquid black, same fine tip, same profile, just a lot shorter to better fit into my pocket. The Pilot G2 Mini is my everyday carry. — KK

Write in the dark

Ideas always hit me right before I fall asleep. So I bought these Glovion LED Light Pens ($15/3pk) to write them down without waking up my husband. The light is bright enough to write under, but not bright enough that it pulls me out of my half-awake state. I love that I no longer have to fight that nagging urge to get up and write something down before I forget. – CD

ART SUPPLIES

Pocketable watercolor kit

This small watercolor kit by Sakura is perfect for the occasional wannabe artist like me. It comes with a brush that stores water, so you can always be ready to paint. It was so easy to incorporate this into my journaling/sketching routine. — CD

Blendable color markers

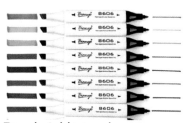

For sketching and painting I favor alcohol-based markers. They let you blend colors like a watercolor brush, but with the convenience of a felt marker. The preferred premier markers are the extremely expensive Copics.

An inexpensive equivalent for blendable markers with dual tips (fat or point) are Bianyo. I can paint quickly and easily in a notebook using a travel set like these 72 Bianyo markers. — KK

Brush pens

Tombow Fudenosuke Brush Pens come in a 2-pack for less than $5. They look like pens, but instead of a nib they have a brush, which allows you to draw lines of varying widths. They're a lot of fun to use. — MF

High-quality drawing pens

The Sakura Pigma Manga Basic Set comes with 5 pens: 4 Pigma Microns (sizes 005, 01, 05, 08), a black brush pen, and a white ink gel pen. The ink is waterproof and very dark. At $8, it's a good deal. — MF

Great sketching pen

My friend Bob Knetzger is a toy inventor. He uses Paper Mate Flair felt-tip pens to sketch out his designs. I bought a dozen for $7 and was reminded why I liked them so much in the 1970s. The lines are smooth and you can vary the line weight by changing the angle between the pen and paper. — MF

Sketch pad for all media

My art student daughter has been using these spiral-bound Canson Mix Media 7x10 drawing pads. I started buying them for myself, too. The heavy paper easily handles ink pens, watercolor, and Copic markers, and has a nice texture for pencils. A 60-sheet notebook is only $7. — MF

Opaque white ink

In my workshop and studio, I label boxes, shelves, drawers, cases, bins, and parts with a very dense white "ink" which is really white correction fluid in a stubby pen. White is usually much more legible than black, but white ink is much more difficult to apply heavy enough to cover any surface. These Pentel Presto Jumbo Correction Pens do a fantastic job applying thick, non-drippy white paint via a fine point tip, and are small enough to carry in my workshop apron. They draw perfectly opaque white on any surface, instantly, even vertical surfaces. I have not found anything else that will do that. — KK

Erasable highlighters

These erasable highlighter pens really work as advertised, at least on non-glossy books. The eraser is smooth and by rubbing on the paper, it produces heat which causes the highlight mark to vanish completely. — MF

Prevent hand pain

I can't handwrite for long periods of time without some discomfort. These pencil grips are designed for kids and adults with arthritis, but they help me out a lot too. I bought a 6-pack for $11. — CD

Better pen holder

A while ago I recommended a pen holder strap that I was really excited about (and still am because it's French and pink), but thanks to Rayan Parikh sharing what's in his bag, I've now discovered these adhesive pen holder loops ($6/5pk). I've stuck these on all my notebooks so that I always have a pen ready. — CD

Hard pencil case

My daughter, an art student, bought this small hardshell pencil case ($7) to hold a few pens and an eraser. It's just the right size for a small messenger bag or backpack. I ended up getting one for myself. — MF

Favorite pencil case

I bought this $8 Japanese pencil case a couple of years ago and my daughters liked it so much I ended up buying one for each of them. Despite its small size you can pack a lot of art supplies in it, thanks to its book-like middle "page" that holds pens and pencils on one side and small items on the other side. — MF

LISTENABLE

Russian mystery

A fantastic two-part podcast episode from *Reply All* (Russian Passenger, Part 1 + Beware All, Part 2) delves very deep into the mystery of how producer Alex Blumberg had his Uber account hacked by Russians. Could it

be malware, phishing, man-in-the-middle exploits, or what? Arriving at a solution required the participation of the full technical teams of Google, Uber, and independent security experts over several weeks, and still the final aha was surprising. Along the way, it's an entertaining detective story, dishing out a serious but still understandable education in global cyber security. The bottom line: You need a password manager right now. My family and I use 1Password, which has been great. — KK

Reply All

My favorite podcast these days is *Reply All*. It's sort of *Wired* in audible format.

Smart, surprising stories about the culture around digital technology. They are especially good in chasing down internet "mysteries." Just for example, listen to episode #76 which is about the Google ad scam around lost phones; it goes way deep. Each episode never fails to enlighten and entertain me. — KK

The story of the once-viral trivia app

I binge listened to all 8 episodes of Boom/Bust: The Rise and Fall of HQ Trivia in one day. I was obsessed with the viral game back in 2017, but eventually lost interest and didn't follow the demise of the trivia startup. This documentary podcast series

gave me an insider glimpse into what really happened and helped me better understand the very fickle attention economy. — CD

S-town

I'm totally hooked on *S-Town*, an amazing 6-hour audio documentary from the folks that brought you the hit podcast *Serial*. Although it starts out like *Serial*, *S-Town* takes off as a deep dive into another America most listeners like me have never experienced. Plenty of plot twists amid a parade of local character and colors: Southern Gothic, redneck, and Trump country blues. But at its heart it's a story of one person's attempt to make sense of his life. — KK

Revisionist History

A new podcast I am enjoying is Malcolm Gladwell's *Revisionist History*.

You get typical Gladwellian reporting, voiced by Gladwell himself. His theme is the re-telling of things everyone knows, so that these "official" stories are inverted, reversed, undermined, or in some way seen new. It's contrarian by design. If you like his books, you'll like his podcast and vice versa. — KK

Vital podcast

Supreme Court decisions can be monumental in their consequences, but they often hinge on very specific, sometimes messy cases. *More Perfect* is a super podcast from the folks at Radio Lab that burrows deep into the specifics of Supreme Court cases in order to illuminate their logic and meaning. All the episodes are fantastic, but a recent one on the Commerce Clause in the US Constitution — One Nation, Under Money — is especially great. I was shocked how little I knew about this clause, and consider this audio lesson to be essential listening for any American. No matter what your political tilt you'll be perturbed and educated. Afterwards, listen to the rest of the shows. — KK

A fantastical factual podcast

I am thrilled by this new quirky podcast that is both fictional and factual. In "Everything Is

Alive," the host interviews inanimate objects, like a pillow or bar of soap. By any logic, this should be flat-line boring, but unexpectedly, each episode is brilliant, funny, informative, and remarkable. Other than the fact the objects talk, everything they say is true. Just listen to the can of cola talking about his life in the first episode and you'll be hooked. — KK

The Gateway by Gizmodo

I was on edge weekly waiting for the next episode of Gizmodo's 6-part podcast *The Gateway*. Journalist Jennings Brown investigates the dangerous effects of YouTube guru Teal Swan on her loyal Facebook followers. Teal, who has no degree or professional experience, admits to using SEO and tags to target depressed and suicidal people and has created her own therapy practices to treat them. She is hypnotic and alluring and adamant she is not the leader of a cult, although her followers do call themselves the Teal Tribe. There's much more to this story that I can't give away, and it made me wish this podcast would never end. — CD

Listen to intimate couples therapy sessions

My favorite podcast is "Where Should We Begin? with Esther Perel." I always find myself choked up with emotion while listening to these anonymous couples therapy sessions. Esther Perel is so professional and progressive and such a master at guiding couples toward the light. It's both voyeuristic and enlightening. Season 1 and 2 are free to listen to in your podcast app, but Season 3 "The Arc of Love" was just released as an Audible exclusive. — CD

Learning from death

Frank Ostaseski has accompanied over 1,000 people as they died in hospice, and in this 60-minute podcast (recorded at a Long Now seminar), he distills what lessons the dying — and death — have taught him. Their wisdom is deep, complex, potent, intimate, and unexpected (not cliche). It will shift your relationship to life. Listening (or watching the video) will be one of the best hours in your life. — KK

Long-term thinking

To encourage me to take a long-term view, I'm a regular at the Seminars for Long-term Thinking hosted by the Long Now Foundation (where I am a founding board member). The hour-long talks (plus 30 minute Q&A) happen once a month in San Francisco. The topics are surprisingly diverse, ranging from ancient history to speculative futures, from food to nuclear power, from Silicon Valley to the Silk Road — all with a slant to the next 10,000 years. Several hundred past talks are archived and available to the public as free podcasts. For those outside San Francisco, or disinclined to travel unnecessarily, a membership to the Long Now gives you access to a real-time streaming version of each talk; you can even ask questions live. — KK

Long conversations

A "long conversation" is a new format for a conference. Two speakers begin a conversation on stage. After 15 minutes one of the two speakers is replaced by a new speaker and the conversation continues, and every 15 minutes for the next 8 hours a speaker is swapped out. (Each speaker converses for 30 minutes.) The day is engaging, unpredictable, passionate, diverse, informative, and entertaining. It's a format invented by the Long Now Foundation that is worth stealing. For an example, here are highlights from a long conversation held at the Smithsonian. — KK

The Power of Vulnerability

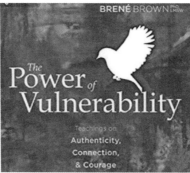

"No one reaches out to you for compassion or empathy so you can teach them how to behave better. They reach out to us because they believe in our capacity to know our darkness well enough to sit in the dark with them." This quote comes from Brené Brown's *The Power of Vulnerability*. Her talk and teachings on authenticity, connection, and courage, based on 12 years of research, inspired me to be a better friend to those in my life — to show up and be present and hold a space of empathy for those in need. Available as a 6-hour audible download or audio CD, listening to her is like listening to your funniest friend, who's also a doctor. — CD

Big ideas in conversation

The economist Tyler Cowen has been a prolific blogger; he is now a prolific podcaster, and one of my favorite interviewers of big thinkers. A really great example of his craft is his interview of David Brooks, the political pundit and op-ed columnist at the New York Times. Their fun public conversation, recorded as a podcast, about the necessary moral dimension of life, and the role of religion in modernity, is super important, but often not talked about. But any Conversation with Tyler is engaging. — KK

Life-changing questions

A really great podcast episode well worth listening to is *17 Great Questions That Can Change Your Life*, by Tim Ferriss. This is an audible extract from his book *Tools of Titans*. In this session he lists the 17 questions that he asks himself on a regular basis in order to get the most from his life. They are very effective probes. This podcast is a good introduction to his book, which is also very useful. — KK

FOCUS MUSIC

Workable flow music

When I am in the flow for work, headphones on, I like to put on any of the annual 2-hour tracks recorded by the DJ Tycho at Burning Man sunrise. Each set is upbeat, trancy, mellow. If you like this year's Waypoint 2018 sunrise set, Tycho's previous years are also available on his Soundcloud site.
— KK

Non-stop music as a soundtrack to your day

At 3PM on a Thursday afternoon I'm one of 41,875 other people listening to the livestream of the ChilledCow lofi hiphop radio station on YouTube. Over 5 million people subscribe to ChilledCow, and I imagine the vast majority of them are students. I learned about it from my 16-year-old daughter who plays it on her headphones while she does her homework. I find that I can listen to the relaxing music for hours and hours while I work (that is, when I'm not in a Zoom meeting.) — MF

Interactive soundscapes

Here is another free ambient sound website to add to our ever-growing list of musical streams we enjoy — myNoise. net. There are hundreds of different noise generators available for free listening that you can adjust to your sound comfort level. What I really like about myNoise is that once I calibrate the soundscape to my liking I can create a custom URL that I can save and go back to. — CD

Productivity trance

I discovered a number of years ago that playing one track of music in an endless loop helped me write the difficult first draft. Some writers and coders use white noise, but another group (I am one) prefer a single musical track in a loop. The kind of music varies by person (I use one specific Russian choir hymn); after a dozen loops the music disappears and what I get is a feeling of comfort, which helps me focus for hours while it repeats. Try it with your song. — KK

Focus music that works

After months of using different email addresses to access free sessions of Brain. fm, I have finally signed up as a paying customer. I've tried classical music, brown noise and other ambient sounds when I need to focus, but Brain.fm's Focus music works best for me. I can put on a two-hour loop and forget to get up from my desk to stretch. They have different genres of focus music, like atmospheric, chimes & bowls, nightsounds, as well as Relax and Sleep stations that I have yet to explore. But now that I am a paying customer, I can listen to all their music on both my laptop and phone. They offer five free sessions, then it's $7 a month or $50 per year.
— CD

Instructional listen

I greatly enjoyed this episode of my long-time favorite BBC podcast, *In Our Time: The American Populists*.  It describes an earlier rise of populism in America around 1880, an era I knew nothing about, but one that has a few parallels with and lessons for the current outbreak of populism in the US. — KK

A terrific podcast about Artificial Intelligence

I started listening to Sleepwalkers a couple of weeks ago. The hosts talk to software developers, ethicists, artists, doctors, military professionals, and other people who are creating, using, regulating, and thinking about AI and how it's affecting every aspect of life on Earth. Instead of inviting guests into the studio, the hosts go into the field and talk to their guests where they live and work, which makes all the difference. — MF

A golden podcast hour

I've long been a fan of Ken Burns' epic documentary series about American history, such as The Civil War, Jazz, Baseball, National Parks, The Vietnam War, and his most recent, Country Music. Each are essential watching. But after listening to a deep interview of Ken Burns on Tim Ferriss's podcast, my admiration for Burns increased two notches. In a short hour he managed to be informative, helpful, entertaining, romantic, creative, moving, wise, and spiritually enlightened — a Remarkable Being. It was one of the best hours I've spent. — KK

Transformational talks

Most of my audible credits tend to be spent on audio from the Sounds True library. I've listened to all the Brené Brown training talks they offer (like condensed versions of her books) and am working my way through the Clarissa Pinkola Estés collection of healing stories and myths. But right now what I'm really enjoying is the very trippy 14-hour-long Out of Your Mind: Essential Listening from the Alan Watts Audio Archives. It makes my commute mind-expanding. — CD

X-ray into music

You know about *Song Exploder*, yes? It's this amazing podcast that takes one well-known song each week and explodes it into its separate components. The musicians who wrote and perform the song take it apart track by track, sometimes beat by beat, explaining what they were thinking as they created the pieces: what challenges and dead-ends they met along the way, how the song changed as they worked on it, and why they like the final version. It's the x-ray into music I always wanted. — KK

Exploratory music stream

For the past decade David Byrne, the legendary rock musician, has operated his own "radio station," which is really the curated playlist of his own musical explorations. Every month on his website David Byrne Radio, Byrne streams another 100-minute loop of new, old, classic, weird, wonderful, surprising, themed music he's discovered and loves. He writes a short introduction, and supplies the full playlist. I've discovered (and bought) a lot of great music I first heard here. (In Nov. 2018 he streamed a notable playlist of eternal protest songs.) — KK

Old-time radio plays

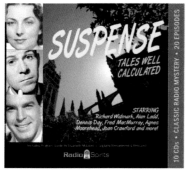

Now that we are stuck at home, we have a lot more time to relax at home. My family of four is using the living room together in the evenings. My wife does a crossword puzzle and my two daughters and I sketch. At the same time, we listen to a terrific old radio drama series called "Suspense." Archive. org has 911 episodes, which may or may not last until the stay-at-home order is lifted, depending on how many episodes we listen to each night. — MF

Tales from the hacker underground

Much of our digital technology is built simply to prevent the harm created by a very few bad actors, mostly kids making mischief. The Reply All podcast episode 130 "The Snapchat Thief" is a marvelous, head-scratching, world-opening, deep dive into this invisible alien hacker underworld that rewards every second of your listening. Highly technical and emotionally satisfying. — KK

Long-form listening

"A novel of the first order, a work of extraordinary art, a thing of exceptional beauty." —Pat Conroy

SHANTARAM

A NOVEL

GREGORY DAVID ROBERTS

One of the best books I ever listened to is *Shantaram*. This very long story — 43 hours! — is the fictionalized autobiography of an Australian outlaw who hides out in the slums of Bombay, is thrown in Indian prison for drug dealing and eventually follows his guru to fight for the muhadjin in Afghanistan. He is a holy thief, a wise sinner, a coyote trickster, and this meld of the sacred and profane is what gives the story its epic rousing power. The narrator in the audible version does hundreds of foreign accents pitch-perfectly and captures the enthusiasm of the Indian sub-continent. Even after 43 hours I wished the story-telling would never end. — KK

Ready Player One audio

I liked the movie, I liked the book, but the best format for *Ready Player One* is to listen to this fun science fiction story as narrated by the actor Wil Wheaton. He tells it fast, with gusto, humor, emotion, and tons of nerdy details. I listened to it once and then re-listened as my wife audited it as well and realized it's one of the best audible books ever. It's 15 hours of joy. Available on Audible. — KK

Advice book on Audible

tiny beautiful things

Advice on love and life from Dear Sugar

Cheryl Strayed
Bestselling author of *Wild*

Read by the Author
Introduction written and read by Steve Almond
An Unabridged Production

At the behest of my best friend, I finally downloaded the Audible version of Tiny Beautiful Things, advice on life and love from Cheryl Strayed's column Dear Sugar. The book is a collection of the most heartbreaking and honest letters seeking help and the advice given. Strayed's thought-out responses pull from her own life experiences dealing with her mother's death, drug addiction, divorce, and now as a happily married wife and mother. They are beautiful written and incredibly moving. This book elicits empathy, laughter and at times, lots of tears. There were a few times I was literally sitting in traffic and sobbing listening to her stories. I highly recommend. — CD

Acappella choir

I'm late to the party, but I've been enjoying the sweet sounds of the now popular group Pentatonix. It's a five-voice acappella choir. One voice is a great beat-box artist who supplies the instrumentation. Somehow their arrangements get everything right. They do originals and covers and I can listen to them for hours. They found their audience on YouTube. — KK

Enjoy the boss radio sound of KHJ 93 Los Angeles

One of my favorite things about Quentin Tarantino's Once Upon a Time... in Hollywood was listening to clips of 93 KHJ, a radio station that pioneered the "boss radio" sound in the 1960s. The DJs were all vocal virtuosos, and the most talented of the bunch was a guy by the name of "The Real Don Steele." Almost all of these broadcasts have been lost to time, but fortunately, some people recorded KHJ on their tape recorders in the 1960s, and the recordings found their way to the Internet. The Internet Archive has a couple of recordings from the 1960s of Steele's show on KHJ. If this kind of thing interests you, you can dig up more by searching "khj airchecks." — MF

World Radio

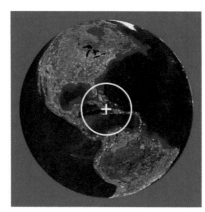

Radio Garden is a website that presents you with a spinnable globe of the Earth. The green dots represent radio stations. Rotate the globe, click a dot and you are suddenly listening to live radio in that part of the world. Right now I'm listening to Radio Seaside Wave in Nakhodka, Russia. — MF

Time machine for music

If you pick a year from your past (1951-2015), The Nostalgia Machine will warp you back musically and link you to videos of the top Billboard Hits of that time. 1996 takes me back to sixth grade and TLC and Alanis Morissette and a lot of weekend nights spent at the rollerskating rink. (Note: Some readers replied that this website did not work for them. One reader suggested that that if you type in "year:1992" in Spotify, you'll get hits from that year.) — CD

Another musical time machine

Last week I recommended The Nostalgia Machine, and some readers reported that it was glitchy and did not work on their browser. Reader Micael suggested if you have Spotify, try searching for "year:1992" to get song and artist results from that year, and @ JMWander recommended Radiooooo.com which lets you customize a music stream based on decade, country, and slow, fast or weird music. Thanks! — CD

PODCAST DIRECTORIES

The Listener

The Listener is a meta-podcast. Each episode of the Listener presents great individual podcast episodes selected from all the other podcasts out there. I listen to it to hear the best podcast episodes on the internet as curated by the same folks who do the Browser; the best articles on the internet. No need to subscribe to hundreds of podcast channels. You'll get the best full shows with original intros and ads, but you only subscribe to one uber podcast, The Listener. The variety and quality are awesome. — KK

Podcast search engine

One way to find new podcasts is a website called Listen Notes — a search engine for almost all podcasts around the world. You can search for topics or a specific person and find related episodes. Or set alerts for keyword mentions. I'm not a daily podcast listener but every once in a while I'll want to hear what people are saying about a certain news story or random topic on my mind, and in those cases Listen Notes is very useful. — CD

Good podcasts

This is a curated list of great podcast episodes aired in 2017, mostly from podcasts you haven't heard of, but should. — KK

Best podcast episodes

I've been using these two lists of the "best podcast episodes from 2018," one from Vulture (10 picks), and one from IndieWire (50 picks), to listen to some great individual shows and to discover new podcasts to potentially subscribe to. — KK

Increase your consumption of podcasts

I found a great way to increase my consumption of podcasts without adding more time — by playing the episodes at 1.5 times speed. Most podcast players will give you this option. You quickly get used to the speedy talk (there is no change in voice pitch). Try it. — KK

Four favorite tools podcast

Every week Mark and I interview a maker on our Cool Tools podcast. We ask them to rave about four of their favorite tools for 25 minutes. The range of tools they recommend is surprising and refreshing; we are always expanding our possibilities. You can subscribe to the Cool Tools Podcast from the usual platforms. (We have 220 episodes!) If you know of a remarkable person who is into tools, send us an introduction, and we'll try to have them as a guest. — KK

READABLE

The Inevitable

NEW YORK TIMES BESTSELLER

THE INEVITABLE

UNDERSTANDING THE 12 TECHNOLOGICAL FORCES THAT WILL SHAPE OUR FUTURE

KEVIN KELLY
AUTHOR OF WHAT TECHNOLOGY WANTS

I unabashedly recommend my book *The Inevitable*, available in paperback for $12, as a clear vision of 25 years in digital technology. It's an optimistic explanation of how we can use this tech for our mutual benefit with the least harm. Years after I finished writing it, I wouldn't change a word. I think it nails the big trends. — KK

Design sourcebook

Every time I return to the masterpiece *A Pattern Language* by Christopher Alexander, I am

rewarded deeply. It's a source book for architectural heuristics (guidelines), such as "A balcony less than 6 feet wide will never be used" or "Make a transition between street and front door" or "Vary the illumination. Aim for pools of light." These design patterns are illustrated with photos and explanations and they serve as remarkable fountainhead for designing any kind of space, whether a room, building, or town. — KK

Fantastic science fiction trilogy

I'm blasting through the last book in Ramez Naam's fantastic science fiction trilogy about technological telepathy. Start with *Nexus*, then onto *Crux* and *Apex*. He fleshes out not only the benefits of a global mind meld but also its problems, so as the series proceeds he keeps changing my mind on

whether I want this invention or not. That's great reading. — KK

The economic benefits of mobility

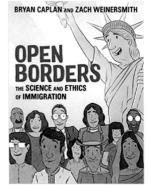

Open Borders is a comic book written by an economist. It's also a comic book about one of the most seriously radical ideas you may ever hear: that all countries, including the US, should have open borders, allowing anyone on the planet to live anywhere they want if they obey local laws. The book carefully runs through the reasons why this is good economically for countries like the US, counters all the obvious and non-obvious objections one by one, and then goes through compromises and partial solutions for those objections. All while keeping it light, fast, easy, fun, and crystal clear. While there are moral arguments, these are mostly economic arguments why open borders are a winner for all involved, especially the US. I am already giving copies of this book away. — KK

How to be cozy

To prepare for the holidays I've been reading *The Little Book of Hygge: Danish Secrets to Happy Living* written by Meik Wiking, CEO of The Happiness Research Institute in Copenhagen. Wiking shares tips on how to light your home (aim for pools of light), what to wear and eat (mostly wool and warm drinks), how to create a sense of togetherness, as well as other things that Danes do to be happy all year round. An idea I plan to adopt is to link purchases with good experiences or an important milestone in life so that I'm reminded of it each time it's used or seen. — CD

Black Voices on Black Futures

Black Imagination is a collection of voices curated by

conceptual artist Natasha Marin, who sought out Black individuals, including youth, LGBTQ+, incarcerated, and unsheltered people and asked them three questions: What is your origin story? How do you heal yourself? and Describe a world where you are loved, safe and valued. The result of which are these deeply moving testimonies/prose/dreams/ poetry. This book has cracked my heart wide open and I'm honored to experience this literary space that expands beyond its bound pages. Here are three excerpts or three possible worlds from Black Imagination. — CD

Victorian-era novel

The Crimson Petal and the White, Michel Faber's 922-page novel about a Victorian era prostitute and a soap-and-perfume industrialist, was a full-sensory immersion into 1875 London. I haven't had this much fun reading a novel about Merrie Olde England since *Pillars of the Earth*. — MF

How to fake influence

I blurbed this self-published book, Under the Influence, which explains how popular influencers on social media make a living by buying fake followers, fake likes, and fake comments. It will tell you how to do all that. It was written by Trey Ratcliff, a photographer who has actual followers and real influence. I blurbed the book because it is more than just a take-down of the dark side; it's about how to have real, enduring, positive influence by being creative, producing real engagement, and being honest. — KK

Changing your mind

You are only as young as the last time you changed your mind. Cass Sunstein compiled 10 great books. Here are 5 books to change liberal minds. And 5 books to change conservative minds. Read and see if you can change your mind. — KK

READABLE

Great read after a break-up

A long time ago after a bad breakup I read *If the Buddha Dated* by Charlotte Kasi. By the time I had finished the book, it was covered in notes and dog-eared pages, and I felt healed and ready to move on. Now, as a newlywed, I am enjoying listening to *If the Buddha Married* on Audible. So many great insights and communication tips. — CD

Easy Electronics

Charles Platt's growing series of electronics learning books are the best I've come across. He explains concepts very clearly, and his illustrations are excellent. His latest book in the series is called *Easy Electronics*. It covers voltage, resistance, capacitors, transistors, integrated circuits and more. No tools are needed to make the projects. — MF

Psychedelics revisited

Michael Pollan's new book, *How to Change Your Mind*, is fantastic on many levels. It charts the recent rehabilitation of psychedelics as a therapy for many mental ailments, and in the right settings, as a reliable aid for spiritual experiences. Pollan is an open-minded skeptic who brings a clarity and balance to this long-controversial subject. He changed my mind and will probably change your mind. — KK

Five good crime books

On the excellent Five Books website Author Simon Brett is interviewed about his five favorite crime novels. Three of his picks (*A Kiss Before Dying*, *The Big Sleep*, and *The Talented Mr. Ripley*) are among my favorites, so I added his other two picks to my wish list. — MF

Short meditations on Love

I bought *How to Love* by Thich Nhat Hanh on Kindle, read it in one sitting and often go back to it for short, helpful reminders on how to be more loving. Two of my favorite passages are: "You are part of the universe; you are made of stars. When you look at your loved one, you see that he is also made

of stars and carries eternity inside. Looking in this way, we naturally feel reverence," and "There's a tradition in Asia of treating your partner with the respect you would accord a guest. This is true even if you have been with your loved one for a long time." — CD

New ways to work

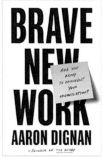

I am not into management or business books, but this one is an exception: Brave New Work. It's an intelligent and readable summary of the best practices (so far) in remaking what we used to call "work." Aaron Dignan evaluates all the crazy ideas (open books, no bosses, etc.) to see which ones are effective in creating organizations that get us to do our best. He distills practical advice, too. — KK

ARTICLES & THREADS

100 Fantastic Articles

I'm working my way through this outstanding collection of over 100 articles from around the web, curated by Conor Friedersdorf, a staff writer at The Atlantic. He included an article I wrote for Wired about losing my bitcoin password. — MF

Changing historical perspective

Every American should read at least the introductory essay in the NYT's 1619 Project, which documents the central role that slavery had in America's rise. Entitled "Our democracy's founding ideals were false when they were written. Black Americans have fought to make them true," it is a strong, tight argument that inverted my own ideas. The whole 1619 package is a seminal work. — KK

Inspirational read

This list of "20 Essential Truths That Women Over 50 Want To Share With Younger Women" seem like no-brainers and things I should already be doing daily, but unfortunately for me, I forget. I made a shorter, more personal version of this list for myself and if I'm ever feeling agitated or unbalanced, I read it again to gain perspective and make everything all better. — CD

Unusual articles

Wikipedia's "Unusual articles" page has links to hundreds of eclectic and offbeat articles. Learn about the Korean invasion of Normandy, happy numbers, and the Phantom time hypothesis (it's really 1719, not 2016 as we've been led to believe). I'd love this as a multi-volume hardbound illustrated set. — MF

Industry secrets

I crave insider knowledge. This Reddit thread feeds my desire to hear what's really going on in everyday businesses. It simply asks people "What's an industry secret in the field you work in?" There's a couple hundred responses, like: Goodwill throws away most of what is given to them; in vodka, the bottle costs more to make than the vodka; it's easy to get library fines waived; bouncers make up the rules; there is way more butter than you think in almost every dish at fancy restaurants; etc. — KK

The best writing on the internet

The Browser is by far the best guide to great writing on the internet. It's a newsletter that recommends 4 or 5 great pieces a day — both new ones or those years old — that are worth your time (and it indicates the pieces' length). Although there is a paid daily version, the free weekly version is a good place to start. I find this newsletter dangerous because the wide variety of subjects is intoxicating and every single article is superb. It's the most potent distraction in my life, but I don't regret a minute of it. — KK

Bad Blood

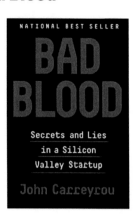

My wife and I tore through John Carreyrou's Bad Blood. It's the story of Theranos, the fraudulent Silicon Valley startup that promised to revolutionize health but instead perpetrated a potentially murderous scam. The founder surrounded herself with ultrarich powerful people who were blind to obvious warning signs because they were so enamored with the idea that they were going to make billions of dollars. This real-life tale beats any fictional corporate thriller. — MF

The value of goofing off

The premise of this book, Time Off, is that you can't maintain a great work ethic without having a great "rest ethic." You have to take time off, vacation, go on sabbatical, pause, rest, sleep, slack, play, and goof off in order to be and do your best. I've long been

a champion of slack time and mandatory time off, and I am delighted all the arguments and evidence for this take are presented in this hefty book. It includes examples of very productive people, and the latest scientific evidence. Time off is not only essential to a good life, it is something you can get better at. — KK

Get comfortable with uncertainty

I've had this book (Comfortable with Uncertainty by Pema Chödrön) for years but find myself pulling it off the shelf more in the last month than ever before. You don't need to be a meditation expert or Buddhist to appreciate

the message. Each chapter is a short lesson in self-compassion and awareness, designed to make you comfortable with uncertainty. It is one of those books you can open to any page and find wisdom. There is a Kindle version, but I think it belongs in everyone's library. — CD

Old but still new

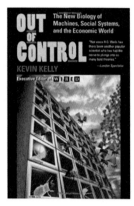

Twenty-five years ago I published my first book Out of Control. In celebration of this anniversary, I re-read the whole gigantic thing and picked out 100 passages to tweet, which you can find at #OoC25. I have to say, the book is still a great read, and probably more informative today than 25 years ago. I recommend it as an easy entry into robotics, artificial life, cryptocurrency, simulations, evolution theory, and the nature of decentralized systems like the internet. If you like the tweets, you'll want to read the book. — KK

Award-winning Chinese science fiction novel

A science fiction novel I really liked is *The Three-Body Problem*. It is the first Chinese-written novel to win a Hugo award. It is making waves in China and, in a new English translation, with the rest of the world. Complicated, deep, and steeped in a different view of China, it's a masterpiece. — KK

More Chinese science fiction

A red-hot area in science fiction these days is China. Like many fans who enjoyed The Three Body Problem, I wanted more. So the translator of that mega hit, Ken Liu, has translated two volumes of Chinese short stories with a sci-fi/fantasy focus. The first anthology, Invisible Planets, is a sampler offering lots of magical realism, fantasy and a few hard-science pieces. The second, Broken Stars, has more speculative fiction, and

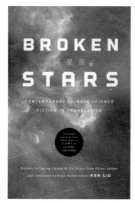

feels more Chinese. As in any anthology, the quality is uneven, but a few stories are standouts and I got a solid feel for this embryonic movement. — KK

The 250 best adventure novels of the 20th century

Voracious adventure novel reader Josh Glenn put together a list of 250 of his favorite adventure novels of the 20th century, with a capsule review of each book. I've already added a bunch to my reading list. Many are available on Project Gutenberg and other public domain book and audiobook websites. — MF

Library of America

The Library of America publishes high-quality hardbound books with multiple novels per volume. I'm reading *Ross Macdonald: Three Novels of the Early 1960s*, which contains three excellent novels about fictional Los Angeles detective Lew Archer. These tightly-written page-turners have kept me up way past my bedtime. — MF

My favorite $1.71 paperback novel

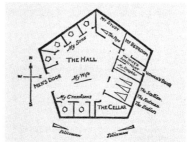

Flatland is a novel by Edwin Abbott Abbott, published in 1884. It's written as a biography by "A. Square," a two-dimensional creature who is literally a living square, thinner than a sheet of paper. He lives with other two-dimensional creatures on a surface called Flatland. In the book, Mr. Square tells of his adventures in worlds of different dimensions: Pointland (zero dimensions), Lineland (one dimension), and Spaceland (three dimensions) all inhabited with creatures suited for their respective worlds. Abbott does a wonderful job of world building, explaining how the society (a satire of the Victorian society) and infrastructure of Flatland works. Even though the book was written 135 years ago, I found it very easy to read. Amazon is selling the Dover edition of Flatland for less than the price of a cup of coffee. I just bought it for my daughter. — MF

DIGITAL HIGHLIGHTING

Remember what you read

If you read books on Kindle or iBooks you should be using Readwise. I got turned on to Readwise by Recomendo readers Chris Galtenberg and Len Edgerly almost two years ago, and it's become an integral part of how I read and retain the words and ideas that grab me. Every passage I highlight in my Kindle is auto-imported and sent back to me in a thrice-weekly email (you can choose the frequency and number of highlights you receive). This service is free for a trial period. I pay $4.99/per month for the upgraded version that allows you to import highlights from other sources, like Medium and Twitter. And I also have it synced to my Evernote account, so that anytime new highlights are imported, my Evernote is updated immediately. Using

Readwise makes me want to read more and highlight more, I've even started inputing the highlighted passages from my favorite paper books. You can read a random selection of my highlights at: https://readwise.io/@claudia. — CD

Readwise update

Claudia recommended Readwise a while back, but since then this powerful ebook and article highlighting app has added a lot of new useful features. You can highlight excerpts from Pocket and Instapaper, and even grab clips of podcasts, which are automatically transcribed into text (using the new airr podcast player). Best of all, I can browse and search all my ebook, article, and podcast highlights on the Readwise website or Evernote. It's an indispensable tool. — MF

Your Kindle highlights

As you read a Kindle you can, with some effort, highlight a passage. The best way to extract those passages so that you can cut and paste them later, or so you can insert the text into an article, or otherwise use a highlight as text, is to go to this page and login with your Amazon credentials. You'll see your highlights book by book. There you select texts and copy them. Or on that page use Bookcision, a browser bookmarklet, that will download each book's passages as a text file. — KK

Kindle hack

I often want to read a long PDF someone sends me on my Kindle. Here is the hack to get it loaded. Use your Kindle account name to create a Kindle email as yourname@ free.kindle.com. In the subject line of an email message put

< convert >. Enclose the PDF and hit send. Amazon will convert the PDF to their Kindle format and it will show up in your library. Then you can select it to download to your device. The PDF on a Kindle is clunky but readable. — KK

Further refinements on the Kindle hack by two readers:

I was trying to read Ellul's Propaganda. I downloaded it from archive.org (which is now crucial to my PDF kindle hack, including old Arthur Koestler books and other hard-to-find titles). Sadly it was 30MB, and the emailed file couldn't upload. For days I sat there frustrated. Then I realized the hack: I split the PDF into two files of 15MB each and named them Propaganda Part I and Propaganda Part II. Wham, solves it. — Bryan Campen

There is an even easier way to transfer a PDF to Kindle. If you download the Kindle app for Mac or PC you can drag a PDF to the app icon (which I keep in my dock on the Mac). You can configure the app to convert to Kindle format or keep the file as a PDF. You can also choose which of your Kindle/Fire devices you want it sent to. — Len Edgerly (The Kindle Chronicles Podcast)

300-page tool recommendation book

Kevin and Mark host a weekly podcast called Cool Tools. For more than 5 years now

they have invited notable and creative people to talk about their favorite tools. This year, I took the transcripts from the best 150 episodes and pulled text, added images, and laid it all out in a 300-page book titled Four Favorite Tools. It is now available on Amazon in both color ($39.99) and B&W ($12.99) versions. Inside the book are hundreds and hundreds of recommendations for apps, gadgets, tools — but my recommendation is the book itself as a handbook for inspiration. — CD

The handmade life

Many folks dream of being self-sufficient on a half-acre homestead somewhere. The person I know who's come closest to that goal is Lloyd

Kahn, who has evolved a do-it-yourself lifestyle near a city that really works and is not a fantasy. He's put his 46 years of building his own homes, foraging for wild foods, raising plants, traveling in a van, working from home, self-publishing, and all-around DIY into one photographic book. The Half-Acre Homestead is not how-to; it's a visual demonstration of what an integrated handmade life looks like, for real. At 85 years young, Lloyd Kahn is still doing it! He is one of my heros. — KK

Population heresy

A book that recently changed my mind is Empty Planet: The Shock of Global Population Decline. In great scholarly detail the authors outline the near certainty of a population implosion all around the world in the next 50 years, starting right now in Japan, Europe, and quickly moving into the rest of the developing world in the coming decade. They calculate China will lose half

READABLE

of its population by the end of this century, and Mexico will need to import migrants. This inverts all kinds of political assumptions. The most newsworthy book I've read in awhile. — KK

An honest book about motherhood

The Female Assumption is a raw and honest look at becoming a mother and the pressures on women to reproduce. I couldn't put it down. Mother of 3, Melanie Holmes interviewed mothers from all over to accurately portray what happens behind the curtain of motherhood. She also includes the stories of women who have consciously chosen to not be mothers. This book is a well-balanced pros and cons list for either path, and a reminder that whatever you decide for yourself is the right choice. Every young woman should read this. — CD

You are a strange loop

I recently read I Am Strange Loop, by Douglas Hofstadter, which makes the

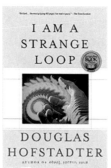

argument that one's sense of self is a mirage that arises out of a cognitive feedback loop. I struggled with many parts of the book, but want to reread it because I believe Hofstadter is onto something. In the meantime, I enjoyed Will Schroeder's 20-minute video, called You Are A Strange Loop, which summarizes the book in an approachable way. — MF

5 life-changing books

I am a very happy user of You Need a Budget (YNAB), a personal finances subscription service. They also have a good YouTube channel and I particularly enjoyed this episode where the host recommended five books that changed her life. Those books are:

The 5 Second Rule

You Need a Budget

Daring Greatly

How to Manage Your Home Without Losing Your Mind

Getting Things Done.

— MF

Popular books in 12 minutes

I recently got a subscription to 12min, a library of condensed non-fiction books (audio and text). New titles are added all the time. I've found it especially useful to refresh my memory on books I read years ago, like Richard Dawkins' The Selfish Gene, Yuval Noah Harari's Sapiens, Nassim Nicholas Taleb's Fooled By Randomness, and Tim Ferriss's *Tools of Titans*. A lifetime subscription to 12min is $39. — MF

Read first pages of novels

When you go to Recommend Me a Book you are presented with the first page of a novel, but you are not told the name

of the book or the author. If you don't like what you've read, click "Next Book." If you do like it, click "Reveal Title & Author," and buy it from Amazon. I wish it let you buy a book without finding out who wrote it, so it was a surprise when it arrived in the mail. — MF

Find out the order of books

Amazon does a poor job of presenting book series in order. I wanted the chronological order of Raymond Chandler's Philip Marlowe novels. The website Order of Books had it, along with many other book series. — MF

Find out how long to read any book

Before you pick the next book on your reading list you should check out How Long to Read. Their search engine includes more than 12 million books and their speed reading timer will calculate

approximately how long it will take you to read the book in its entirety. — CD

Find a book by asking questions

Google's Talk to Books uses experimental AI to browse book passages that respond to your questions. I asked "How can I time travel?" and got back a rabbit hole of responses. It's pretty much a dream come true. — CD

Library vs Amazon

Remember libraries, where content is free? Library Extension is a browser extension that will tell you

whether a book you are looking at on an Amazon page is available in your local library. If it is you can click on the button to put a hold on the book, or find which branch has it. Very nicely done. Like libraries it's free. Works on Chrome and Firefox. — KK

Sampling books

Several power users of the Kindle turned me on to a great tip: load up your Kindle or phone with free sample chapters of any and all books you are interested in. Read the sample (usually the first) chapter and then decide if you want to buy the book. In fact, don't buy any book until you've read the sample chapter. The "Send free sample" button is under the "Buy Now" button on the book's Amazon page. — KK

Page turner aid

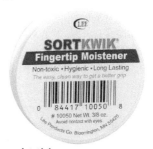

I bought this Sortkwik fingertip moisturizer so I could do card tricks better, but it turns out to be excellent for separating sheets of paper and turning book pages, too. If you have dry fingers, give this stuff a try. It's not greasy or sticky, it just adds a little extra grip. — MF

eBooks

Lovingly produced ebooks

Standard Ebooks is a labor of love. They take public domain texts (from Robert E. Howard to Bertrand Russell), scour them for typographical errors, add great cover art, and format them for Kindle and other e-readers. The online catalog is a pleasure to browse, with a synopsis for each book. Join the mailing list or subscribe to the RSS feed for updates on new books added to the catalog. — MF

Revisiting Standard Ebooks

A year or two ago I recommended Standard Ebooks as a resource for free reading. They have since updated their catalog with a lot of new titles, so I thought it was time to re-recommend them. They take public domain texts

(by authors such as Robert E. Howard, Edith Wharton, Sarah Orne Jewett, Bertrand Russell), scour them for typographical errors, add excellent cover art, and format them for Kindle and other e-readers. Join the mailing list or subscribe to the RSS feed for updates on new books added to the catalog. — MF

Advance reader ebooks

If you are a "person of influence," particularly when it comes to books, and you'd like to read books before they are published (so you can rave about them when they are), you can sign up at NetGalley and get digital "advance reader copies (ARC)" of upcoming books. This is an early ebook edition used to promote the book. Most titles are available to all members, but some books need to be requested. For avid readers who like to talk about what they are reading, NetGalley is a handy service. — KK

Free bestselling ebooks

If you are an Amazon Prime member, you are entitled to two free Kindle ebooks per

month from a selection of 9 popular bestselling books chosen by Amazon that month. This same program, called First Reads, also gives you access to free short stories and Audible readings for listening, commissioned as Amazon originals. I can usually find at least one book I am interested in each month, and since it is free, why not? —KK

Check out library books from your phone

I feel like an idiot for not discovering OverDrive sooner. It's a free mobile app that lets you check out ebooks, audiobooks, and videos from your local public library. To use it, you need a local library card. I got a Los Angeles Library e-card by signing up online and a couple of minutes later I was reading A *Burglar's Guide to the City*. — MF

FOLLOWABLE

Instagram cliches made beautiful

Insta_Repeat is an Instagram account that beautifully highlights common cliches on Instagram. Like view through tent hole, or standing on white van. Hey, travel and outdoor Instagramers, don't do these! Try something different. Yet I follow it because arrays of the cliches are mesmerizing in their nearly identical images. — KK

Gallery of magazine covers

I don't read many paper magazines nowadays, but I appreciate good magazine covers. I've been working for magazines for decades and have learned that coming up with eye-grabbing, meaningful covers is the most challenging

aspect of publishing. *CoverJunkie* collects the best covers from magazines all over the world. They have an Instagram account, which is the best way to browse the gallery. — MF

Accidental Wes Anderson

A delightful Instagram account I enjoy: Accidental Wes Anderson. It's a curated collection

of still images in the style of a Wes Anderson movie. Same symmetry, colors, and tone. The way Wes Anderson would view this Instagram is not in a stream but in grid view. — KK

3D animation treats

One of my favorite Instagram follows is Esteban Diácono. He's a motion graphics designer who posts spellbinding "animation experiments" of humanoid dancing figures made of feathers, metal plates, outrageously long fur, and vegetation. They look real and impossible at the same time. — MF

Science fiction art

For the past year I have really been enjoying Sci-Fi Daily on Instagram which floats out one beautiful piece of science fiction artwork each day. Some of the images contain an entire movie within them. — KK

Marriage Minute

marriage minute
from The Gottman Institute

Sleepless in Seattle

In the film "Sleepless in Seattle," Tom Hanks plays a widowed man (Sam Baldwin) whose son calls a radio talk show (Dr. Marcia Fieldstone) in an attempt to find his dad a new wife.

Dr. Marcia Fieldstone: Tell me what was so special about your wife?

Sam Baldwin: It was a million tiny little things that, when you added them all up, they meant we were supposed to be together, and I knew it. I knew it the first time I touched her. It was like coming home, only to no home I'd ever known. I was just taking her hand to help her out of a car and I knew it. It was like magic.

His response gets at our motto of "small things often."

On their own, a million tiny little things don't seem that important, but when you add them all up, they make a big difference.

I really look forward to getting the twice-weekly Marriage Minute by The Gottman Institute. The advice given is based on more than 40 years of research and the emails are always a quick read. It's definitely inspired me in my first year of marriage. Here's an issue I really appreciated about self soothing. — CD

Cartoonist instagram

Cartoonist Danny Hellman did a lot of illustrations for "Boing Boing" when it was a zine in the 1990s. His Instagram feed reveals his fascination with European cemetery statuary, and his photos reveal some striking examples. — MF

LiarTown USA

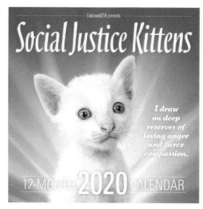

Designer Sean Tejaratchi's website LiarTownUSA contains Sean's profoundly absurd (and occasionally R-rated) parody book covers, TV show credits, collectible plates, store signs, and advertising ephemera. He's a genius. — MF

A month of curiosities

Every December means it's time for blinry's Advent Calendar of Curiosities. Every day of the month, Sebastian "blinry" Morr will post interesting bits of little-known history, culture, or trivia. You can browse earlier years by altering the URL (it goes back to 2011). — MF

The Journal

Most of the email newsletters I subscribe to go unread. Kevin Rose's "The Journal" is one I always read. Kevin points to interesting science articles (The brain starts to eat itself after chronic sleep deprivation), finds provocative quotes ("Give me six hours to chop down a tree and I will spend the first four sharpening the axe."), and reviews products and apps that he finds useful. — MF

Newsletter about the Art of Noticing

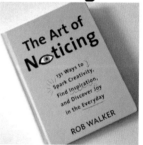

Writer and New York Times columnist Rob Walker has a book coming out in May called "The Art of Noticing: 131 Ways to Spark Creativity, Find Inspiration, and Discover Joy In the Everyday" and he has relaunched his wonderful grab-bag newsletter of cultural signals, trends, and curiosities to promote it. I look forward to every issue. — MF

1970s sci-fi art

I'm enjoying this stream of old science fiction art, mostly from the heyday in the 1970s. Comes as an Instagram, Twitter, Tumblr, or RSS feed. — KK

Stunning travel instagram

Instagram encourages envy. I am totally envious of the photography of Jord Hammond on Instagram. He travels to the kind of remote places I go, but he gets stunning images on a regular basis. Each one is a classic, requiring a lot of work, and captures the spirit of a place. — KK

Video treats

These little video experiments from Dirk Koy are fantastic. They are short kinetic loops, like a long gif, that explore perspective shifts, new POVs, and re-framing motion graphics. Quick surprises. — KK

Literary inspiration

Belletrist

My favorite newsletter right now is from actress Emma Roberts' female-focused book of the month club called *Belletrist*. Weekly emails include interviews with women authors who share their favorite books and articles, among other things. Here's a link to their archive to check out. I'm also loving the Belletrist Spotify playlists featuring songs that inspired authors while writing their books. — CD

Make 100 things

Project We Love

The Tiny Type Museum and Time Capsule

A tiny museum of authentic type and printing artifacts from letterpress to the present; a prized possession...

by Glenn Fleishman and 391 backers

The crowdfunding platform Kickstarter has become so successful that it's also become a big deal to succeed by it. Big projects, big productions to launch, and big sums raised. To scale things back, Kickstarter launched the "Make 100" campaign to encourage makers to simply make one hundred of something. A multitude of makers have responded with limited editions of low-budget cool things, without a lot of fuss. I've backed a handful of them. It has also inspired me to make my own 100 of something. – KK

Fond follower

Someone I started following on Twitter who I enjoy is Noah Smith as @ Noahpinion. Wide range of interests, topical but unexpected opinions, likes to hunt for data and evidence. — KK

ASIAN TRENDS

Extreme street fashion

Japanese youth have more fun with fashion than anyone. When I need a dose of pick-me-up, a bit of fresh thinking, or a smile, I head over to the Tokyo Fashion Tumblr, which features the latest eye-popping street-fashion finds on the streets of Tokyo. Never dull. — KK

Japanese trends

The curiously named blog "Spoon & Tamago" is the best way to keep up with the latest art, design, fads, and lifestyle innovations from Japan. They also offer a nice feature: curated "guides" to Tokyo via interesting long-term residents. A well crafted well-designed site, as might be expected. Add 'em to your RSS feed. — KK

Traditional life in China

In China, Li Ziqi is a huge online star. She is sort of a hippy young Martha Stewart — a DIYer and maker, as well as ancient lifestyle guru. Dressed in traditional garb, Li Ziqi posts hundreds of videos about making traditional Chinese rural things from scratch with traditional tools — in an extreme way. She'll make a silk comforter by first raising silk worms. She'll make her own soy sauce by first growing soy beans. She'll make some bamboo furniture in a day, starting with harvesting the bamboo. Plus she plays guitar and sings! To her 50 million followers in China, her idyllic and blemish-free videos are soothing and an antidote to their overworked urban lives. She delivers nostalgia for the country life they left — without the drudgery and starvation. To her 8 million foreign followers, like me, watching her on YouTube, her impossibly romantic videos are cinematic glimpses of vanishing arts and crafts, of amazing and ingenious ways millions of people thrived in the past. I could watch them for hours. — KK

Only in Asia

I get my LOLs by following the "Only in Asia" Twitter feed. They pass along all the weird and crazy stuff from Asia. Clips from Japanese game shows, web cams from China, funniest phone videos from Indonesia. You can't make this stuff up. — KK

Time travel in Asia

With shameless self-promotion I recommend you follow my new Vanishing Asia Instagram. Every day I post one amazing photo I have taken of an exotic part of Asia that is disappearing because of modernity. The images are a few of the many thousand that will appear in my Vanishing Asia book later this year. In the meantime, enjoy this ride in a time machine. — KK

If You High (and even if you aren't)

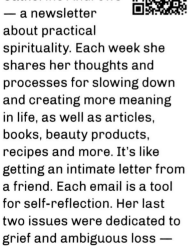 The ifyouhigh Instagram account has 3.4 million followers, but I recently stumbled on it and am hooked. It's an endless scroll of strange and beautiful short videos of natural phenomena, machinery in motion, slo-mo, time-lapse, art, and other "Whoa dude!" moments that you don't need to be high to appreciate. — MF

Sunday Soother

 I love reading The Sunday Soother by Catherine Andrews — a newsletter about practical spirituality. Each week she shares her thoughts and processes for slowing down and creating more meaning in life, as well as articles, books, beauty products, recipes and more. It's like getting an intimate letter from a friend. Each email is a tool for self-reflection. Her last two issues were dedicated to grief and ambiguous loss — which I learned is a particular type of loss that lacks a definition and closure. She solicited stories from her readers and here is what was shared. — CD

9 Eyes

This blog is called 9-Eyes because the cameras on cars that take photos for Google's Street View maps have 9 lenses. The anonymous curator of this site posts unusual photos they come across on Street View. Most of the photos are of people being people: acting silly, fighting, eating, pulling leashes attached to livestock, soliciting prostitutes, taking drugs, nursing their young, etc. Endlessly fascinating. — MF

Kottke

Not enough people know about Jason Kottke's blog, *Kottke*. Jason's official full-time job is to surf around the web looking for truly interesting stuff, which he posts along with a paragraph of why he found it remarkable. He creates a handful daily, and has for 18 unbelievable years!

No clickbait, no barrage of ads and no soap box. Just old-school blogging about neat things. — KK

Old music Twitter feed

 Dust-to-Digital is a record label specializing in early, hard-to-find music. They have a terrific Twitter feed with videos I've never seen of performers like Sister Rosetta Tharpe, Papa Jo Jones, Eddie Cochran, and Koko Taylor. I spent an enjoyable couple of hours watching the videos. — MF

See what's in people's bags

 We have a new weekly newsletter called What's in my bag? Each week, one interesting person shares four favorite things they carry in their bag. Last week Mark shared the four things he always travels with, which he keeps in Japanese see-through zipper bags. Check it out! — CD

Nerdy makers

Wheelhouse #12: With Spencer Wright
Toolboxes, Organizing, and Cutting
Joshua Schachter
Aug 10

Wheelhouse #11
Print Transfer, Press Forming, and Typing
Joshua Schachter
Aug 1

Wheelhouse #10: Wiring Edition
Wheelhouse is a newsletter for makers that covers new materials, techniques, and tools. Crimping vs Soldering Those that come from an electronics backg...
Joshua Schachter
Jun 19

As someone who makes things, I am very interested in new materials, cool ways to hack off-the-shelf products, and innovative techniques for constructing stuff. All these subjects are covered in an occasional free newsletter, Wheelhouse, written for nerdy makers. Wheelhouse also hosts a Discord community whose discussions generate content for the newsletter. — KK

NextDraft

NEXTDRAFT
THE DAY'S MOST FASCINATING NEWS **FROM DAVE PELL**

enter email address   SUBSCRIBE

I'm enjoying Dave Pell's legendary free daily newsletter NextDraft. Each day he writes up to 10 short summaries of newsworthy items (in the broadest terms). Often unexpected, usually interesting, and always well-written. In a former time, this would have been a blog (and it is), but I am delighted to get it in my mail stream. — KK

Advice for the sane prepper

I'm not a prepper. I did zero prep for Y2K; didn't even fill my gas tank. A lot of prepper talk is sheer nuts, and even damaging. However in an emergency I aim to be a help not a burden, so some degree of being prepared is needed. The least insane prepper site is The Prepared, which dials back a lot of the paranoia and nuttiness, and is more Wirecutter-style reviews of gear. Their intensity is two notches above mine, but at least their advice is sane. I got some good tips about being responsibly prepared. — KK

Interesting miscellany

Digital strategist Laura Olin has a newsletter with interesting miscellany that contains links to useful tips, thought-provoking quotations, and links to articles and

LAURA OLIN

Girls racing sheep in Wales, 1965

videos. If you like Recomendo, you will like Laura's newsletter. — MF

Advice from books

PEAK
SECRETS FROM
THE NEW SCIENCE
OF EXPERTISE
Book Freak #65: How to Push Past
Your Comfort Zone

I recently started a weekly newsletter called Book Freak. Each issue has three short pieces of advice found in books. Here's an example, from issue 7: "If you want the law to leave you alone, keep your hair trimmed and your boots shined." Louis L'Amour, The Man Called Noon (1970) — MF

Delightful Twitter feed

For my Twitter feed I like following people who surprise me, and ideally, delight me. (Outrage is exhausting.) No one reliably surprises me with delight as much as Kurt

FOLLOWABLE

Kohlstedt, director of the 99% Invisible podcast. His Twitter feed delivers a steady stream of unexpected discoveries and insights. — KK

Following the unexpected

I like to follow people who consistently surprise me. Tyler Cowen's blog Marginal Revolution is a prime source of the unexpected. He collects surprisingly interesting papers and posts he unearths from different corners, plus trivial oddities, and profoundly insightful essays, and all of it thought-provoking. He posts at least a handful of items per day. (I follow his blog via my RSS reader.) — KK

FOR FUTURISTS

Futurism

I follow a lot of blogs on Feedly, the RSS reader. A favorite blog that reads well in RSS is *Futurism* — it's a steady stream of new ideas, inventions, and experiments from a wide range of sciences and technology. Their headlines are long and descriptive (often sufficient) rather than click-baity.— KK

Daily futurology news

Reddit's "Futurology" subreddit features news stories that point to our future. Stories such as "New antibiotic found in human nose," "Singapore Scientists Grow Mini Human Brains," and "Should a human-pig chimera be treated as a person?" I visit it daily. — MF

Artificial intelligence news daily

I feel it is important to keep up with the advent of AI, so I subscribe to a daily email one-pager which succinctly reports the news in AI each day. There is a lot happening, but this email is short and to the point. Get it from Inside AI. — KK

News from the Future

In addition to Recomendo, I also write a newsletter for Institute for the Future, called "News from the Future." It comes out twice a week and each issue has four or five short news items that are signals of possible futures that await us. Subscribe here. — MF

The long view

In a time of great complaints about new tech, I am encouraged by the Pessimist Archive which goes through historical records collecting end-of-the-world rants about the horrors of such inventions as bicycles, subways, and electricity. Most complaints about modern things could have been recycled from 100 years ago. The Pessimist Archive is a necessary counterpoint to complain wisely today. I follow both their Twitter stream and their podcast. — KK

NEWSFEED

Text-only CNN

CNN | 2018-8-24 | Español

Main Stories

- Pope on Pennsylvania abuse report: We abandoned the little ones
- Read Pope Francis' letter on abuse
- 'Your faith is shaken,' Catholics react to report detailing sexual abuse by
- Pennsylvania AG: Cardinal under scrutiny over report on priest abuse 'i
- Trump rewrites history as Russia probe pressure mounts
- Trump keeps up attacks on Mueller probe following McGahn revelation

This no-graphics version of CNN's website looks like the web circa 1993, and I love it. I think they should run a couple of text ads to monetize it, because I don't want them to stop. — MF

Good news, daily

Here is where I go to counter pessimism. Every day, one piece of good news, made graphically beautiful, is served up by Beautiful News Daily. Available on Twitter, Instagram, Facebook, RSS feed, and the web. It's like breathing pure oxygen. — KK

My best news source

NEWS ITEMS

I get a bunch of email newsletters but the only one I pay for is News Items. Every weekday the one-person wizard behind News Items, John Ellis, delivers a dozen brief paragraphs of global news summarized from 75 uncommon sources, including many behind pay walls. News Items is much more global, more high level, and much more succinct (two pages at most) than any newspaper in the world. It's $90 per year, and there is a free abbreviated version. — KK

Internet on one page

Every day I get the entire internet compressed into a single page. My first stop in the morning is the one-page Upstract (formerly called Hvper, and previous to that, Popurls) Upstract is a super

aggregator that collects the top headlines of every news source out there into ONE single page. I see what's at the top of mind in the both the New York Times and Wall Street Journal, plus HuffPo and Fox News, plus Al Jazeera and the Drudge Report. Plus Reddit, Digg, BuzzNews, Twitter, CNN, ABC, Verge, Wired, and on and on. All of it! The whole news media landscape in a one-page dashboard. Each headline is clickable directly to the source. It is fast, clean (no ads!), free and magical. Must read. Upstract also can deliver a free daily one-page email (formerly called Briefing Day) that lists the top web results voted by subscribers to Upstract. Sort of like Reddit and Digg. It's curated by Thomas Marban who created Upstract, Hvper, and Popurls. I usually click on one or two items each day. — KK

READERS

Best RSS reader

I've come to appreciate blogs more and more. They are reliable sources of informed enthusiasm and news that stays new. I've been surprised how few people use an RSS reader to subscribe to their select choices of blogs because a great RSS reader like Feedly is a tool I use every day. With Feedly, I can read the newest posts of any blog I subscribe to on my laptop or phone in a smooth, intelligent form. It is MUCH easier to read a blog on RSS than it is to go to the website, and it also strips away all ads and other marginalia, so I only see the core text and images. Feedly isn't the only RSS reader, but it's stable and highly evolved and I love it. — KK

Social media digest

More people should know about Nuzzel. It's the sane and

efficient way I consume social media without having to read it. Nuzzel displays the six most recommended links each day among all the people I follow on social media. So instead of reading those endless feeds, I read my one page Nuzzel digest and get the six best articles that are most read by my friends. — KK

Narwhal for Reddit

If you have an iPhone, Narwhal is the best app to access Reddit. It's snappy, highly customizable and much easier to use than Reddit's own app. — MF

Best news app

Smartnews is a free, lightweight, mobile app for iOS and Android. It presents

the top news stories in different categories and is updated frequently. You can add your favorite news sites to it, too. When I want to find out what's going on, it's the first place I go. — MF

Use Feedly for real-time keyword alerts

I've been a long-time user of Google Alerts to help me track internet mentions of anything work-related like "Recomendo." Google Alerts are free and easy to set up, and every week I get an email digest of new results. And if you're a paying customer of Feedly Pro like me, you can fine-tune your keyword searches to get real-time alerts and create your own custom newsroom. 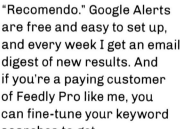 These Feedly tips will help you refine your keyword searches, discover more results and weed out whatever is irrelevant. — CD

Insider industry news

I've become of a fan of Inside newsletters. Once a day I get a brief summary of what's been reported in a narrow specialized field, like AI, or VR, or Space, or Robotics. Succinct, select, in depth, and free. Inside also offers newsletters focused on each of the big tech companies, like Amazon or Google. And they now offer inside industry news on fashionable sectors like Cannabis or Beer. – KK

Trend spotter

A free newsletter I find valuable is Exploding Topics. The weekly emails spotlights about 5 words or phrases that are quickly rising in popularity among web searches and social media mentions. The terms might be a product, a company name, a bit of slang, a Millennial catch phrase. It's a nice easy way to track what's rapidly trending. (Explanations of the trends are included in the newsletter but not the website.) — KK

China cultural news

TECH BUZZ CHINA BY PANDAILY

Ep. 76: Lufax IPO and the end of P2P lending in China

In episode 76 of Tech Buzz China, co-hosts Rui Ma and Ying Lu take advantage of the recent Lufax IPO filing (Chinese name: 陆金所 lùjīnsuǒ) to talk about the P2P...

Rui Ma and Ying Lu

NÜVOICES

Hong Kong media, redefined

Beijing's enactment of sweeping national security legislation in Hong Kong spurred fresh fear for the territory's cherished freedoms as authorities sought to quash months of...

NüVoices

MIDDLE EARTH — CHINA'S CULTURAL INDUSTRY PODCAST

China's board game industry

China's card and board games market size was valued at \$580 million in 2018, and is projected to reach \$1.6 billion by 2025. Minlu Chen, co-founder...

Aladin Farré

CAIXIN

The Caixin-Sinica Business Brief, episode 133

This week on the Caixin-Sinica Business Brief: Shenzhen will provide approximately \$1.5 million of coupons to residents to test the digital yuan, China's virtual currency;...

Kaiser Kuo

My two favorite sources for what's happening in China are these two blogs. Say I want to know, what are Chinese youth watching, reading or listening to? SupChina is a big sprawling website with auxiliary podcasts and newsletters, that comprehensively covers China's culture and politics. Based in NYC, it's slick and professional. Sixth Tone is a smaller publication based in Shanghai, with a slower rate, often deeper pieces, more off-beat and less headline-driven. Both give me a good pulse of a rising China and can be subscribed to via RSS. — KK

Stay up-to-date on most-edited Wikipedia articles

I've found another way to keep up with what's happening in the world that doesn't

the **WEEKLYPEDIA**

A list of the most edited Wikipedia articles and discussions from the last week.
Delivered every Friday by email.

Next issue: September 16, 2016 (Issue 131)

Join a list to receive a weekly email with the top twenty Wikipedia articles and top five Wikipedia discussions from this weekk, available in English and more languages.

SIGN UP!

Last week, in Issue 130: 109,974 users made 800,878 changes to 372,648 articles on English Wikipedia. The top articles for the week:

1. Birds in the Trap Sing McKnight (439 changes by 30 authors)
2. Deaths in 2016 (341 changes by 66 authors)
3. Events at Madison Square Garden (332 changes by 4 authors)
4. 2016 US Open (tennis) (324 changes by 21 authors)
5. Art Deco (293 changes by 9 authors)

Read the full issue

MORE LANGUAGES & ARCHIVES

involve "doomscrolling," and that is signing up for The Weeklypedia. Once a week, I'll get an email summarizing the top 20 Wikipedia articles with the most changes, the 10 most actively edited articles created in the past week and most active discussions on Wikipedia. — CD

Neighborhood network

Neighborhood

♡ Recommendations

◇ For Sale & Free

% Offers New

26 Events

⌂ Real Estate

! Crime & Safety

? Lost & Found

When you sign up for Nextdoor it's like instantly joining your

SOCIAL MEDIA DIET

News Feed Eradicator

I've been slowly weaning myself off Facebook. I still type it into my browser on autopilot, but now instead of getting lost in the bottomless feed, this chrome extension replaces it with a random quote. The quotes are repetitive, but you can add your own. Even so, I'm sure this helps my mental health in some way. — CD

Instagram advice

Slowly working on this piece of advice: "Unfollow IG models and influencers.

Start following artists and designers. Your entire outlook on life will change." Found this in my weekly Unreadit newsletter: Self Improvement. The curators of Unreadit pull all the best content from related subreddits and send you an email once a week. I've spent zero hours rummaging through Reddit in the last month because of this. — CD

Fake follower audit

None of us have as many followers as we think we do. Up to half may be bots or shills. Every now and then

I give myself a reality check by seeing how many fake followers I have on Twitter. I enter my twitter handle into SparkToro. Ouch, 21% are fake. — KK

Quickly access delete account pages

I began the year with a purging of accounts I no longer use like Facebook, Snapchat and LinkedIn. This Consumer Reports article has direct links to Delete Account pages for the major platforms. It spared me the hassle of navigating through settings in search of a delete button. — CD

---

neighborhood watch group. Plus you get local business recommendations from neighbors, classifieds and events. — CD

Keep informed of emergency activity

Whenever there is a swarm of firetrucks in our neighborhood, I check my Nextdoor app in case

anyone has posted any info, and it was there that one kind neighbor pointed me to the PulsePoint Respond app, which informs you of real-time medical and fire emergencies near you. If you're CPR-certified, you can also sign up to receive "CPR-needed" notifications if someone nearby is having a cardiac emergency. Unfortunately, it's not available in all areas yet, but definitely worth checking out. — CD

NEWSLETTER DIRECTORIES

Newsletter App

I've been using the Stoop app to discover and read new newsletters. It's great to have them all in one place where I can let them pile up and read when I have the time. I'm really enjoying the Clearer Thinking newsletter, which offers tools for better decision-making. You can also find Recomendo on there! — CD

Subscribe to newsletters with one click

I'm frequently on the lookout for new newsletters and I found Letterlist to be a great website to discover interesting new content. You can browse their curated collection of newsletters for free, but if you sign up (also free) you can subscribe to the ones you want with their 1-click button instead of having to type out your email address over and over again. — CD

Discover newsletters by subject

Newsletter Stack is a directory of newsletters grouped by learning topics like COVID-19, Philosophy, Design, Wellness, etc. The website seems to be updated frequently. I signed up for all the Creativity topic newsletters. My favorite one is The Creative Independent, which explores the emotional facets of "creating" with a different working artist each weekday. — CD

Article saver

Whenever I come across an article online that I want to read later, I click the Pocket icon on my browser toolbar. It adds the article to a list so I can read it later on my phone when I have time. Pocket also stores the articles offline and presents them in a stripped-down, easy-to-read format. I use the free version, but there's a pro version with additional features for $5 per month. — MF

Sort by reading time

Read Ruler is a must-have if you use Pocket. It sorts all the articles you saved to read later by how long it takes to read. Most of my saves take 5-minutes, so I try to knock them out during my work day when I need a mental break. — CD

WHAT TO WATCH

Swedish funny

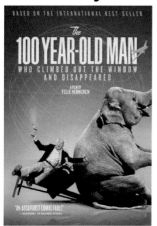

Deep in the basement of Netflix is a very funny Swedish movie called *The 100-Year-Old Man Who Climbed Out the Window and Disappeared*. Subtitled in English, I found the humor translated well into American. It's sort of a Swedish version of *Forrest Gump* meets *Mr. Bean*. This big hit in Sweden was playing on Netflix streaming but now is on Netflix DVD only. However, last year they made a sequel that is almost as good, *The 101-Year-Old Man Who Skipped Out on the Bill and Disappeared*, and this one is currently streaming on Netflix. — KK

Funny watchable

Ronnie Chieng makes me laugh. Might be because most of my relatives are Asian American, but I think his humor is much broader than that. You can catch him on Netflix's stand-up special Ronnie Chieng: Asian Comedian Destroys America. — KK

Completely improvised comedy special

Before I watched Middleditch and Schwartz, the very little improv I was exposed to was not enjoyable. I get anxious when jokes don't land and then I sympathy laugh and the whole thing is awkward. But now I'm stuck at home and in desperate need of laughs, and this has been the best comedy special I've seen. It's like they've harnessed the superpowers of a childlike imagination and then threw it into adult situations, and it's hilarious and magical to watch. — CD

Silicon Valley

A series I am binging on is *Silicon Valley*. I know all these people and every detail of their lives and situations is pitch perfect right on. The producers get the tiniest details exactly right, from the technology to the mannerisms, as well as their bigger narrative. I haven't laughed so much in ages. At the same time, it's a remarkably fantastic advanced class in what technology companies are *really* like. Whether you want to work in one, or start one: watch this series. — KK

SCIENCE-FICTION

The Expanse

The best science fiction series now going is *The Expanse*. It's set in a plausible 200-year ahead horizon, a period where Earth, Mars, and Asteroid Belters are in conflict. The everyday details of life in 2200 are well defined and worn convincingly; the characters nuanced and realistic, with no glaring villains. The science is sound, the production values high, and the plot is a detective thriller. The first two seasons are free to watch on Amazon Prime. — KK

Serious lockdown viewing

To have a research station on another planet, we have to figure out how to recreate a tiny biosphere for humans. That's what the Biosphere 2 project in Arizona was trying to do in 1991. I was so interested in this experiement that I spent time locked inside their test module. But this $150 million structure was built by a theater group instead of scientists, and therein lies the drama worthy of a film. Skip the comedy (Biodome, 1996) and watch Spaceship Earth (2020), a new sympathetic documentary on this remarkable project. What they learned, of life support and human dynamics, should be better known. (Imagine being really locked down for 2 years.) — KK

Binge watch TV: Colony

I'm eagerly looking forward to season 3 of *Colony*, a science fiction thriller about a world under lockdown after aliens arrive and take over. We never see the aliens — the oppressors are the humans who have cut a deal with the aliens to administrate repressive and cruel martial law in exchange for better living conditions. The story centers on a family trying to survive in a militarized, walled-off Los Angeles, where the smallest infraction is punishable by death. — MF

A Year in Space

I am a huge fan of spending big bucks to explore space scientifically. But I bet humans won't settle (live long-term) on Mars, or the Moon, or in space willingly. To get a glimpse of why not, watch the Netflix mini-series, A Year in Space. This documentary follows two astronauts as they subject themselves to the harsh punishment of living off our planet. We'll keep improving the process of space fitness, but this documentary is very sobering about the steep cost of doing without the things we get for "free" on this planet. — KK

Chinese sci-fi movie

Chinese science fiction has arrived. A recently translated sci-fi trilogy, The Three Body Problem, by Cixin Liu, won the Hugo award and a popular following in the US. It is worth reading, and re-reading. Another of Cixin Liu's stories, The Wandering Earth, is a mega-hit movie in China, and is now streaming on Netflix. In Mandarin, with English subtitles, I'd call it a science fiction blockbuster with high-production values, special effects, and Chinese characteristics. It's not a great movie, but I recommend it as a great window into modern China and its vision; it is more about China than the future. Watch it. We don't have too many chances to see non-Hollywood science fiction. — KK

BattleBots

My mother-in-law is 90, doesn't speak English, and lives with us. She and I enjoy watching the new season 3 of BattleBots on Amazon Prime. This mindless machine-on-machine violence of robots demolishing other robots is universally entertaining, and spectacular. No language needed. — KK

Quirky series about marriage and afterlife

I stumbled across Forever on Amazon Prime having never heard of it. The show stars Fred Armisen and Maya Rudolph as a married couple stuck in the same old routine who then die, only to reunite in the afterlife and pick up right where they left off. It's so funny and unexpectedly romantic. There may or may not be a season 2. Fingers crossed there is, but even if not this 8-episode series feels complete and worth binge-watching. — CD

Russian Doll on Netflix

In Russian Doll, a video game programmer finds herself in an endless loop of dying and

repeating the same day. Each reboot requires her to dig deeper into her own existence, relationships, and trauma to figure out the purpose of the paranormal glitch and try to fix it. It is Groundhog Day meets Twilight Zone meets a life-coaching session from hell. It's great — I finished it in two days. — CD

Entertaining whodunnit

For sheer summer-movie enjoyment, we really liked Knives Out. This is a fun murder mystery constructed with fantastic, vivid characters, great acting, clever plotting and pitch-perfect editing. It's a real page turner, if you know what I mean. Now streaming on Amazon Prime. — KK

Perfect Blue

My family watches an awful lot of anime. We also like horror and thriller movies, so we enjoyed Perfect Blue, a violent, disturbing, R-rated psychological thriller from 1997 about a former pop idol who loses her ability to distinguish between fantasy and reality. If you like the films of Darren Aronofsky (Requiem for a Dream, Black Swan) you'll like Perfect Blue, because Aronofsky is a fan of the anime and even recreated a scene from it in Requiem for a Dream. — MF

French supernatural series

Les Revenants (The Returned) is a French supernatural television series (with English subtitles) that my wife and I are enjoying. The first episode opens with a terrible school bus accident in the Alps that leaves 38 children dead. Four years later, some of the children return home, un-aged and unharmed. Spooky and fun. — MF

Glitch

In a sleepy Australian town, a group of long-dead people come to life and dig themselves out of their graves. Unlike traditional zombies, they are intact, both mentally and physically. They are as confused as the good-natured sheriff who becomes their protector against people who wish them harm. Can't wait for the next season of Glitch, this intriguing Netflix original series. — MF

Laughing at evil

For something completely different in movies, I recommend the intensely dark comedy The Death of Stalin. As the New Yorker said, its humor "is so black you could pump it out of the ground." Normally trivializing evil is not

something I could enjoy, but this story, loosely based on historical facts, is so over the top and well done, it was funny. Laughing at the horrifying atrocities seemed the only sane response. The movie skirted the soul's edge, but it worked for me. Available to rent on YouTube. — KK

Zero Days

I am not worried about much, but I do worry about cyber war. There is no consensus on what is acceptable in cyber warfare and all countries, including the US, are deploying cyber attacks. The best documentary to inform this worry is Zero Days, available on demand on Amazon, iTunes, GooglePlay, etc. It shows what cyber war is. Not sci-fi, but what is already here yesterday. With more to come! — KK

HISTORICAL

The Story of China

We are entering the century of China. Our collective future is dependent on its future, and China's future is highly constrained by its past. By far the best history of China so far is a 6-part BBC experience now running on Amazon Prime by the peripatetic historian Michael Woods. *The Story of China* boasts incredibly high production values, filmed in China. A thousand-year history is grounded in visits to the actual places where it happened, making it visible and intimate. More importantly this program presents an understandable history that sadly even most Chinese today are ignorant of. Woods is a likeable host who will make you smart. I consider *The Story of China* essential viewing. (His *Story of India* is likewise great.) — KK

Musical travel

Latcho Drom is a 25-year old French documentary that explores the historical migration of (and connection between) music from the nomads of western India to the Roma deep in the heart of Europe. It has no narration, and essentially no speaking at all. The film just follows music being played and sung by genuine local musicians in their authentic homes as it travels westward. The film itself is a long song and quite unlike anything else I've seen. You can watch it in full on YouTube. — KK

Vietnam War masterpiece

I'm late in getting to Ken Burn's masterpiece The Vietnam War, a 10-part documentary streaming on Netflix. But OMG, it is electrifying. Even though I lived through that war, I apparently knew nothing about it. It would have been easy (and cheap) to stir up a continuous thread of outrage, but instead this monumental work stirs up a continuous thread of clarity and insights: "Oh, so that is why they did that!" This should be mandatory viewing for all citizens of the US and Vietnam. — KK

Theological fantasy

I've been wow'd by the Netflix series Messiah, and binged all 10 episodes in a few sittings. The initial premise is:

What if a Jesus figure came to the Mid East today and started doing miracles? Would he be declared a fake? A Prophet? By what religions? A potential revolutionary terrorist? All of the above? It goes on from there in unexpected ways, including becoming a CIA thriller. The Messiah's lines are really good. — KK

BOLLYWOOD

Recomended Bollywood

I recommend this long movie for a stay-at-home visit to India. This 2009 Bollywood hit is called 3 Idiots (a better title would be 3 Renegades) and was the all-time bestselling movie in India in its time. Besides being fun and campy, almost a parody of a Bollywood hit, it is a brilliant depiction of the ongoing tension between tradition and innovation in this most populous country on the planet. Here's what a billion young Indians are contending with. Although it is almost 3 hours long, I've seen it three times. This version on Amazon Prime is in Hindi. You need to turn CC on for subtitles. — KK

Social mission Bollywood

Two notable Bollywood films give you that special dose of outlandish song, dance and

rom-com drama that you expect with a Bollywood extravaganza, plus they advance a vital social cause. And they will give you deep insight into today's India. Both films are about a maverick who takes it upon himself to undo an entrenched detrimental Indian custom. Interestingly, the same Bollywood super-star, Akshay Kumar, plays the protagonist in both films, which are based on true stories. Toilet: A Love Story is the movie version of a real guy who tried to put toilets in his home against the wishes of the village, and his wife is pressured to divorce him for this affront, and how this became a national campaign. Padman is the true story of a guy trying to get Indian village

women to use sanitary pads instead of being quarantined outside during menstruation. He invents a way to make the pads cheaply, which he tests on himself. (!!!) His wife also divorces him. But all ends well in both films — it's Bollywood! There is a third film, a straight documentary about the real Padman, called Period. End of Sentence. This won an Oscar this year for a documentary short. Quite inspirational. All three films can be streamed on Netflix with English subtitles. The first two are painless entryways into Bollywood. — KK

Epic Bollywood spectacle

If you have never seen a Bollywood movie, the action epic Bahubali is a great one to start. The plot revolves

around a mythical demigod, Bahubali, who must reclaim his throne.
This 2-movie 5-hour extravaganza is part Lord of the Rings saga, part kung-fu spectacle, part crazy soap opera, part Saturday morning cartoon, part LSD trip, and unlike anything you've seen. It is ridiculously corny, absurdly fictional, un-ironically campy, and immensely cinematic. It's a lot of fun, all 5 hours of it. It streams on Netflix in 4 different languages. (The films are technically Tollywood, filmed in Telugu language, not Hindi.) The first movie, Bahubali: The Beginning has an English-dubbed audio version, while the second movie, Bahubali: The Conclusion, has an English subtitle version. These films are the highest-grossing films in India. Once seen, they cannot be unseen. — KK

Quiet masterpiece

Do yourself a favor and watch Shtisel, a two-season (24 episode) series on Netflix. It's an incredibly written Isreali drama that is now a world-wide hit. It just happens to take place in an ultra-orthodox Jewish family. Ironically, it is a big hit in many conservative Muslim countries because these two traditional cultures overlap so much. Part of Shtisel's charm is the full immersion into a world that is as alien as Mars to most moderns, but the main attraction in this global gem is its universal humanism and real people characters. (Shtisel should not be confused with Unorthodox, another recent good Netflix series taking place in the same orthodox Jewish community, but with a very different ambiance and different artistic mission.) Shtisel is not loud or flashy; it is a quiet, low-budget masterpiece that leaves you feeling like you encountered something remarkable. — KK

The Mask You Live In

The Mask You Live In is a heartbreaking glimpse into

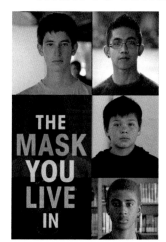

how the media and ideals of masculinity are affecting young boys in America. The most poignant part of the documentary for me were the interviews with San Quentin's Juvenile Lifers. They shared their experiences, and regret, about how being unable to articulate and share emotions as a child contributed to their rage and subsequent crimes. — CD

Tony Robbins documentary

My preconception of the mega-speaker Tony Robbins was shattered by a Netflix documentary on him. For decades I had the image of Robbins as an over-the-top motivational speaker, a fast-talking get-rich salesman, a new-age be-yourself booster. But he is more of a fast-talking therapist or shrink. I really enjoyed the streaming doc I Am Not Your Guru and learned some things, although I still feel no need to attend his seminars. — KK

Happy Happy Joy Joy Tragedy Tragedy

By the early 1990s, television cartoons had hit a depressing nadir. The stories, art, characters, and animation were terrible, and the cartoons existed for the sole reason of selling toys and merchandise. Then along came Ren & Stimpy, a hyperkinetic, rubbery, explosive, hilarious, and beautifully animated cartoon that harkened back to the era when Bob Clampett and Tex Avery were producing insanely great work for Looney Tunes. Ren & Stimpy changed the course of animation. The documentary Happy Happy Joy Joy recounts the tragic history of Ren & Stimpy and features extensive interviews with everyone involved, including its creator, John Kricfalusi, a supremely talented animator, a sadistic tyrannical boss, and sexual predator of teenage girls. — MF

Failing, while being right

Icarus is a Netflix streaming documentary that starts out small. The director has the idea of documenting how elite bicycle racers elude doping tests by doping himself and getting tested. This leads to Russian doping experts, which in turn stumbles into the Russian doping underground, which eventually breaks into the Russian doping scandal, and as the director gets involved with newspapers and the FBI, his investigations lead directly to the ban on Russian athletes in the Olympics and an international diplomatic crisis. All the while the director is filming everyone, including the Russian whistleblower, who is put into the US federal witness protection program for fear of Russian assassination. It's a mind-boggling Oscar-winning documentary that expands bigger and bigger as it proceeds. — KK

Thrilling documentary

While failure is to be avoided, no teacher is as powerful. The tech startup General Magic failed big time, but it was also one of the most influential companies of all time that no one has heard of. Its all-star team of tech wizards invented the smartphone 15 years too early. General Magic is a fantastic documentary about the dilemma of dreaming big versus paying attention to reality. It's now streaming on Amazon Prime ($0.99). — KK

Inspiring livelihood documentary

Shorebreak is a fast, 60-minute doc on Amazon Prime about this surfer who found a special niche in photography. His thing is standing at the scary point where giant waves break onto the beach while he photographs whatever crazy surfers are in the wave, before he ducks under the pummeling mountain. The doc is well done, and his photography is stunning. But what I love is the lesson of focus, enthusiasm, mastery, and foolish individualization. His relentless enthusiasm, going back to the shorebreak day after day to see if he could make something new again and again, has improbably earned him a living doing this. What a treat! — KK

FOR THRILL-SEEKERS

Exquisite documentary

I've watched my share of mountain climbing documentaries. A new one, Meru, streaming on Netflix, is among my favorites. Meru is a stone fishtail peak in the Himalayas that had remained unsummited until recently because it required climbers to haul their own 200 pounds of gear for the final overhang wall routes. The lure of this doc is that it includes an intimate record of two attempts by the same team, the first one failing within 100 meters of the summit. It also documents unbelievable disasters and horrors the climbers endured before starting the second. Because two of the three ace climbers happened to be world-class photographers (one works for National Geographic), no other high adventure has been this well documented, or as beautiful. The climbers are intelligent, warm and humble — and obsessed. Meru is a stunning experience, expertly crafted, comprehensive in capturing all moments, yet briskly edited, and a joy to watch. It entails the most innovative, thorough, and brilliant photography I've seen in any documentary. — KK

Maniacal performance

The fantastic documentary Free Solo deserves all the praise it has received, including its recent Oscar. The film follows one guy's attempt to climb the vertical face of Yosemite's El Capitan without ropes. A single slip and he dies. I could barely watch it, it was that crazy good. As the climber's friend put it: this demands an Olympic gold medal performance, except here, if you don't get the gold, you die. The film has suspense, drama, emotion, and explores maniacal obsession and perfection. Five stars. Now streamable. — KK

An impossible ascent

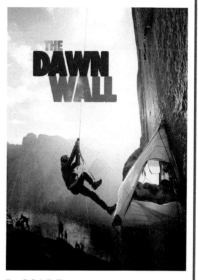

In 2015 Tommy Caldwell and Kevin Jorgeson embarked on a multi-week attempt to free climb a 3,000 foot, nearly featureless rock face in Yosemite National Park, called the Dawn Wall. This documentary (on Netflix), called The Dawn Wall, bounces back and forth between Caldwell's tragic past and his thrilling ascent. I've seen a lot of climbing movies and this is my favorite. — MF

TRAVEL

A dollar a day

A few years ago, two gringos travelled to Central America and attempted to survive for 2 months on a dollar a day — as the locals do everyday. A diary of the visitors' struggle is available on Amazon as a pretty eye-opening documentary, *Living on One Dollar*. Turns out it requires great *skill* to live on this little; the attempts illuminate the lives of the world's majority in a vivid way I've seen nowhere else. — KK

Street food stories

I really love street food, and I'm enjoying Street Food, a series streaming on Netflix. It plays out in the same format as the

Chef's Table series: food and culture are focused into mini-biographies of the cooks themselves. So we see the ordinarily unseen lives of street food vendors in Asia (in Season 1) and in Latin America (Season 2). It's about the people, not the food; brilliant and delicious. — KK

Craft in action

Everyone knows Anthony Bourdain's various travel/food series, but in 2015 Bourdain did his hanging-out thing with master craftsman and craftswomen, going to their shops, watching them work with their tools, and at times trying his own hand at their craft. I can watch masters work all day.

Their obsession with details is astounding, and their extreme excellence is captured in 14 episodes of Raw Craft. The art ranges from hand-tailored suits to a traditional letter-press printer, all sponsored by a whiskey company, and available on YouTube. — KK

Global gardens of culture

There are legions of TV shows using food as an excuse to travel, more focusing on history and architecture travel, but only one that I know about features gardens of the world. The host Monty Don, who is an institution in England, travels the world and in a deeply personal and sympathetic manner, uses gardens as his lens into cultures. His Netflix streaming series Italian Gardens and French Gardens are eye-opening and totally refreshing. His previous series Around the World in 80 Gardens is likewise mind-expanding. You won't look at gardens the same. — KK

The importance of play

Andy Goldsworthy is an artist I pay attention to. Goldsworthy is famous for his playful, intricate rearrangements of leaves, twigs, ice, and stones in natural settings. An incredibly enchanting documentary about his work, Rivers and Tides, shows him as he works outside overcoming pieces that keep failing, so for a brief moment I see the world as the artist does, as invisible flows revealed by play. Recently the same documentarian made a second film recording a more mature Goldsworthy working on more ambitious projects. This doc, titled Leaning into the Wind, accomplishes the same trick of helping me see the world differently, and via Goldworthy's example, to take play seriously. – KK

Relive the 1980s personal computer revolution

I've been watching *Halt and Catch Fire* on Netflix, a TV series that ran for four seasons, from 2014 to 2017. It's like a non-comedic Silicon Valley and is about a team of misfits (led by a guy who looks and acts like a psychotic Don Draper) who are trying to build a 15-pound portable computer during the PC computer revolution of the 1980s. Each season is better than the previous one. — MF

Going transparent

I really enjoyed Dave Eggers' fictional book The Circle, but the movie is even better. This is a disturbing forecast of where always being on social media will take us. A place so transparent, it may be too clear. Much like a *Black Mirror* episode, but more plausible. The villain, deftly played by Tom Hanks, is likeable and relatable. I have said some of the things he says. Set in today's Silicon Valley with perfect pitch, the story seems inevitable. If you are clicking on your phone more than 3 times a day, you should watch this. The Circle is now streaming on Amazon Prime. — KK

YOUTUBE TIPS

YouTube shortcut tips

YouTube keyboard shortcuts are handy, especially when watching how-to videos. For example pressing the 1 key will make the video start playing at the 10% point, pressing 2 takes you to the 20% point, and so on. The space bar pauses the video, and then you can press the period key to advance one frame at a time. — MF

Fast life

Just as I zip through podcasts at 1.5x speed, I recently learned I can speed up YouTube videos too. So now I go through twice as many tutorials. Just click on the gear-circle at the bottom right corner of the YouTube frame, and in the pop-up menu select Speed and your choice up to 2x. — KK

More YouTube shortcuts

I can't believe I didn't know these YouTube shortcuts before! To pause a video press K. To fast forward press L. To rewind press J. To watch frame by frame forward or backward, press the period or comma key. — CD

WHAT TO WATCH

Netflix viewing activity

iMore

Netflix bases its recommendations on what you watch. If you want to change what its algorithm sees, or if you are just curious to see everything you've watched on Netflix, go here. You can delete a show from the list by clicking the X next to it. I was surprised to see that the oldest item on my list was *Phineas and Ferb the Movie: Across the 2nd Dimension*, which someone in my family watched on 12/12/11. — MF

Instantwatcher.com

I'm a Netflix subscriber, but the built-in title browsing isn't great. I use instantwatcher.com, which lets you browse and search shows and movies in many different ways. — MF

Never run out of things to watch

This database of secret Netflix genres will help you out when you can't find anything to watch. Otherwise how would I ever realize I was in the mood to watch a Mother-Daughter Relationship Thriller if I never knew it was an option? Some of the category codes currently have no movies that fit the description, but that's understandable when they're so specific. — CD

Find out where a show is streaming

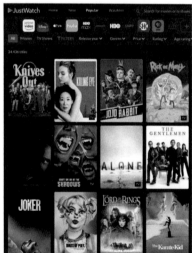

In the mood for a particular movie or show but don't know which streaming service it's playing on? That's where JustWatch comes in. Just enter a title and this site will list all the services that offer it, along with prices. — MF

Excellent indie movies for free

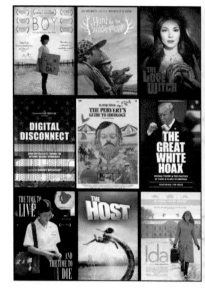

My Los Angeles Library card entitles me to 8 free movies on Kanopy a month. Your local library probably has a similar Kanopy offering. It's like Netflix for classic, foreign, documentary. and indie films. Visit the site to see what they have. — MF

Endless movie trailers

I love getting to the theaters early enough to watch all the movie trailers. Trailernite.com is

non-stop trailer watching. If you don't like it, just hit next. — CD

Discover the inspiration behind a movie

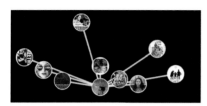

This year I've watched more movies at home than I thought possible. When I finish a movie I enjoyed I always check the "more like this" tab to find related films to watch, and now as an alternative discovery engine, I've been searching Cinetrii, which pulls any mention of influences or inspiration from movie reviews to suggest films with similar moods. — CD

Get the average of film ratings

Flixmetrix is a website that combines film ratings from Rotten Tomatoes, IMDB and

Metacritic and gives you the average. What I find the most helpful is that I can filter my movie search by genre, and limit results to only those available on Amazon Prime and/or Netflix Watch Instantly. That way I don't waste time flipping between services searching for a movie. — CD

Read movie spoilers

I stopped watching horror movies a while back, because they seemed to be getting more and more graphic and I couldn't cut it. Instead, I enjoy reading scene-by-scene spoilers for all the films I am too scared or lazy to watch. The Movie Spoiler is not the best designed site, but it's been around for a long time and all the reviews are well written. — CD

Funny film recaps

I've been a long time fan of The Editing Room for their hilarious

rewrites of movies in screenplay format. They make fun of movie tropes and call out every cliche. Reading their abridged scripts is like watching a movie with a funny friend. — CD

Unconsenting media

Unconsentingmedia. org is a searchable database of movies and TVs show for the purpose of finding out whether or not sexual violence is depicted. You can filter by rating. Green means there is none. Orange means it is implied and Red means it is on-screen. — CD

Scary movie tip

Fargo is probably my favorite thing in the world right now, but watching it makes me very tense. Some life-changing advice when watching something scary or suspenseful: root for the villain. Once I decide I want the bad guy to win, I actually get happy when he pops up out of nowhere or kills someone off. — CD

HEALTH

Good small first aid kit

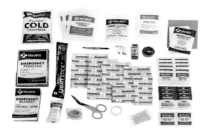

This first aid kit comes in a small bag, but it's loaded with stuff. Besides the usual bandages and sterile gauze pads, it comes with sting relief pads, an instant cold pack, a light stick, a poncho and blanket, splinter tweezers, a compass, a whistle, and a lot more. At $11, it's a great deal. — MF

Superglue first aid

I use superglue (cyanoacrylate) to close small cuts and stop them bleeding. Dab it dry, apply glue, hold together. You can use any kind of "krazy glue" occasionally for first aid; it's really handy in a workshop. Sometimes instead of stitches doctors use an expensive variant of cyanoacrylate called Dermabond, which is medical-grade glue. Second best is cheaper vet-grade glue, Vetbond, which some also use to heal skin cracks. — KK

Stop the bleeding

When I first started shaving in high school my dad gave me a stytptic pencil. When this chalky stick is touched to razor nicks and cuts, it immediately stops the bleeding. One stick seems to last forever. Two new stytptic pencils cost $3.50. — KK

Home blood type test

My 15-year-old daughter learned about blood types in school and was curious to learn her blood type. I ordered two of these kits (each $12 kit has two tests) so our whole family could find out what our blood types are. The included auto-lance makes it easy to draw blood (it hurts just a little, not much) and it was interesting to see how our blood types clotted differently. — MF

Easy blood pressure

The last time I visited my dentist, her technician took my blood pressure with a small cuff that fit around my wrist. My results appeared in about a minute on the LCD. Very convenient. As soon as I got home I ordered a similar model on Amazon (Automatic Wrist Blood Pressure Monitor) for less than $15 — MF

Best blister remedy

The second-best thing to use for foot blisters is duct tape. It's way more sticky than a bandaid or moleskins or adhesive tape, and when I hike I always carry a tiny bit of duct tape rolled around a pencil in my bag anyway for all kinds of emergencies. But the very best thing for blisters is a bit of flexible kinesiology tape (which is not its intended use). This is even more sticky on skin, but with less residue than duct tape, and also conforms wonderfully to curves and shapes and toes and heels. There are tons of brands. My walking pal Craig Mod, who walks for weeks at a time and has tried every type of tape or pad made, recommended this variety: Laneco Kinesiology Tape, which is what I now use. One roll is a lifetime supply. — KK

Reusable hot and cold gel wrap

I don't get aches and pains often, but I'm very grateful to have this hot and cold compress on hand for when my muscles

are sore ($18/2pk). We used to use clay ice packs but they all cracked open in the microwave and these gel packs are better at holding heat longer. — CD

Reduce lower back pain

I bought this 13-inch balance disc ($14) to help reduce lower back pain. I use it for about 4 hours a day when I'm sitting at my desk. It keeps me from slumping forward and helps perfect my posture. — CD

No more car sickness

My daughter was nauseated during a long car drive, and fortunately my sister had a couple of Bonine motion sickness tablets in her purse. In a matter of minutes, the nausea

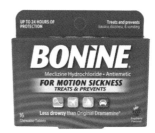

dissipated, and my daughter felt fine for the remainder of the 10-hour drive. It's highly rated on Amazon. — MF

No more clogged ears

Air travel with a head cold leads to excruciating ear pain when the plane descends, followed by three days of plugged ears. Neither the Frenzel maneuver or the Valsalva maneuver work for me. Last week I had to fly to Switzerland with a cold. I found out about this $60 gadget called Eustachi, and I brought it with me on the plane. It worked! It delivers little bursts of pressurized air through your nostril, and when you swallow, your ear will "pop." This is a life changer. — MF

BETTER EYESIGHT

Cheap and fast glasses

If you happen to live in the Bay Area or in Southern California, I highly recommend getting your next pair of prescription glasses from JINS. At first I was overwhelmed by their huge selection, but lucky for me my best friend was there to help me pick out frames — and that was the most difficult part! Then I just showed them my prescription, checked out and came back in 30 minutes to pick them up. I was out the door with a new pair for just $80 including lenses. Faster than Warby Parker and way cheaper than LensCrafters. — CD

Reading glasses in bulk

I'm rough on my reading glasses. I roll on them in bed, snap them in carrying bags, and leave them at airports. So I buy them cheaply and in quantity. I like these retro horn rim readers, which are less than $10 for a six-pack. — MF

Home vision test

EyeQue Personal Vision Tracker®

This Personal Vision Tracker Lets You Measure Your Eyesight With Your Smartphone

About six months ago I bought an EyeQue Personal Vision Tracker for $25. It looks a bit like a microscope and attaches to a smartphone. After installing the app I was able to check my vision with it. The app gave me the same information as an optometrist's prescription, which I used to buy inexpensive prescription eyeglasses online. I still plan to get eye health exams from an ophthalmologist from time to time, but this is a cheap and convenient way to find out what kind of lenses you need, especially in the middle of a pandemic when going into an optometrist's office poses an infection risk. — MF

Mini pharmacy

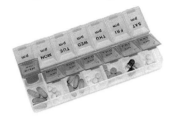

I travel with a mini-pharmacy in my day pack, particularly overseas. I use inexpensive pill organizers to hold common non-prescription remedies. These small plastic strips are sold as "7-day" containers for folks who need to take multiple pills per day, but I put just a few doses of different medicines in each slot. I carry remedies for semi-emergencies like motion sickness, allergies, colds, diarrhea, pain, sleep aid, coughing, upset stomach, etc. I stick a tiny label on each compartment with the name and dosage, which is enough. I restock the few doses before each trip. Off-the-shelf medicines are not rare abroad, but language and branding differences often make it a chore to secure them. Using these light and compact containers I (and traveling companions) have access to a wide range of immediate treatments. — KK

Cheaper than insurance

Sometimes you can purchase a prescription drug yourself for less money than paying your insurance co-pay. And when you buy, drug prices vary wildly between retailers. Go to GoodRx website to find the cheapest source for a drug, including online pharmacies. They also supply coupons at steeply discounted prices, up to 80% off (their biz model). It's free, no account or personal info required. — KK

Hay fever relief

I've been taking nettles leaf capsules for over 20 years to deal with my allergies to dust and pollen. My wife and daughter use it too. All of my dubious friends who try it also become true believers. I buy the 100-capsule bottles of Nature's Way and take 4-6 every few hours during allergy season. — MF

Respirator subscription

Anytime I go into the attic or near dust of any kind, I put on one of these 3M Cool Flow respirator masks. They are comfortable and they really help prevent me from having a sneezing fit. My daughter uses them for her art projects. Amazon sells a 10 pack for $15, but I use Amazon's Subscribe and Save and get a 10 pack sent to me every six months for $14. — MF

DIY facemask

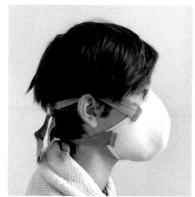

There's a lot of back-and-forth about the effectiveness of facemasks to prevent the spread of Covid-19. The ragmask is one you can make on your own by following the PDF instructions. It looks more comfortable than wrapping a bandana around your face. — MF

Treating nasal congestion

I struggle with sinus issues, and it's easy to mistake a sinus infection for a cold. When over-the-counter meds aren't working for me, I go back to using a nasal rinse. It instantly relieves pressure and makes me feel better. Dr. Hana's Nasopure Nasal Wash. — CD

Wedge pillow for sleeping

When my sinuses are acting up, the thing that gives me the most relief  is using a wedge pillow like this FitPlus Bed Wedge. It keeps my head elevated and prevents post-nasal drip while I sleep. I always wake up better rested without a blocked nose or phlegm. — CD

Get birth control without insurance

I was recently in between health insurance providers and couldn't get in to see the doctor before my birth control pills ran out. I signed-up for Nurx (took less than 10 minutes), and within 3 days, they sent me a 3-month supply in the mail — no charge. For those without insurance, options start at $15 per month. — CD

Favorite period tracker

The simplicity of Period Tracker (iOS, Android) makes it an ideal app for logging and tracking my menstrual cycle. I appreciate the minimalist monthly calendar view and ability to add journal entries to each day. — CD

HYGIENE

Favorite body scrubber

Last year I started using a Salux Japanese Nylon washcloth, and I won't ever go back. No other product has made me feel this clean before. It exfoliates, but it's not as rough as some gloves or loofahs I have tried, and I use the one labeled "super hard." — CD

Facial sonic cleansing brush

I've been using the Clarisonic Mia2 for a couple of months now and I've seen a definite improvement in the appearance of my pores and brightness of my skin. It does a really great job at removing

my makeup and exfoliating. I can't imagine living without it now. — CD

Shower with fresh Eucalyptus

I've been hanging fresh Eucalyptus in our shower because it's said to reduce sinus inflammation, which I struggle with, but mostly because it

makes showering feel like a spa experience with its soothing scent and how it looks so pretty. I've tried both the Silver Dollar Eucalyptus, which Whole Foods often has in stock, and the more aromatic Baby Blue Eucalyptus, which I order on Good Eggs. Here is a good how-to article. — CD

Best flushable wipes

I've installed inexpensive bidets in the toilets at my house, and I'm sorry I can't bring them with me when I travel. But I have recently started carrying a DUDE Wipe packet in my pocket. The packet resembles a condom packet, but it contains a flushable single wipe. It's unscented and is treated with vitamin E and aloe. — MF

Favorite travel razor

This small $15 electric razor from Philips Norelco uses 2 AA batteries. I bring it with me when I travel and have started using it at home too, because it works so well. — MF

Ocean-friendly sunscreen

Many sunscreens contain ingredients harmful to coral reefs. Hawaii announced a ban on sunscreens containing oxybenzone or octinoxate, which goes into effect in 2021. Our family switched to zinc oxide sunscreen, which doesn't hurt coral reefs. We like Thinksport SPF 50+ ($10.25 per tube). — MF

CLEAN TEETH

Clean teeth for travelers

For a variety of reasons, most hotels don't supply toothpaste in rooms. (Here's an article from *Slate* that explains why.) And you can't take a standard-sized tube in carry-on luggage because the toothpaste police at the airport will confiscate it. I stock up on 12 packs of 0.85-ounce tubes of Crest. — MF

Flossing better

The civilized way to floss is to use a long-handled floss bow so you don't keep putting your fingers deep into your mouth. I've been using a Reach Access Flosser for many years, now rebranded as Listerine Ultraclean Reach. Rinse after use, and replace the cheap tiny bow as needed. — KK

Travel floss

GUM Soft-Picks do a better job than toothpicks or floss for cleaning food and plaque from between my teeth. The soft green brush pushes out all the gunk without hurting. I buy the version that comes with the travel cases. — MF

Hand Mirror for online meetings

Hand Mirror is a one-click camera check (free, Mac only). If you are about to join a Zoom or other video meeting, just click the icon on your menu bar and make sure you look presentable before you go live. — MF

Oil-absorbing sheets

Blotting sheets are a savior when my face gets oily and I don't want to ruin my makeup. Clean & Clear Oil-Absorbing Sheets are cheap and portable. But if you find yourself in need and without, just use a sanitary toilet seat cover — they work just as well. — CD

HAIR CARE

Winter shampoo routine

It's wintertime, which for me means my skin and scalp get itchy. Lotion helps my skin, but I don't want to put lotion in my hair. Instead, I've been using a J.R. Liggett's Tea Tree & Hemp Oil Shampoo Bar ($7) and a $6 hair scalp massager to thoroughly shampoo my hair. This shampoo doesn't seem to remove all the oil from my hair, so my scalp doesn't get dry and itchy. — MF

Stylish shower cap

Some days I skip out on washing my hair. After my reserve of complimentary hotel shower caps ran out, I needed to buy my own. These are cheap and long-lasting, but the prints are what sold me — nostalgic and fun. Reminds me of my grandmother in Mexico. — CD

Best hair towel

I bought an Aquis Microfiber hair towel and I use it every day. It's probably shaved off a minute or two of blowdrying, but what I really appreciate is that my hair is breaking less, and is visibly smoother and less frizzy. Also, it's much more comfortable to wear a lighter, less heavy towel on my head. — CD

Hair timesaver

Dry shampoo works great at absorbing oil and making my hair look clean when I skip out on washing it. All brands pretty

much work the same, and you could even use talcum powder. I prefer Batiste Dry Shampoo because it comes in "brunette," which spares me having to aggressively comb out the white powder from other shampoos. — CD

DIY haircuts

I've been cutting my own hair since I was in college. I've used a lot of different electric hair trimmers, but just

recently I got one that has ceramic coated blades. It clips hair much more efficiently than plain steel blades. As a bonus, this one is cordless, making it easier to maneuver. — MF

Painless hair brushing

Because of the Tangle Teezer, I actually like brushing my hair after I shower. Just a few, quick strokes and my hair is super smooth and detangled. I've used the Tangle Teezer on my 10-year-old niece, who has really long hair and hates getting it brushed, and there was not one complaint. A tip for brushing long hair painlessly: gather all hair in a fist and brush in sections from the bottom up. — CD

Spikiest hair gel

If I don't spike my hair, I look like Captain Kangaroo or Moe Howard. Bangs may have worked for those two august gents, but it doesn't for me.

The best styling gel I've come across is Got2b Ultra Glued Invincible Styling Gel ($8 for a 2-pack as an Amazon Prime Add-on Item). A little dab does the trick, and it lasts all day. — MF

Get rid of frizz and flyaways

My favorite quick-fix hair product is Bumble and Bumble Brilliantine. The product description says it's unique and hard to define, and it's true. I use it when I don't have enough time to heat style my hair. I rub a dime-size amount between my palms and pat it through out my hair to smooth it out, create shine and get rid of flyaways. — CD

Keep your hair in place while sleeping

I use my satin pillowcase ($10) on nights before "no-wash" hair days. The silky pillowcase prevents my hair from getting tangled up or matted so that I barely have to brush it or style it. Beauty blogs claim that these pillowcases also prevent

face wrinkles while you're sleeping, which would be an added bonus if true! I just like how it makes my hair look and how cool and soft it feels. — CD

Cheap hairdryer

I'm always amazed and slightly annoyed when the hotel hair dryer works better than my more expensive one back home. This hair dryer is cheap, portable and works just as well as any $50+ dryer. — CD

Hair bun pins

These spin pins are essential for holding your hair in place in a perfect little bun. They never loosen or fall out, even while working out. My only problem is that I'm always losing them and rebuying them. — CD

FITNESS

Inexpensive upper body workout

In 2012 I bought an $25 pull-up bar that hangs from a door frame. When I started, I wasn't able to do a single pull-up. After a week I could do one pull-up. A couple of months later I was able to do over 10 pull-ups. I still can. — MF

7-minute workout

I am a minimalist. What is the least amount of exercise I can do with max benefits? Answer: Just seven minutes of calisthenics. For the past several years I've been using a 7-minute workout app on my phone, which is also great for traveling. There are many versions to choose from, but my favorite app is free, no upsell: Johnson & Johnson's Official 7-Minute Workout. — KK

Yoga studio in your phone

Yoga Studio by Gaiam are like mini-yoga classes in your pocket. You can choose from 65 videos, varying in duration of 15-60 minutes. I'm still in beginner mode and the 15-minute videos go by so fast! The app is available on Android and iPhone. — CD

Relaxing deep stretch video

This deep stretch for hips YouTube video by Sara Beth Yoga is 20-minutes long, but flows so well and it's easy to follow

on my phone. It's relaxing, rewarding and always helps me get rid of the tightness in my hips. — CD

Muscle map

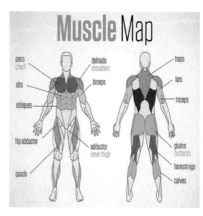

As a casual exerciser, I really appreciate this muscle chart from the DAREBEE website. It's straightforward and I think, "hey, I can do that." The website has other cool posters and printables to inspire you to workout. — CD

Back stretcher

I feel great after I stretch my back with a foam roller like this one. It loosens me up right away and using it in the morning helps me be mindful of my posture all day long. — CD

Foam roller alternative

I bought this orthopedic Stretch Mate more than five years ago and I still use it weekly to stretch out my back and alleviate soreness. For me, this works better than a foam roller because my clothing and hair don't get caught up in it. It's stiff and plastic, and not a one-size-fits-all solution, but I recommend it if you're not a fan of rollers and want to try something else. There's an option to add on a padded cover which I have yet to try but ordered this week. Note: The Stretch Mate is $40 today without the pad, I paid $22 for it back in 2013. — CD

Handheld heated massager

We bought this heated Shiatsu Massager more than a year ago, and it has definitely been put to good use. We keep it plugged in right next to the couch and use it every night. The arm handles allow you to adjust and place the massage nodes directly on hard-to-reach muscles. — CD

Inexpensive neck massager

My husband has suffered from chronic neck pain for a few years. He does posture

exercises and uses a cervical pillow, but could not find a way to massage the pressure points that radiate pain up and down his neck. Then he found this cheap and wonderfully designed neck massager ($12) and can not stop touting its effectiveness. He loves it so much he even packed it and brought it on our current overseas trip. — CD

Mindful eating tips

In a now-deleted Reddit LPT that stuck with me, I read that in France people do not eat to the point of being stuffed or rarely say "I am full," instead they say "Je n'ai plus faim" which translates into "I am no longer hungry." My French neighbor couldn't verify if this was true, but even so it's a good mindset to have when eating. Especially when dining out or in a friend's home where I feel pressured to finish everything on my plate. — CD

A new habit I've picked up is to put my fork down between bites. Originally this was a weight-loss tip — and it has helped me eat less — but also it's helped me relax while eating, and I enjoy my meals more. — CD

MIND

What is your reason for being?

Ikigai
A JAPANESE CONCEPT MEANING "A REASON FOR BEING"

Ikigai is a Japanese word that can be roughly translated into English as "a reason for being." I appreciated this graphic, which shows how ikigai is at the intersection of what you love, what the world needs, what you can be paid for, and what you're good at. — MF

50 life-changing ideas

Writing instructor David Perell wrote about the 50 ideas that changed his life. Here's one: "Competition is for Losers: Avoid competition. Stop copying what everybody else is doing. If you work at a for-profit company, work on problems that would not otherwise be solved. If you're at a non-profit, fix unpopular problems. Life is easier when you don't compete. (Hint: don't start another bottled water company)." — MF

Self-review questions

The lifehacking guru Tim Ferriss compiled 17 questions he frequently asks himself, which I find useful to review myself every now and then. They are meant to help ensure that I spend my time on the right things. You can download them as a "17 Questions That Changed My Life" PDF. — KK

Find out more about yourself in 5 minutes

This Personal Values Assessment takes only 5 minutes to complete and it peers right into your soul. I felt naked after reading the report of what matters to me the most and essentially, what drives me. I don't know much about where it originates from but it seems to be used as a tool for leadership and career training. Personally, I think it's far too personal to share with just anyone. With that said, I did ask my closest friends to take the test and send me their results. It helped me understand them so much better. — CD

The Alien Exercise

In Jen Sincero's book, You Are a Badass, she describes the Alien Exercise for rebooting yourself and getting some clarity. Imagine you are an alien and you've just landed on Earth — into your body and life. Take notice of all the connections, opportunities, skills, possessions and people who love you and can help you. What would you do and how would you feel? I think this is great for brainstorming projects, ideas and new ways to enjoy your day-to-day life. — CD

DEATH REMINDERS

Death reminder app

> To get out of your anger, you can close your eyes and visualize the other person in 300 years. What will they become? Ash. And you too.
>
> Thich Nhat Hanh

WeCroak (iOS, Android) is a bit morbid but I love it. At random times throughout the day I get a notification banner that says "Don't forget, you're going to die," with instructions to open the app for a quote. All the quotes are about dying. The app is inspired by Bhutanese culture where one is expected to think about death five times a day to achieve happiness. So far my favorite quote to contemplate is a question from Pema Chödrön: "Since death is certain, but the time of death is uncertain, what is the most important thing?" — CD

Write your own eulogy

Anne-Laure of Ness Labs has a great post on the exercise of writing your own eulogy as a blueprint for your future. The process of writing down the exact values and accomplishments you want to be remembered for can provide clarity as to the small steps you can take today to create that narrative. Her post provides example questions to help you draft a eulogy and it's up to you to work backwards to take action. I also spent about 25 minutes using this free step-by-step guide to writing my own obituary (angstrom. life/goals) and when I was done I was given a mission statement to create

the imaginary legacy I want to leave behind. My life goals are very simple: write more poetry, which is something I yell at myself every day, and to perfect my poor drawing skills so that I can create the stories that won't stop gnawing at me. — CD

Countdown to your death

I hacked up a death countdown clock to show me how many days I have left to live. I went to the actuarial tables for life expectancy to determine how old a typical person my age will live to, and then input that date into the Date Countdown website. It shows me that I have an estimated 6,300 days to live. Each day that small sum really focuses me. (BTW, your longevity increases over time because of science, so every few years you need to adjust your death date.) — KK

Give advice to your younger self

I love the concept of Hey, From the Future, a website that lets you share advice you wish you had at specific ages. I encourage everyone to contribute. I read all the advice that is posted from age 35 and up, and from what I gathered I need to spend more money traveling and more time with my parents and the people I really like. Also, it's not too late to [fill in the blank]. Whatever you've always wanted to do. You can still do it. — CD

List of truths

This list of 88 important truths are all aha moments for me. My top three are: 5. Everyone likes somebody who gets to the point quickly. 16. Cynicism is far too easy to be useful. And 86. Wishing things were different is a great way to torture yourself. — CD

Pain management skill

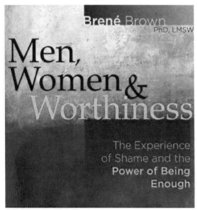

I love Brené Brown's exercise of repeating "Pain, pain, pain, pain, pain," to instantly release yourself of the fight or flight mentality. I first heard it in her Men, Women, and Worthiness talk (which I highly recommend), but the full embarrassing story behind it can be read here. — CD

Autocorrect your negativity

I've developed this small habit of editing my internal monologue when I catch myself saying something negative or absolute. If the thought "This sucks — it's never any fun," pops into my head, I immediately correct myself with "This sometimes sucks. It might be fun." If I don't autocorrect myself I stay stuck in a negative mood, but when I do, I let go of the negative outcome and just roll with whatever. — CD

How to deal with difficult emotions

Practicing mindfulness is easier said than done. This chart breaks it down into six easy steps to make sense of your difficult emotions. I find that visualizing my emotion as a little tangled mess that lives outside of my body makes it less likely I will react impulsively. — CD

How to stop taking things personally

Sometimes my obstacle is when I've taken something

personally that shouldn't be. Like when my husband asks me if I unloaded the dishwasher "yet" and I interpret it as an all-out attack on my productivity. My therapist has advised me to listen to the request, not the tone. But that's easy to forget. Here is a good printout to keep nearby if you also struggle with the same thing. — CD

Danish word for stressful situations

"Pyt" is now in my vocabulary thanks to this Fast Company article. It doesn't have an English translation, but Danes use it as an interjection to frustrations or mishaps. It means something like "Oh, well," and is used as a reset button to accept the situation

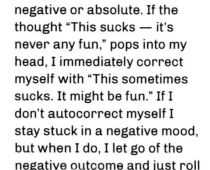

and refocus rather than react. I like it because it sounds like a cute short curse word. — CD

Critical thinking cheatsheet

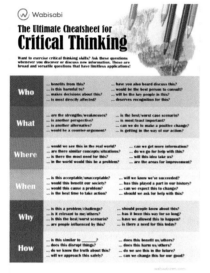

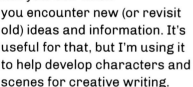

This Ultimate Cheatsheet for Critical Thinking is a set of questions to ask yourself when you encounter new (or revisit old) ideas and information. It's useful for that, but I'm using it to help develop characters and scenes for creative writing. — MF

9 common thinking biases

I'm sure I'm afflicted by a lot of cognitive biases, but I like this list of 9 common biases because of the short advice on how to overcome them. I'll admit that I struggle with the halo effect — "when your overall impression of someone

is influenced by one part of their character" — but I'm working on it and trying to appreciate humans in all their complexities. — CD

Classify your emotions

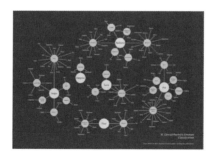

I am hoping I'll get better at communicating my emotions by studying this chart. It is a mind map of the 6 core emotions we feel and all the other emotions that branch off of them. — CD

Inspiration for Overthinkers

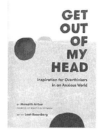

I love this small, illustrated handbook for easing anxiety: Get Out of My Head: Inspiration for Overthinkers in an Anxious World. It has become a roadmap to help me navigate out of my anxieties and distortions, and it's so much more magical than it is clinical. You can pick it up and start anywhere in the book at any time, and you'll find playful ways to reframe your thinking and easy actionable advice to try now. My favorite part of the book is that it comes with an even smaller pocket book inside, with soothing illustrations, that acts as a visual tool to help you, "when something is wrong, but nothing is wrong." — CD

Daily self-care newsletter

Tiny Spells is a daily self-care email that feels like it's sent from your best friend. Every day Joan Westenberg sends out three simple things you can do for yourself to make your day and self better, like reminders

to take a stretch break, make the doctor's appointment you've been avoiding, buying yourself fresh flowers, or finding something that makes you laugh. It has a magical effect and I look forward to it every day. — CD

81 resources for your mental health

Greatist has gathered an extensive list of websites, hotlines and apps to help find support when you are in need. All the resources are either free or cheap. This list was published in 2015, so it might be a little outdated, but I have yet to find a more recent, comprehensive list like this. — CD

Free therapy

Earlier this week book author Caroline Moss tweeted, "If you go to therapy quote tweet this with the best thing you learned at therapy that way everyone else can get free therapy." The hundreds of replies are filled with excellent advice. Examples:

• Don't react. Sit with it until you know what you feel. Sit with it.

• It's ok to not be busy and to not offer to others a reason I do or don't do each thing.

• Don't beat yourself up for not knowing things that you hadn't learned yet.

• Anxiety causes me to put things off a lot and in group therapy we worked on "the 15 minute rule". If something feels impossibly overwhelming I set a timer to work on it for 15 minutes and that takes away that "I'm about to swan dive into a bottomless hole" feeling.

• The only things I owe people are straightforwardness and kindness.
— MF

Free confidential crisis text line

If you're in the United States and need someone to talk to you can text 741741 any hour of the day and be connected with a crisis counselor (For Canada text 686868, and for UK text 85258). I tested it out to make sure it works and the first text was automated, but I was connected with a live person in less than 2 minutes. I hope I don't need it, but I'm relieved to know that it's there. For more info check out their website: crisistextline.org. — CD

A helpful relationship app

I like the Gottman Card Decks app because it requires minimal effort to use, it's not awkward and it actually helps me get to know my husband better. There are 14 decks to choose from. Some of them have interesting questions to help you start a conversation, others have ideas for improving your relationship, or there are phrases to help you word what you're having trouble expressing. It's free and a great way to connect with your partner and work on your communication skills. — CD

Cool down phrases

This Gottman Institute blog post has some examples of phrases to help de-escalate arguments with your partner. I wish it wasn't so hard to say "I'm sorry" when I'm in the wrong, but these workarounds help steer heated conversations back on track. — CD

BETTER RELATIONSHIPS

Find your apology language

I consider myself well-versed in figuring out people's love languages, but I was surprised to find out that there was such a thing as an apology language. I took this free quiz and discovered that I am most receptive of apologies that "Accept Responsibility" meaning simply saying "I was wrong." The other types of apology languages are "Genuinely Repent," "Expressing Regret," "Make Restitution," and "Request Forgiveness." — CD

Apologize effectively

I often refer back to this Reddit LifeProTip that describes the three parts of an effective apology. (1) Acknowledge how your action affected the person; (2) Say you're sorry; (3) Describe what you're going to do to make it right or make sure it doesn't happen again. Don't excuse or explain. It's amazing how easy this is to forget so I have it saved and pinned in my iCloud notes. — CD

How to comfort someone

C CLEARER THINKING

The Four States of Distress: how to comfort someone when something bad happens to them.

I think being able to make someone feel better is a superpower and one that I often fail at when I go into problem-solving mode too soon. This article outlines "The Four States of Distress" — 1. Shocked. 2. Feeling bad and not wanting to feel better. 3. Ready to feel better. 4. Feeling better and needing solutions. — and suggests the most helpful actions you can take to comfort someone at each state. It also shines a light on "comfort languages," and after some thought, I recognized my comfort language is having someone help me explore and understand my feelings (and distraction helps too!). — CD

Become a mind reader

A good practice in empathy I like is copying someone's body language to get a glimpse of what they're feeling. Sometimes taking notice is enough, but if you mimic a person's posture or positioning you might be able to understand them better. — CD

Advice for connection

This YouTube video about Oprah breaks down her magical ability to make people comfortable with their raw emotions. She does this by not trying to defuse tension, and instead validating people when they are the most vulnerable. There's a bunch of other tips for having meaningful interactions, but the narrator suggests that the most important thing to focus on is to discover what moves people emotionally. — CD

MEDITATIONS

Walking meditation

I find that walking a labyrinth is a much simpler way for me to meditate than sitting. I stand at the entrance and contemplate my issue or question, then after some deep breathing and when I feel ready, I enter. As I walk through the winding path toward the middle, I imagine myself shedding all fears and doubts, so that when I arrive at the center I physically feel lighter and open for clarity. — CD

Morning meditation

I try to set aside time to meditate every day. The easiest and quickest way for me is to play positive affirmations in the morning while I shower. My favorite is a gratitude meditation that helps me focus, remember what's important and gets me excited for the day. The

narrator's accent makes it very soothing to listen to and the 9-minute length helps me keep my showers short. Here is a free version on YouTube. — CD

Mountain meditation

One of the most effective visualization techniques to quickly destress is to imagine I am a mountain and every annoying, stressful thing is just floating past me like clouds or momentary bad weather. I remind myself that I am a mountain and my purpose is to just sit and be myself and nothing can sway me. You can find a lot of these "mountain meditations" on YouTube. Here is a short example I like and found on Aura. — CD

Fall asleep faster

When I have trouble sleeping, listening to the Autogenic Relaxation by Meditation Oasis

usually knocks me out. The audio guides me through relaxing all my limbs starting with my feet. I rarely make it past my neck. Here is a link to download the meditation. — CD

Meditation app bundles

I'm a meditation-app junkie and have spent many dollars and downloads searching for the perfect one. I would recommend any app by Meditation Oasis. I use iSleep Easy (there is a free version) at night, which lets me create playlists of guided meditations and pair it up with either a background instrumental or nature sounds, with separate volume controls for each. My emergency go-to for quick and re-energizing naps is the 13-minute Deep Rest meditation, available

on the Relax and Rest app. I usually start to doze off at around minute 10, but I come to feeling as if I had taken a super long nap, and without that awful groggy feeling. Individual apps range from $1.99-$5.99, but you can purchase bundles, which I suggest, because once you try one you'll definitely want the others. — CD

Meet your future self

I tend to use meditation to help me slow down and ease into discomfort

or when I feel my anxiety flaring up, but I came across this 30-minute Life Visioning meditation on my Aura app and felt completely transformed after it. At first the breathing exercises and noises felt hokey, but it helped to put me into an almost hypnotic relaxed state, and then the narrator took me down a dark tunnel to meet my "future self" and I was able to see her so clearly! I was so moved by this whole practice. I've done it three times since, and each time I discover some new desire or goal that is buried within me. — CD

Relaxing float in water

After each session of floating in a sensory deprivation tank I find myself walking out deeply relaxed, with zero tension in my body and a slightly-high feeling. Here's a directory of float tanks near you. — CD

Free guided breathing

Calm your body and mind in seconds.

Hello, James

Calm | Sleep
Awake | Recharge

This free iOS app called Breathwrk makes it incredibly easy to start a consistent habit of daily breath exercises. I schedule to practice different methods of breathing for different times of the day. Like "Awake" to get energized at 7AM, and "Unwind" to

reduce stress at 5PM. This is one of the few apps from which I enjoy receiving reminder notifications. What I appreciate the most about this app is that there are different sounds played for the duration of breathing in and exhaling, and this lets me just close my eyes and focus on breathing. — CD

Mood tracking

How are you?

Swipe up or down

There are a lot of mood tracking apps out there and most are free, but I have yet to find one as easy to use and well-designed as Moodnotes ($4.99, iPhone). You can customize the app to check in with you as many times a day as you want, and your level of participation can be as little as adjusting a smiley face from frowning to grinning, to journaling and learning about common "thinking traps" and practices to avoid them. It also provides insights/stats about your moods over time. — CD

Favorite habit tracking app

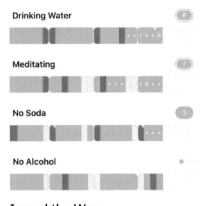

I used the Way of Life app (iOS, Android) to make a habit of making my bed. The simple app lets you set up a list of habits you want to make or break. Once a day you touch a red X or a green checkmark to record your success or failure. It took me about two years to get to the point where I don't think about making my bed. I just do it. It's free if you track three or fewer activities. The full version, with unlimited activities, is $5. — MF

Favorite iOS habit tracker

The only habit tracker that I have consistently used and enjoy using is Tally: The Anything Tracker (iOS only).

You can color code and group habits by type, set targets, track by day, week, month or year and have them reset whenever you want. You can track 3 habits with the free version and upgrade for more. There are a lot of other features too, but what I like the most about it is the cool, colored grid view and that I am able to add notes for the tallies I make. I am trying to read at least 20 books per year and I use the notes to track titles. I've been using this app for almost a year now and I like being able to see the historical data — like of my miles hiked per month — because it motivates me to outdo myself. — CD

Send yourself a future email

FutureMe is a tried and true free service for sending yourself letters in the future. I use it to remind myself of goals I have or enlightening quotes I want to be reminded of. — CD

Book excerpts about Happiness

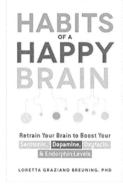

Excerpts from the book, Habits of a Happy Brain: Retrain Your Brain to Boost Your Serotonin, Dopamine, Oxytocin, & Endorphin Levels, by Loretta Graziano Breuning:

"Finding threats makes you feel curiously safe. When you know a lion is near, you feel safer when you can see it. We keep seeking evidence of threats, and we get a dopamine boost when we find what we seek. You may also get a serotonin boost from the feeling of being right, and an oxytocin boost if the evidence bonds you to those with similar concerns. This is why people seem oddly pleased to find evidence of doom and gloom."

"Happy chemicals were not meant to create constant ecstasy. They were meant to steer us toward things that

HAPPINESS TRICKS

promote survival. When we try to get constant happiness from them, disappointment is likely."

"Celebrating small steps triggers more dopamine than saving it all up for one big achievement."

"Your brain will never stop trying to promote your survival. It will take what you have for granted and look for ways to get more – more rewards (dopamine), more physical security (endorphin), more social support (oxytocin), more respect (serotonin). Seeking more is risky. Your brain is constantly deciding whether it's worth giving up some of this to get more of that."

— MF

1 simple trick

This article titled "1 simple trick to be happier" is not clickbait — it's sound advice.

It suggests that because your happiness level is more dependent on the frequency of positive events, rather than the intensity, you should be creating a daisy chain of happiness-inducing events all day long. "Think of some of the small delights that bring you joy — whether it's a certain song, a photo from a gathering with friends, or even a pen that writes like a dream — and try intentionally placing them throughout your day." I have a running list of 100 things that bring me joy that I pull up when needed. On the top of my list is hugging my dog and cuddling (mostly bugging) my cat. — CD

Joe Rogan on Happiness

I enjoy the occasional Joe Rogan rant, because he can be very enlightening. Thankfully, this video on Happiness is short and straightforward, and surprisingly uplifting. Personally, I struggle with "[Happiness is] not having all your ducks in a row," so this video is a good reminder. — CD

Science of Happiness

INCREASE YOUR HAPPINESS IN THE LONG RUN BY...

Nurturing relationships · Having new experiences · Helping others · Being grateful for what you have

Get even more happiness out of a good experience by savoring it

Use all your senses: pay attention to sights, sounds, smells, etc. · Pay attention to the little details of the experience

Share it with someone else · Linger! Dwell on the moment

This infograph by Happify is a great reminder to check in with yourself and your current priorities. It lists 5 instant ways to boost happiness, and the one that always works for me is to send a quick note to someone thanking them for something they did. Always puts me in a better mood. — CD

Happiness practices around the world

I've stumbled upon these ten little drawings of happiness practices all over the internet, and they still make me happy. I like learning untranslatable words that stretch the imagination. My favorite from this set is the idea of forest bathing. — CD

Look and sound more confident

Keep your hands visible

Don't: Put your hands in your pockets.

Do: Use your hands to make gestures with the palms facing upwards.

Why: Hiding your hands suggests uncertainty or nerves, while keeping them open conveys honesty and poise.[1]

Make eye contact

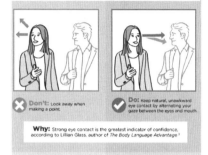

Don't: Look away when making a point.

Do: Keep natural, unawkward eye contact by alternating your gaze between the eyes and mouth.

Why: Strong eye contact is the greatest indicator of confidence, according to Lillian Glass, author of *The Body Language Advantage*.[2]

End phrases on a falling tone

Don't: End sentences with a higher pitch.

Do: Create a vocal full stop by dropping your voice at the end of the sentence.

Why: Communications expert Dr. Laura Sicola says 'upspeaking' makes you seem unsure, so saying every point like you mean it helps you assert yourself and adds finality.[3]

Project your voice

Here's a chart to remind you of the small things you can do to appear more confident. Speaking slowly is one that I'm always working on. When I'm on the phone, I tap the desk for each word I say to avoid uhms or uhhs. — CD

STRESS TECHNIQUES

Self-care checklist

It can be very hard to check in with yourself when you have anxiety or are having a bad day. This is a very simple checklist for self-care that I found floating around Reddit. — CD

Everything Is Awful and I'm Not Okay: questions to ask before giving up

Are you hydrated?
If not, have a glass of water.

Have you eaten in the past three hours?
If not, get some food — something with protein, not just simple carbs. Perhaps some nuts or hummus?

Have you showered in the past day?
If not, take a shower right now.

Have you stretched your legs in the past day?
If not, do so right now. If you don't have the energy for a run or trip to the gym, just walk around the block, then keep walking as long as you please. If the weather's crap, drive to a big box store (e.g. Target) and go on a brisk walk through the aisles you normally skip.

Have you said something nice to someone in the past day?
Do so, whether online or in person. Make it genuine; wait until you see something really wonderful about someone, and tell them about it.

Have you moved your body to music in the past day?
If not, jog for the length of an EDM song at your favorite tempo, or just dance around the room for the length of an upbeat song.

Have you cuddled a living being in the past two days?
If not, do so. Don't be afraid to ask for hugs from friends or friends' pets. Most of them will enjoy the cuddles too; you're not imposing on them.

Have you seen a therapist in the past few days?
If not, hang on until your next therapy visit and talk through things then.

Have you changed any of your medications in the past couple of weeks, including skipped doses or a change in generic prescription brand?
That may be screwing with your head. Give things a few days, then talk to your doctor if it doesn't settle down.

If daytime: are you dressed?
If not, put on clean clothes that aren't pajamas. Give yourself permission to wear something special, whether it's a funny t-shirt or a pretty dress.

If nighttime: are you sleepy and fatigued but resisting going to sleep?
Put on pajamas, make yourself cozy in bed with a teddy bear and the sound of falling rain, and close your eyes for fifteen minutes — no electronic screens allowed. If you're still awake after that, you can get up again; no pressure.

Do you feel ineffective?
Pause right now and get something small completed, whether it's responding to an e-mail, loading up the dishwasher, or packing your gym bag for your next trip. Good job!

Do you feel unattractive?
Take a goddamn selfie. Your friends will remind you how great you look, and you'll help fight society's restrictions on what beauty can look like.

Do you feel paralyzed by indecision?
Give yourself ten minutes to sit back and figure out a game plan for the day. If a particular decision or problem is still being a roadblock, simply set it aside for now, and pick something else that seems doable. Right now, the important part is to break through this stasis, even if it means doing something trivial.

Have you over-exerted yourself lately — physically, emotionally, socially, or intellectually?
That can take a toll that lingers for days. Give yourself a break in that area, whether it's physical rest, taking time alone, or relaxing with some silly entertainment.

Have you waited a week?
Sometimes our perception of life is skewed, and we can't even tell that we're not thinking clearly, and there's no obvious external cause. It happens. Keep yourself going for a full week, whatever it takes, and see if you still feel the same way then.

You've made it this far, and you will make it through. **You are stronger than you think.**

No two people are the same; you are encouraged to customize this document to your own needs, abilities, and resources. Copyright Sinope (eponis.tumblr.com), 2015. This work is licensed under a Creative Commons Attribution 4.0 International License. Original: http://eponis.tumblr.com/post/113798088670/everything-is-awful-and-im-not-okay-questions-to

Quickly de-stress with deep breathing

exhale

Doing breathing exercises is easier for me if I can focus on something visually. Xhalr. com is perfect for that. It's also helpful if you want to discover different types of yoga breathing. — CD

60-second worry soother

Put a stressful thought in the star

Pixel Thoughts is a simple website that just wants to help. Type whatever you're stressed about into the star and watch it fade away into the universe, while relaxing music is played and you're reminded that everything will be okay. Works better on desktop, but there is an app. — CD

Worry later list

I got the idea to make a worry list from this Forbes article on organizing your feelings. I keep a sticky note on my laptop and when something is bugging me I add it to the list and mentally shelve it until later. By the end of the day, most of it doesn't matter and then I get to cross it out and that feels great. — CD

Strikethrough stress note

I started a "stress note" in my Notes app where I keep a list of whatever I'm anxious about. Anytime I add something new I reread my past worries and if they no longer matter (which is usually the case), instead of deleting them I apply the strikethrough style. There is something very calming and self-affirming in doing this, and as the list grows I actually find it very beautiful to look at. — CD

Relax your jaw

Every once in awhile I will be scrolling through Reddit and come across a short reminder or tip post that simply says: Relax your jaw. I'm not sure at what moment it became second nature to me, but I noticed in the last week I've started relaxing my jaw at the first sign of anxiety or discomfort, which is great, because I then check-in with my entire body and relax my shoulders. Just that in itself is an instant mood booster. So I would like to pay it forward with a reminder to relax your jaw. — CD

Swipe through care cards

This simplistically designed website lets you quickly swipe through cards with kind suggestions meant to uplift your spirits when needed. It works well on both your phone and desktop (on your desktop you press spacebar instead of swiping). — CD

Weighted blanket alternative

If you've ever had a panic attack or are prone to anxiety, a weighted blanket can be helpful but pretty pricey. A free alternative if you're ever in need is to take a shower with a towel wrapped around you. The towel will be made heavy by the water and the calming effect is that it feels like a warm hug. — CD

LEARNING

Wikipedia tool

V for Wikipedia recreates the childhood joy of getting lost in my old Encyclopedia

set. One subject would inspire me to look up another and I'd end up flipping back and forth between pages and indexes for hours. Now I can use my iPhone and seamlessly jump to the next subject with a quick tap. Honestly, this app is so easy and enjoyable to use — totally worth the $4.99. — CD

$1500 Sandwich

A reminder of the progress we all enjoy. A curious fellow decides to spend six months growing his own wheat and vegetables, making his own cheese and meat, and evaporating his own salt in order to make his own sandwich from scratch. He spent $1500 on this lunch, and in this short, *How To Make A $1500 Sandwich*, he gives the particulars of what is really involved in our everyday consumption. Like the Toaster Project, which was an earlier attempt by an artist who spent a year to make a $30 electric toaster from scratch (iron ore, petroleum plastic), it conveys in concrete terms the huge subsidy we get from modern civilization. I repeatedly return to these brilliant examples. — KK

The best learning videos

YouTube is way underrated as an educational institution. You can learn literally anything, including how to do surgery. The challenge is the uneven quality of the average video. One solution is YouTube's own channel called The Learning Playlist. YouTube hired experts to curate the best learning videos they could find on a particular subject, and make a playlist for it, all on one channel. I am a happy subscriber. It's also a good place to begin a search for how to study for a test, to how to organize a community group, and so on. — KK

Explainer videos

I love good explainer videos. The best are made by Kurzgesagt. Their 5-minute videos are stunningly animated and cover topics such as automation, genetic engineering, gamma ray bursts, and ebola. They often leave me in awe about our universe. — MF

Best virtual museum

Google hosts one of the best virtual museums in the world. They've

scanned many thousands of the world's masterpieces at super-high resolution. So from my home I can visit their "Arts and Culture" site and by scrolling get very very close to the art — much closer than I could in a physical museum. I've seen many of the originals in their home museums, and I feel I was seeing them for the first time here. — KK

Painless history

My favorite example of how video is displacing much of what books used to do is this short YouTube video on the History of Japan. In only 9 minutes it covers the complex, twisted, obscure history of Japan but with insight and clarity. (One of its subtle tricks is to use nicknames instead of proper names for people.) The clip has racked up 30 million views because it teaches so well. — KK

Tour historic sites

During entire month of May, the National Trust for Historic

Preservation is sending out a daily email unlocking one historical site that you can explore virtually. On Friday, I toured Frank Lloyd Wright's Pope-Leighey House in Virginia and fell in love with the Mayan-inspired motif, and yesterday morning, the National Trust released a 27-minute concert video filmed at Nina Simone's childhood home in North Carolina. — CD

Learning videos for kids

The website The Kid Should See This gathers the best short videos that explain how the world works. Subjects includes nature, science, technology, art, and politics. So far they have collected 2,600 videos that "are not made for kids, but are perfect for them." The videos are really great for any do-it-yourselfer, and for any life-long learner. In fact, the site might be called "The Adults Should See This." — KK

Vintage Kids Book about the Human Body

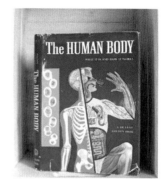

I love the old large format Golden Books about science, math, and technology. The color illustrations are stunning, and the text is accurate and still valid, decades after they were originally published. You can get "The Human Body: What It Is and How It Works" from 1959 for about $6. — MF

Lynda for free

Lynda.com has an excellent collection of training videos for learning programming, design, bitcoin fundamentals, bookkeeping, and much more. Lynda charges a monthly fee, but if you have a library card, the chances are you can become a Lynda member for free. Here's a link for L.A. residents to use Lynda (and other great stuff, like the digital edition of the *New York Times*) for free. — MF

LEARNING AIDS

The Learning Toolbox

SPORE
To help me organize my ideas to write stories.

S etting
P roblem
O rder of Action
R esolution
E nd

The Learning Toolbox website has a bunch of useful tips for getting the most out of studying. It was created for students with "mild disabilities," but I think it's useful for all students and non-students too. As someone who gets distracted easily, I appreciated the tips on how to focus on lectures and while reading. — MF

Flashcard learning

Anki is a free flashcard program that uses the Spaced Repetition System (SRS) to present words or facts you have trouble remembering more frequently than ones you can recall easily. I'm using Anki based on the advice in the

anthology

n. book of literary selections by various authors.

Soon	3.2 months	6.9 months	9.5 months
Again	Hard	Good	Easy

Remaining: 0 **107** 69 | ETA: **14.1 minutes** | 00:24

book *Fluent Forever: How to Learn Any Language Fast and Never Forget It*, which I highly recommend. — MF

Better test scores

For high-schoolers: The Khan Academy, the premier free online classroom, will tailor an SAT study course to your personal abilities based on your PSAT scores. They claim to be able to increase scores by 115 points. Sign up at Khan Academy, give PSAT permission to share your completed test, and Khan will create a free course designed for you personally. It will focus on your weak areas. BTW, they found that students who study together learn 2.5x as much as those who study alone. — KK

How to understand difficult subjects

THE FEYNMAN TECHNIQUE

1 CHOOSE A CONCEPT
2 TEACH A TODDLER
3
4 REVIEW + SIMPLIFY
IDENTIFY GAPS

FARNAM STREET

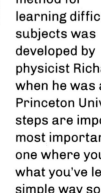

This four-step method for learning difficult subjects was developed by physicist Richard Feynman when he was a student at Princeton University. All the steps are important, but the most important step is the one where you have to teach what you've learned in a simple way so a new student can understand it. If you can't do that, you don't really understand it yourself. — MF

Analogies about technology

Sideways Dictionary uses analogies to explain technology. You can contribute your own, upvote those you like or downvote those you don't find helpful. Here's one to describe API: "It's like a LEGO brick. An application without an API is like a LEGO brick without nodules (are they called nodules?) – it's not much fun and you can't build anything new with it." — by Nick Asbury. — CD

Animated mechanical movements

When making toys, I refer to 507 Mechanical Movements. This old book is sort of a periodic table of known mechanical movements, first published in 1868. The book has been scanned onto the web, with many of the gears animated into looping gifs so you can see exactly how their ingenious mechanisms work and what

movements they create. Just paging through this amazing 507 Movements website fills me with ideas. — KK

Search engine for comparing measurements

I like having The Measure of Things handy for those really random moments when I want to visualize the size of something, like how big or how much, in units I might understand better. For example 4 fluid ounces is about three-fourths as big as a tennis ball, and 500,000 acres is 1.075 times bigger than the size of Maui. — CD

Python Tutorials

One of the things I miss about the 1980s was writing programs for fun in BASIC. A couple of years ago I started playing around with Python. It's easy to learn, and powerful enough to do anything I would want to automate. Christian Thompson's YouTube channel has wonderful Python tutorials for beginners. Check out the one on how to program a Pong clone. — MF

Hands-on introduction to machine learning

My 16-year-old daughter and I are interested in learning about artificial intelligence, and we found a YouTube series produced by Google that has easy-to-understand examples that you can program yourself using the Python programming language. The first program we wrote was only 6 lines long, but it can tell the difference between an apple and an orange. — MF

Best knot tying instructions

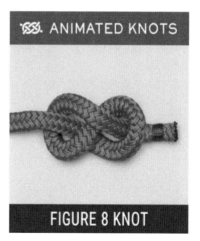

FIGURE 8 KNOT

The best way to learn how to tie a knot: visit Animated Knots. Choose left- or right-handed, any direction. — KK

LANGUAGE

Memorize Japanese

Shi has shiny hair
Think of a girl with long hair

Dr. Moku's Hiragana and Katakana apps use mnemonics to help you memorize the Japanese syllabaries. Within 60 minutes I had all the syllables memorized (roughly 100). — MF

Language learning with Netflix

I study Japanese, so I use this plug-in to watch Terrace House in Japanese. It allows me to read the kanji and kana as they are spoken by the characters and use the control buttons to play sentences over and over again if I'm having trouble understanding what someone is saying. I can also click on a kanji to translate it into English. I can also configure it to pause at the end of every subtitle so I can study them before moving on. This is a language learner's dream. — MF

Kanji tutor

In the last six months I've learned over 500 kanji characters and Japanese vocabulary words using WaniKani, a "spaced repetition system" flashcard website. The first 3 levels are free, after that you can pay by the year or buy a lifetime account. (Disclosure, my wife used to work at WaniKani's parent company). — MF

Kanji Practice Pad

The Beginning Japanese Kanji Language Practice Pad looks like a daily calendar. On each tear-off page is a different Japanese kanji character, along with its definition, pronunciation, sample use, stroke order, and space to practice writing it. — MF

A website of untranslatable words

I enjoy browsing this website of 500+ words that don't translate, because I'm always intrigued by the concepts I had no idea existed, like "qarrtsiluni," a North Alaskan Inupiatun word for sitting in the darkness, waiting for inspiration to strike you, or " razbliuto," a Russian word to describe the feeling for someone you used to love but no longer do, or "vellichor," which I think may be made up but is a much needed word to address "the strange wistfulness of used bookstores." It's weird how once I learn a word for something I was hardly aware of before that I can instantly recall feeling it in the past. I would like to know the word for that. — CD

Learn to negotiate

A great one-episode podcast that taught me a lot about negotiation that I wished I had learned decades ago: "How Creatives Should Negotiate," run by Ramit Sethi on the Tim Ferriss podcast. As the title suggests, this 1.5-hour seminar is aimed at creatives such as photographers, musicians, designers, and the like, but really the advice is useful to anyone. — KK

Skill builder

Your Salary, and How to Raise It
Episode 10 of *Slate*'s Negotiation Academy on negotiating for your salary.
Jill Barshay and Seth Stevenson

Two Slate journalists attended a class on negotiation skills at Columbia Business School and created a 10-episode podcast called *Negotiation Academy*. After listening to the series, I feel like I can negotiate a better deal for myself from now on. — MF

How to persuade, distilled

A whole book ("Influence" by Robert Cialdini) on the key scientific principles of how to persuade people — get them to change their mind

SECRETS FROM THE SCIENCE OF PERSUASION BY ROBERT CIALDINI & STEVE MARTIN

or behavior — has been expertly compressed into a 12-minute doodle video. It's so compressed you might need to review The Science of Persuasion more than once. The principles work! — KK

The only thing you need to know about public speaking

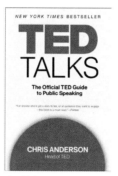

NEW YORK TIMES BESTSELLER
TED TALKS
The Official TED Guide to Public Speaking
CHRIS ANDERSON, Head of TED

"The only thing that truly matters in public speaking is not confidence, stage presence, or smooth talking. It's having something worth saying." This is from Chris Anderson's book, TED Talks: The Official TED Guide to Public Speaking. — MF

Social media manipulation explained

This well-done 3-part YouTube series by SmarterEveryDay

will make you smarter about how/why social media algorithms are exploited, why it is so difficult to remedy, and why this will be an on-going arms race. — KK

Don't be the mark

You can't win fairly at carnival games, because they aren't fair. Here's a great fun tutorial that teaches you a few tricks for the ones you might win. — KK

Learn a new skill

COPYWRITING BEGINNERS

I signed up for a free 30-day trial of Skillshare because I wanted to improve my drawing skills, and I did. There's more than 16,000 video classes to choose from. A monthly subscription is $15 per month, but I opted to cancel before the trial ended — they make it really easy and in fact, when I went to cancel they extended my trial another month! They also offer classes in photography, film, cooking and writing. — CD

SCIENCE

Understanding technical papers

The best way I've found to understand a very technical or scientific paper is to search YouTube for someone to explain it. The ideal is to find a journal club report. Journal clubs are informal groups who share the task of explaining an interesting paper to each other. Each member rotates in picking a paper to explain to their peers. This is 100 times better than having the author explain it, because authors assume too much prior knowledge. It is better to have a newbie who just figured it out. If you are lucky, a journal club will video their reports and post. Search YouTube with the paper's title or topic and add the term "journal club." — KK

Quick research explainers

Two Minute Papers is a YouTube channel featuring short videos (sometimes 5 minutes long) created by a professor who reviews new research papers in visual programming, artificial intelligence, machine learning, computer graphics, simulations, and other state-of-the-art computer science. He explains the research's significance, while running very cool graphics demo-ing the results. I find it a painless way to keep up in this fast moving field. — KK

Free academic papers

For the past 8 years Sci-Hub has been the Napster of academic papers. It's a pirate site that serves up scholarly journal articles usually stashed behind paywalls. You copy and paste the link from the official journal site (or its DOI) into the Sci-Hub website and it immediately gives you the PDF. I have no qualms using it. Many researchers who have legitimate access to the journals prefer to use Sci-Hub because its interface is easier, consistent, and better designed. — KK

Science news

A good Reddit thread I learned a lot from, and one I hope will keep going: "What are some recent scientific breakthroughs/discoveries that aren't getting enough attention?" — KK

Beautiful star-gazing app

Last week my friend texted to tell me that 4 planets were visible and I should go outside to check them out. I was only able to see 3, but I found them quickly with the beautifully designed

SkyView app ($1.99). I just held my phone up to the sky and SkyView pinpointed where they were precisely. For the occasional stargazer this app is more than enough. — CD

Step-by-step solutions to math problems

Scan almost any textbook math problem with your phone's camera and Photomath will generate a step-by-step solution instantly. The app works for iOS and Android and it's free. — MF

An app to teach you about the fourth dimension

This iPhone/iPad app does just one thing — it gives you a feel for the fourth dimension by moving from 0 dimensions to 4. I've had this jewel of an app on my phone for years and still open it from time to time. — MF

Learn from Nature

Asknature.org is a free online tool where you can search thousands of nature's solutions to various challenges. Like how a decentralized society helps ants to recover from a food shortage or how maple tree seeds twirl in a tornado-like vortex to increase the reach of where their seeds are planted. You can also discover nature-inspired ideas like this design for a thermos inspired by polar bear fur. Just ten minutes a day exploring this website will get you thinking differently. — CD

Identify nature app

There is utility and pleasure in being able to identify wild creatures and plants. But it's a steep learning curve. The fastest way I found to learn is via the iOS app Seek, which will identify flowers, plants, fungi, animals, and bugs instantly. It's kind of magical. You point your phone at the specimen and it tells you the species about 95% of the time (in North America). The other 5% it can often identify the family. Someone called it Shazam for nature. The app is patient; you can keep asking it to ID the same thing you asked about before and it will will answer again with no judgement. Seek is free; it was developed by folks who did iNaturalist, an app that uses crowdsourcing to identify species, but Seek uses machine learning to render the ID instantly. I've been impressed by how well this magic works. Kids and teachers love it. It gives them a superpower to name everything around them. — KK

Learn to play blues guitar in 10 minutes

I've been building 3-string guitars for about 10 years. It's easy to do and they sound better than you probably think. Learn how to make one at Cigar Box Nation. They are even easier to play. Here's a 10-minute video that will have you sounding like you know what you're doing. — MF

Learning to draw

This hand-drawn book is the best course on art and drawing I've seen.

The cartoonist Lynda Barry has been teaching non-artists to draw, and she has somehow magically captured her class into this book called Making Comics. This guidance is particularly aimed at people who think they can't draw. It will teach you how to draw, more importantly how to see, and even more importantly how to create with originality, by taking yourself out of the way to see what shows up. It refreshed my very concept of art. I've already given two copies of it away. — KK

Shrink the quantum of experience

I came across some great advice on a Twitter thread which asked "What are some non-obvious ideas that can change your life?" @noahlt answered: "Shrink the quantum of experience: instead of reading a book, read a wikipedia article. Instead of eating a cup of ice cream, eat a spoonful. Decreases turnaround time, which both reduces procrastination and also allows me to decide whether I want to go deeper." This tip encourages me to follow my curiosity, but reminds me to start with small bites. — CD

QUOTABLES

Kevin's favorite quotes

To achieve great things, two things are needed: a plan, and not quite enough time.
— Leonard Bernstein

No, no, you're not thinking; you're just being logical.
— Niels Bohr

Seeing is forgetting the name of the thing one sees. — Paul Valery

Life is full of obstacle illusions.
— Grant Frazier

If you are not embarrassed by the first version of your product, you've launched too late. — Reid Hoffman

Babies are such a nice way to start people. — Don Herold

You aren't wealthy until you have something that money can't buy. — Garth Brooks

I've always been very careful never to predict anything that has not already happened.
— Marshall McLuhan

I think I speak for everyone when I say no one can speak for all of us. —Glenn Fleishman

The question isn't who is going to let me: it's who is going to stop me. — Ayn Rand

What looks like tomorrow's problem is rarely the real problem when tomorrow rolls around. — James Fallow

The cure for boredom is curiosity. There is no cure for curiosity. — Dorothy Parker

Decisions are made by those who show up. — Jennifer Pahlka

If at first the idea is not absurd, then there is no hope for it.
— Albert Einstein

Not long ago what we have today was so implausible that nobody bothered to say it would never happen.
— Marc Andreessen

The first 90% of a project is a lot easier than the second 90%." — Tim Sweeney

There will come a time when you believe everything is finished. That will be the beginning. — Louis L'Amour

If you don't like change, you are going to like irrelevance even less — General Shinseki

What you seek is also seeking you. — Rumi

No limit for better. — Harrison Ford

A good book is more intelligent than its author. — Umberto Eco

The time you enjoy wasting is not wasted time. — Bertrand Russell

How to change your behavior

A maxim I am paying attention to is an anonymous quote: "It's easier to act your way into a new way of thinking, than think your way into a new way of acting." This is a handy way to remember that smiling makes me happier, and acting as if I am confident makes me more confident and that changing my behavior is a great way to change my mind. — KK

Be the only

Good advice I keep returning to:

"Don't be the best. Be the only." — Jerry Garcia

Works for individuals and companies. — KK

Are we being good ancestors? — Jonas Salk

You don't have a soul. You are a soul. You have a body. — C.S. Lewis

When I grow up I want to be a little boy. — Joseph Heller

Never take a job for which you are qualified. You won't grow. — Esther Dyson

That we were absent for a great expanse of time in the past causes no fear. Yet, our impending absence in the future is cause for terror. — Brian Greene

Too many people worry about what AI will do to us. Too few worry about what Power will do with AI. — Zeynep Tufekci

Entrepreneurship is the pursuit of opportunity beyond the resources you currently control. — Howard H. Stevenson

The simplification of anything is always sensational. — G.K. Chesterton

I decided to spend my time trying to create the things we need as opposed to preventing what threatens us. — Bill Joy

If you really want to learn how something works, try to change it. — Matt Mazur

For something to be beautiful it doesn't have to be pretty. — Rei Kawakubo

If you find a path with no obstacles, it probably doesn't lead anywhere. — Frank A. Clark

Eighty percent of success is showing up. — Woody Allen

If you're not ready to find exceptional things, you won't discover them. — Avi Loeb

I don't explain — I explore. — Marshall McLuhan

Everywhere I go I find a poet has been there before me. — Sigmund Freud

The genius is the one most like himself. — Thelonious Monk

There is only one difference between a madman and me. I am not mad. —Salvador Dali

Don't be the best. Be the only.— Jerry Garcia

The only interesting ideas are heresies — Susan Sontag

Technology is the reason we get old enough to complain about technology. — Gary Kasparov

Plans are worthless, but planning is everything. — Dwight Eisenhower

If my work is accepted, I must move on to the point where it is not. — John Cage

Remember, you can't be stuck in traffic; you are the traffic. — Kevin Slavin

Best quotes from authors

When starting to read a new author, or trying to recall a favorite author, I use the quote search function at Goodreads to surface the best quotes of a writer. The quotes are ranked by the number of times Goodreads readers "like" them. (This only works for books.) — KK

Kevin Kelly's birthday advice

Personally I know Kevin to be effortlessly wise and warm and honest, and his way of life is something I've strived to copy, so I treasure these 68 bits of unsolicited advice. There are so many sparks of clarity here and great guiding principles to adopt. — CD

These are my favorite:

• Pros are just amateurs who know how to gracefully recover from their mistakes.

• A worthy goal for a year is to learn enough about a subject so that you can't believe how ignorant you were a year earlier.

• The universe is conspiring behind your back to make you a success. This will be much easier to do if you embrace this pronoia.

Claudia's favorite quotes

Loneliness is a sign you are in desperate need of yourself.
— Rupi Kaur

When you say something unkind, when you do something in retaliation, your anger increases. You make the other person suffer, and they try hard to say or do something back to make you suffer, and get relief from their suffering. That is how conflict escalates.
— Thich Nhat Hanh

Your assumptions are your windows on the world. Scrub them off every once in a while, or the light won't come in.
— Isaac Asimov

The cost of a thing is the amount of what I will call life which is required to be exchanged for it, immediately or in the long run. — Henry David Thoreau

We're all going to die, all of us, what a circus! That alone should make us love each other but it doesn't. We are terrorized and flattened by trivialities, we are eaten up by nothing. — Charles Bukowski

The only thing that isn't worthless: to live this life out truthfully and rightly. And be patient with those who don't.
— Marcus Aurelius

We waste our energy and exhaust ourselves with the insistence that life be otherwise. — Frank Ostaseski

What do we live for, if it is not to make life less difficult for each other? — George Eliot

The cradle rocks above an abyss, and common sense tells us that our existence is but a brief crack of light between two eternities of darkness.
— Vladimir Nabokov

Life shrinks or expands in proportion to one's courage.
— Anaïs Nin

Have you ever noticed that anybody driving slower than you is an idiot, and anyone going faster than you is a maniac? — George Carlin

You know, the matrix says, "Pick an identity and stick with it. Because I want to sell you some beer and shampoo and I need you to stick with what you are so I'll know how to market it to you." Drag is the opposite. Drag says, "Identity is a joke."
— RuPaul

Each moment is a place you've never been. — Mark Strand

You're under no obligation to be the same person you were 5 minutes ago. — Alan Watts

Always remember that to argue, and win, is to break down the reality of the person you are arguing against. It is painful to lose your reality, so be kind, even if you are right. — Haruki Murakami

Understanding a person's hunger and responding to it is one of the most potent tools you'll ever discover for getting through to anyone you meet in business or your personal life." — Mark Goulston

Advice? I don't have advice. Stop aspiring and start writing. If you're writing, you're a writer. Write like you're a goddamn death row inmate and the governor is out of the country and there's no chance for a pardon. Write like you're clinging to the edge of a cliff, white knuckles, on your last breath, and you've got just one last thing to say, like you're a bird flying over us and you can see everything, and please, for God's sake, tell us something that will save us from ourselves. Take a deep breath and tell us your deepest, darkest secret, so we can wipe our brow and know that we're not alone. Write like you have a message from the king. Or don't. Who knows, maybe you're one of the lucky ones who doesn't have to. — Alan Watts

The most courageous decision that you can make each day is to be in a good mood. — Voltaire

Let everything happen to you: beauty and terror. Just keep going. No feeling is final. — Rainer Maria Rilke

A good marriage is one in which each spouse secretly thinks he or she got the better deal, and this is true also of our friendships. — Anne Lamott

Things usually happen around us, not to us. — Unknown, found on Reddit

We suffer more in imagination than in reality. — Seneca

If all you did was just looked for things to appreciate, you would live a joyously spectacular life. — Esther Abraham Hicks

Let go or be dragged. — Zen Proverb

Be messy and complicated and afraid and show up anyways. — Glennon Doyle Melton

"No." is a complete sentence. — Unknown

To realize your existence, do the things you know you should do — the duties that echo from deep below. Stop avoiding your life. — u/TheEmployedMoth1 on Reddit

When you are making plans, you are actually not making plans but you are creating reality... — Somewhere on Reddit

A big secret is that you can bend the world to your will a surprising percentage of the time—most people don't even try, and just accept that things are the way that they are. ... Ask for what you want. You usually won't get it, and often the rejection will be painful. But when this works, it works surprisingly well. — Sam Altman

Zuibun nagaku ikasarete itadaite orimasu ne. "I have been alive for a very long time, haven't I?" Totally impossible to translate, but the nuance is something like: I have been caused to live by the deep conditions of the universe to which I a humbly and deeply grateful. P. Arai calls it the "gratitude tense," and says the beauty of this grammatical construction is that "there is no finger pointing to a source." She also says, "It is impossible to feel angry when using this tense." — Ruth Ozeki

Mark's favorite bits of advice

Short bits of advice I've collected — MF

"If you're the smartest person in the room you're in the wrong room."

"Never miss a good chance to shut up."

"Don't argue with a stranger unless you're prepared for them to pull out a gun and shoot you."

"Before buying anything expensive online, keep it in your shopping cart for 24 hours. You may end up changing your mind."

"What got you here won't get you there."

PLAY

Smooth speedcube

I have not yet solved Rubik's Cube, and whenever I used to try, I'd get discouraged because the cube would lock up when turning it. Then I discovered Chinese speed cubes. They are very smooth and a pleasure to use. I'm working on a 2 x 2 x 2 mini-cube ($7) instead of the usual 3 x 3 x 3. Still haven't cracked it! — MF

Japanese toys

Leave it to the Japanese to sell toy models of prehistoric invertebrates. Not fierce dinosaurs, or ancient predators, but spineless slugs and amorphous marine creatures extinct millions of years ago. The Favorite Store offers two of my favorites, inexpensive anatomically accurate soft casts of Opabinia and Anomalocaris. (Use Chrome to translate).— KK

Magnetic block set toy

Magnetic "blocks" are a toy for constructing things. I keep a big pile of these magnetic tiles around our place for small kids visiting. The outline shape of these tiles are easy for toddlers to grasp, yet still satisfying (for a short while) for older kids. Like Magnatiles, embedded magnets along their edges assist in constructing shapes fast. What you can build is far more limited than what you can do with Lego or Kapla blocks, but these are quick and easy. I have bought many different "brands" of what are sometimes called Magnaforms; they are all interchangeable. I am partial to the 100 piece Magnetic Block set. — KK

Beautiful puzzles

Pomegranate's Charley Harper puzzles are beautiful and sturdy. Each piece is glossy and locks well with other pieces, and it's a fun distraction for a few hours. I've bought two so far — Tree of Life and Exquisite Creatures. — CD

Escape room tips

Escape rooms are a blast and are now found in most cities. For maximum fun, a small group of people try to solve a roomful of puzzles in order to escape. Here is a quick solid tutorial on the best tips for successfully solving any escape room. — KK

MAGIC TRICKS

Imp bottle magic trick

I bought this $5 pocket trick in 2015. It's a tiny plastic bottle with a spherical base. It has a weighted bottom to keep it from tipping over. I can make it lie on its side, but no one else can (unless they know the secret, and surprisingly few do). Drive your friends crazy with frustration. — MF

Card magic DVD

I've been interested in card magic for the last five years or so. The best way to learn is not by books (which are confusing), but by videos (which make the sleights and handlings clear).

A great video collection for beginner and intermediate card magicians is the 7-DVD set called Complete Card Magic ($25). Get this and start amazing people. – MF

Anti-boredom

I always carry a deck of cards. Not to play card games, but to practice sleight of hand. It's easy to have a conversation and practice moves at the same time, and it prevents me from fidgeting. This 4 DVD set, The Royal Road to Card Magic is a bargain at $15, and a great way to get started. — MF

So many paper airplane designs

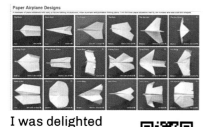

I was delighted to come across this repository of paper airplane designs on Foldnfly. com. I didn't know so many possibilities existed! We had a fun family tournament in the backyard this weekend. There seems to be quick, video tutorials for all of the designs. — CD

Sharpen your skills of deduction

One thing that has helped me unwind at the end of every day is trying to solve logic puzzles on my phone. Something I always loved doing as a kid. I found this free, no ads iPhone app ($2.99 on Google Play) called Logic Puzzles by Egghead Games. There are puzzles for different levels of experience that you have access to, so you can start off easy and work your way up, or alternate between quick and more challenging games. It's been two months since I downloaded it, and I have solved 80+ games, and I still have 16 more to go before I in-app purchase more, which I will, because it really is fun! — CD

COMPUTER GAMES

Make your computer 35 years older

In the summer of 1983 my friends and I became addicted to a role-playing computer game called *Wizardry: Proving Grounds of the Mad Overlord*. It was a lot like Dungeons and Dragons, and had very primitive wireframe graphics to represent a multi-level underground maze filled with orcs, zombie kobolds, bushwhackers, bleebs, bubbly slimes, and many other monsters. We started playing at 9pm every night, drinking beer and sitting around a monochrome PC until 3 in the morning, sleeping for a few hours before going to our summer jobs (installing a sprinkler system for a new golf course) and starting over again the next day. It took us all summer to complete the game. Recently I told my 14-year-old

daughter about Wizardry and she wanted to try it. It's no longer for sale, but the files are available online if you search for them (I don't know if it's legal for these sites to give away the files, so I'm not going to link to them here). In order to play Wizardry on my Mac laptop, I had to download a DOS operating system emulator called DOSBox. It turns my 2017 laptop into a 1983 PC. It's free and works like a charm. My daughter and I are now playing *Wizardry* almost every night. No beer this time around, and we call it quits at 10pm, but it's still thrilling to make the hand drawn maps as we crawl our way through the monster- and trap-filled dungeon. — MF

A fun interactive way to learn about game theory

You have probably heard about the Prisoner's Dilemma, the classic Game

Theory problem. This website, called The Evolution of Trust, lets you play the Prisoner's Dilemma against computer opponents who employ different strategies to maximize their winnings. You also get to see what happens when the computer players play against each other.
— MF

Mysterious text adventure

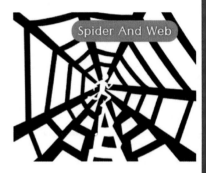

I used to love the old Infocom text adventure games. They were interactive stories where you affected the outcome by making decisions and doing things as you moved around a world described in words only. A friend told me about a free web-based text adventure called Spider And Web and I am enthralled by it. I don't want to say anything about the plot. Just give it a try.
— MF

Zelda: Breath of the Wild

My wife bought me a Nintendo Switch portable game player for Valentine's Day and, on my 14-year-old daughter's advice, the first game I bought for it was Zelda: Breath of the Wild. Much has been written about the beautiful world and fluidity of motion of the game, and once I started playing it I realized why long-time gamers are saying it's freaking amazing. It really feels like there's a planet in there, with weather, varied terrain, plants, animals, and people. I transport myself into the world of Zelda every spare

moment I have. I can't wait for my 18-hour flight to Singapore later this month! — MF

CARD GAMES

Mini-card game

Iota ($10) is a tiny card game in an equally tiny tin, making it perfect for taking on trips with friends. The object is to assemble the colorful cards in a grid so that the colors, shapes, and numbers are all the same or all different. — MF

Werewolf, intense social game

When we meet for family reunions, or gather with friends, our favorite group game is Werewolf. Classrooms and corporate retreats also play Werewolf. It's a deduction/deception game, extremely social, that is as much fun to watch as to play, so it can involve everyone. The games are exhilarating, surprising, and addictive. The only gear you need are some cards. While you can get by with an ordinary deck of cards, a set of dedicated Werewolf cards makes it much easier. After you've played a number of basic games, it's easy and fun to play with variations, which are supported by this deck of Apostrophe Werewolf cards ($11). — KK

Cooperative tabletop game

Most board games have a winner and a bunch of losers. But there are a number of games where users must work with each other to achieve a goal. One of the best cooperative games is Forbidden Island ($18). The goal of this attractively designed card and token game is to recover four life-saving treasures from an island before it sinks into the ocean, drowning all the players. Achieving victory requires players to formulate plans, agree on strategies, and make sacrifices. — MF

Two Rooms and a Boom

I played this social deception/deduction game with about a dozen other people. If you've played Werewolf or Mafia you'll be familiar with this kind of game. In Two Rooms and a Boom, the goal is for team red to blow up the president, and the goal of team blue is to stop them. Each game takes about 15 minutes and if you're like me, you'll end up playing multiple rounds until way past your bedtime. It's addictive — MF

DIGITAL DISTRACTIONS

Random places

I love playing this geography game. Go to Geoguessr.com. It will place you on a random spot in the world in Google Earth/Maps, and you have to figure out where you are by walking around in Street View. Easy clues like words on signs are usually blurred out. It might be hard to even locate the right continent. You get points for how close your guess is to your actual location. Was your guess five miles or 5,000 miles away? It probably appeals to world travellers like myself, but I enjoy the hunt for telltale signs of a different culture. — KK

Travel without moving

I just spent the last ten minutes on Window Swap staring out a window in Villalago, Italy, where I could see the mountains and hear birds chirping and church bells ringing. Anyone is welcome to submit video (and audio) of their window view, and with the click of a button you can bounce around all over the world. — CD

Nature live cams

For a dose of awe and wonder head over to Explore.org and choose from almost 100 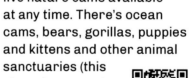 live nature cams available at any time. There's ocean cams, bears, gorillas, puppies and kittens and other animal sanctuaries (this sheep barn can be pretty mesmerizing to watch when they're in for the night). Never a dull moment. — CD

Drive & listen

This cool website, Drive & Listen, pulls dashboard cam videos from YouTube and pairs them up with local music channels so that you can feel like you're cruising around in a foreign city, blasting the radio, all while sitting at your desk. — CD

Deep YouTube

My daughter told me about Astronaut.io. It's a website that plays a few seconds of random YouTube videos with almost no views — like this video of a cafe in Vietnam with 1 view, and this one of goats eating weeds near a freeway in rural Japan with 0 views. After a few seconds, it starts playing another video. It's addictive. Many of the videos aren't in English, which is a plus for me. — MF

Alien humor

In these dark times I need a little lightness, I need some humor, I need a bit of inspiration. I need Inspirobot. Inspirobot is an AI that generates inspirational quotes set on an inspirational photo — you know those posters. Because it is a dumb AI, it generates a lot of nonsense. But every fifth one is foolish in an unconventional way, which is the root of humor. It borders on profundity. Just keep clicking. — KK

Google autocomplete game

Google Feud is a game that challenges you to guess the top ten Google autocompletes for a particular word or term. For instance, the game might prompt you with "my friend is addicted to" and you have to fill in the rest of the query. (FYI, the top ten autocompletes for this example are weed, her phone, drugs, coke, pills, drama, oxycodone, crack, anime, and alcohol.) — MF

Who are you?

Know Yourself is a set of 60 cards to prompt you to examine your beliefs. Example card: "List five things that are important to you in your life. How much of your time do you give to each of these?" The back of each card offers advice to make sure you answer the questions in a useful way. You can use their cards on your own or with another person you feel close to. Be prepared to surprise yourself. — MF

Wise oracle cards

Second to the traditional Rider-Waite deck, my new favorite set of tarot cards is the Tao Oracle. It is the I-Ching, without the coin throwing, in beautifully-illustrated oversized cards. The guide book itself is a sacred text. I often just read random pages for quick, calming wisdom. — CD

Make your portrait a poem

I love poetry, so this Google AI experiment "PoemPortraits" was something I enjoyed playing with. I donated the word "supernatural" which then produced a unique two-line poem, pulling from more than 20 million words of 19th century poetry. Then I took a selfie with my laptop camera and the poem became my face. I am now a part of the ever-expanding and evolving machine-created poem. — CD

Feel connected to the Universe

This helped me get out of my headspace for a bit: NASA's What Did Hubble See on Your Birthday? I entered all the important dates I could think of and went down a Wikipedia wormhole to learn more about the Sombrero Galaxy and light echos. Every image is awesome and uplifting and teleports me out of my mental space to somewhere else. — CD

OUTDOORS

Sturdiest big umbrella

We've had one of the rainiest winters in memory. I normally carry a compact foldup umbrella in my bag, but when I head out from my house in the rain, I grab the Blunt near the door. This full-length umbrella is built like a tank. It is super sturdy, larger than a solo umbrella but not as big as a golf umbrella. There are no pointy corners (they are blunt, hey), and high winds won't faze it a bit despite its large-sized canopy. It would take an actual hurricane to invert it. You'll lose it before it wears out. It's expensive, but worth it. — KK

Four legs

Hiking poles give me two extra legs. They are most useful going

downhill, over uneven or wet terrain. I bring them wherever I hike, especially when I travel, because I use a collapsible set from Black Diamond that folds up to less than 14 inches (36 cm). That not only fits in carry-on luggage, it will also hide away in a day pack, so I can take them out only when needed. The $75 Distance Z-Poles are lightweight aluminum, unfold in a second, and are very rigid. You can get featherweight carbon fiber if you want to pay more. — KK

Find new hikes

I've had the AllTrails app for 4+ years now, but I've been using it more often since I moved from SF to San Jose. I needed to find local hiking routes and I love that I'm able to filter by elevation, distance, and route type (e.g., loop, out & back, point to point). Since it's been around for a while now, there are a lot of reviews for each hike and that's really helpful because I like to avoid any trails where I might run into a mountain cat. — CD

Create local walking routes

Plan routes in seconds **flat**

Footpath is ridiculously easy to use. I missed my weekly hike recently and wanted to find an alternative walking route nearby. I downloaded Footpath for free and traced a route with my finger from my location to the nearest park. The line you trace snaps to roads and trails, and you can choose between a loop or out and back route, and then it displays the distance and elevation if any. I figured out that I would have to walk around the park ten times if I wanted to get 5 miles in. – CD

Low-cost compact prism binoculars

I bought two of these handheld binoculars ($23) for an upcoming Rolling Stones concert my wife and I are going to. They are small and light enough that I could put them in a daypack and not know they are there. The optics are excellent, especially for the price. — MF

Clear vision underwater

If your eyes aren't perfect and you wear corrective lenses, you can purchase inexpensive swim goggles with corrective lenses built in. They make a huge difference underwater. I use TYR Corrective Goggles, about $20. Select your prescription strength, between -2 and -8. — KK

Best pool float

I spent almost four hours lounging in this Papasan float on the 4th of July and it's now my favorite purchase of the year. Half my body stays in the water, so I'm able to stay cool while basking in the sun. The only drawback might be how easy it is to relax — time went by so fast, I got sunburned. — CD

Affordable inflatable kayak

This inflatable two-person kayak is perfect for beginner couples. It's sturdy and easy for one person to steer, and it even survived when we took a scary turn toward some fast flowing water — although it's better for floating down flat water. The best part is it's really comfortable to sit in and it took less than 40 minutes to both set up and deflate. We bought this a month before summer for $80 and right now it's $115. Reviewers say the price fluctuates between seasons. — CD

Best ocean tide app

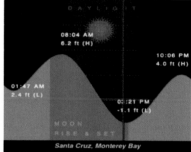

One of my favorite uses for the supercomputer I carry in my pocket is to tell me when high or low tide will be, and how high or low. I live near the ocean, so tide level is important for beach walks. My go-to tide app is TideTrac, $3 on iOS. — KK

How much sun is left in your day?

Sunshine.fyi is a simple webpage that tells you how many hours, minutes and seconds of sunlight are left in your day. I keep it in my bookmark bar, but it's now available as a Chrome extension, so that every new tab serves as a reminder to go outside and make the most of your day. — CD

CYCLING

Electric bike reviews

EBR (Electric Bike Review) is the best place to go if you are thinking of getting an electric bike. One guy, Court Rye, has personally reviewed in depth over 800 ebikes. He has seen and ridden them all, and his knowledge about them is encyclopedic. His reviews are in text and video. These days you can find an e-version of almost any type of bike made, from e-cruisers, electric mountain bikes, folding e-bikes, city riders, cargo bikes and so on. This site will help you sort through them. It respects your attention with minimum selling and maximum helpfulness. — KK

Affordable electric bikes

Electric bikes are improving so fast that they are becoming an option for most people. But the field is young, flooded with startups, and gear changes so fast, keeping up with the best one is hard work. I recommend newbies go to the "Affordable ebike" playlist of the YouTube channel of EBR (Electric Bike Review), and start at the top (most recent) for in-depth, impartial, video reviews of ebikes that cost between $1,000 to $1,500. — KK

Car and bike safety

Anyone can accidentally kill a bicyclist if you open your car door at the wrong time. Learn the "dutch reach" method (Holland is a serious bike country) to open your door mindfully and save a life. — KK

Better road ID

My husband wears a Road ID bracelet on long bike rides, but prefers a necklace so I chose to get him a Crashtag because they have a lot more designs to choose from. It looks cool

and the tag doubles as a bottle opener. I had it printed with our new address and my phone number, but there is enough space to include medical information or multiple lines of text. — CD

Touring by bicycle

I'm a huge fan of bicycles as the ideal way to tour. You see more than in a car, but you cover more than walking. Inexpensive, too. The Adventure Cycling Association is dedicated to encouraging bike touring in the US and offers very detailed maps and guides for many routes, short and long – including those paths without cars. I used their fantastic maps to bicycle 2,000 miles from Vancouver to Mexico along the Pacific coast with minimal traffic, hills, and hurdles. Plus tons of other help for bike touring. — KK

TRAVEL GEAR

Best bicycle tour bags

The best way to tour somewhere, IMHO, is via bicycle. E-bikes make that even easier these days. For overnight touring, you'll need some bags (panniers). The blue-ribbon panniers are classic Ortlieb dry bags. Each is a roomy, rubberized single bag (no dividers or pockets) that seals off at the top to provide an absolutely waterproof container. Not cheap, but because of their simplicity they will last a lifetime. After 2,000 miles of use, I am very attached to mine, in bright yellow. — KK

Best travel day pack

On a recent trip to Tokyo, I brought along the Sea to Summit Travelling Light Day Pack ($33). It weighs 2.4 oz (my iPhone 6 Plus weighs 6.2 ounces) and zips up into a bundle smaller than my fist.

But it holds 20 liters of stuff, and I used it every day to carry water, snacks, sweaters, an iPhone charger, a portable wifi, groceries, and things my wife and I bought while walking around. The material feels indestructible. — MF

TSA-proof knife

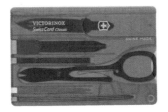

After decades of using a Utili-key as my choice of a small knife to pass through airport security, I lost it in the woods. I replaced it with Victorinox SwissCard. This tool is a mini-Swiss Army knife flattened into a plastic holder the size of credit card but thicker. It has a tiny (1.5 inch) sharp blade, scissors, tweezers, a pen, toothpick, and a pin. You can carry it in your wallet or bag. Goes through security. There

is a knock-off version which remarkably adds a magnifier, a light, and four screwdriver heads in the same size card for half the price at $9 — but you'll need to sharpen the flimsy blade. — KK

Women's travel kit essential

I recently visited my grandmother in Mexico and the first thing I packed was my pStyle,

which helps women pee while standing. It was the perfect travel tool for Mexico, where most public bathrooms have no toilet seat and you have to pay for toilet paper. There was no mess, it was easy to use and I just attached it to my purse in one of these discreet carrying cases. — CD

LUGGAGE

Maximum baggage for basic economy

"Basic economy" is the cheapest way to fly on United. You don't get to select your seat and you can't check any bags or even bring a standard carry-on bag without paying extra. You are allowed one personal item, measuring 17x10x9" or less. That's smaller than most backpacks and is an unusual size. Fortunately, Aerolite makes a bag measuring 16x10x8" (called the 16 Inch Aerolite Carry On Hand Luggage Flight Duffle Bag) and it's big enough for a couple of changes of clothes, toiletries, electronics, and a laptop. — MF

My primary travel luggage

I travel a lot, mostly overseas, often for many weeks at a time, and sometimes in very remote parts of the

world. I pack everything I need for 3 weeks or more of adventuring and business speeches into one carry-on-size luggage. My bag of choice is the Travel Pro Crew, also highly recommended by the intense researchers at Wirecutter. At 20 inches in length it fits easily overhead, has plenty of storage, pockets, and recessed wheelies. Fully packed it won't tip over. This is slightly lighter, cheaper (and shorter) than Travel Pro's Magna 22-inch model, but since I carry on rather than check it, it's held up fine. — KK

Cheap packing cubes

On our last trip my husband and I shared one large suitcase for a week. This 4-piece set of packing cubes by Amazon Basics (I bought two sets) kept it from getting out of hand. Everything stayed organized and folded. I like that they're soft and not rigid, because

they expand as you fill them up and saves space when you don't. The long, slim cube was perfect for my hair styling tools. — CD

Flat toiletry bag

This eBags toiletry bag is the perfect size to fit all essential travel toiletries plus a lot of my makeup. It has four compartments and stays pretty flat, so I can slip it into my large tote if I need to. My favorite feature is the hook for hanging which is great for hotels with little counter space. — CD

TRAVEL PILLOWS

Best travel pillow

My 22-year-old daughter used this Ralthy inflatable travel pillow ($17) to snag 9 hours of uninterrupted sleep on a recent flight to Singapore. You set the pillow on your meal tray or your lap and lean forward into it, placing your head in the hole, like you would on a massage chair. I just bought another so I can use it on an upcoming flight to Japan. — MF

Better neck pillow

I just got back from an overseas trip and this ergonomic Trtl pillow helped me sleep through most of my long flights. It's super soft and supports my head better than traditional neck pillows. The best part of course is that it takes up virtually no space when packing. — CD

Comfortable driving pillow

This car pillow makes long drives, slow traffic, and neck pain more tolerable. The material is so soft and it's so nice to lean my head back on this after work. When my husband drives he can easily adjust it to his height. — CD

WATER BOTTLES

Favorite water bottle

I bought the 32-ounce Takeya stainless steel water bottle last month to bring on hot summer day hiking, and it's now my favorite. The vacuum insulation keeps the water cool for hours. It has a comfortable carrying handle, a drinking spout, and a wide-mouth lid for cleaning/drying. — MF

Collapsible water bottle

You aren't allowed to bring a bottle of water past airport security, and the bottled water sold at airport convenience stores is expensive. But many airports now have filtered water dispensers. I keep a collapsible water bottle in my travel bag. It rolls up to a tiny size and weighs nothing. Free water, what a concept! — MF

Water bottle sling

For walks and short hikes, I've been forgoing my daypack for this ChicoBag's water bottle sling. It's convenient and comfortable to wear and it even has a large pocket for my phone and keys. It folds up and takes up no space, so I just carry it on me at all times. — CD

DESTINATION

World's cheapest destinations

So much to see, so little money. Why not maximize your travel by getting the most per dollar? The World's Cheapest Destinations will guide you to the best least expensive countries in the world, where a small budget will purchase you ten times the joy of a more expensive region. Part of my secret to travel is to visit these countries listed, which are usually the most interesting, too. Now in its 5th updated edition, this succinct guide is one of the best investments in life you can make. — KK

Offbeat attractions guide

Whenever I travel I search for my destination at the Atlas Obscura website. It will yield dozens of very obscure, very offbeat attractions in the area. How else can you find a nearby museum of parasites, or trail of doll heads, or a restaurant of robots, underground tunnels, or a store for time travel? — KK

Explore cities by bike

I used the Red Bike service when I was in Cincinnati recently. A 24-hour pass costs a measly $8. You just grab a bike at any of the dozens of stations (an app shows you how many bikes are available on a map) and start pedaling. The bikes have baskets and locks. It's a lot more fun than Uber! — MF

Caravanistan

I've been exploring the vast territory of Central Asia, sometimes known as the Silk Road. Between the Caucuses in the west, and remote parts of China in the east, these places are exotic, beautiful, vastly varied (deserts to alpine) sufficiently developed to be fun, yet devoid of tourists. In the near future these will be prime tourist destinations. But right now it can be hard to navigate and occasionally hard to get visas. By far the best resource is a website, called Caravanistan, run by a English-speaking couple that has the clearest, most up-to-date information on the practical aspects of traveling along the Silk Road. Not what to see, but how to see it. Highly reliable, immensely helpful, and always inspiring. — KK

Intimate boat tours

A tour in the Galapagos was one of our best vacations ever. There are no hotels so you live on a boat, which travels during the night so you wake up in the cove of a different island each morning. Each island is a different biome (inspiring the idea of evolution for Darwin). You spend the day actively hiking around the islands encountering a myriad of perfectly tame animals and birds. While there are large cruise boats, the key is to sail on a small boat to minimize transit times ashore. Go to Happy Gringo to find diverse small boat tours. They are utterly reliable and 1/3 the cost of others. — KK

Tours by locals

When I want to find an expert to guide me around in a walking tour in a foreign city, I first look up a freelance local guide on Tours by Locals. Rates and experience vary. — KK

Visit culturally significant sites

My first choice when seeking exotic destinations is to check this list of UNESCO World Heritage Sites. These are 1,000 culturally significant places worth preserving, which means they are usually the best places to visit. While many sites are well known, many more are little known gems. Most counties have at least a couple. I've never been disappointed traveling to a World Heritage Site. — KK

Global street foodie

My favorite street foodie is the YouTuber Mark Wiens. He is half-Chinese, lives in Bangkok, but specializes in eating street food around the world. It's no surprise to me his channel has 5 million followers because he is enthusiastic, thrifty, do-it-yourself, and he goes to the places I would go for street food: Pakistan, Ethiopia, Lebanon, Mexico, Sri Lanka, Uzbekistan, China. His "tours" are more useful than say Anthony Bourdain's or Andrew Zimmern's, in part because he doesn't have a crew and stays low to the ground. When I head somewhere remote, I check his extensive archive out. — KK

Find street food tours

Before I travel to new city X, I search for "street food tour for city X." Almost every interesting city these days has someone offering this inside look. I find it a quick, fun, inexpensive, exhilarating way to get to know a place. — KK

Favorite natural destination

My new favorite US national park is Zion. Like Yosemite (my former favorite) it is a walkable valley enclosed in sheer vertical steepness. There's a spectacular view each time you turn, or turn around. Hot in summer, it can be cool-ish much of the rest of the year, and has lots of trails around it. Like Yosemite, they restrict cars, so you get around on shuttle buses. It rewards repeat visits. — KK

National parks lifetime pass

Anyone 62 or older can get a senior lifetime pass to the US National Parks for $80. That's the cost of a regular one-year pass, so it's a great bargain, and a great gift for a relative or friend if you are not 62. — KK

Room of Silence

One of the most profound experiences I've had while traveling was visiting the Raum der Stille, a non-denominational room of silence in the Brandenburg Gate in Berlin. I sat in a clean, nondescript room in a chair facing other chairs with maybe 2 or 3 other people. The room wasn't soundproof, but we were all silent and in our own reflective states. I didn't want to leave. I felt connected to these strangers and I felt connected to myself, which is something I never felt in any church. I was so overwhelmed and grateful for that short experience, and was excited to visit more quiet rooms. I encourage anybody visiting there soon to seek it out. You can read more about it here. — CD

Coolest nature museum

The world's coolest nature museum: The Pitt Rivers Museum in Oxford, England. It's a day trip from London. Take the 1-hour train to Oxford, then walk 15 minutes from the station to the museum, co-housed with the Oxford University Nature Museum. Enter into a lost world of curiosity. You are surrounded by three floors of artifacts collected over centuries by eccentric British explorers. Displays include shrunken heads, voodoo dolls, tomb relics, weird insects, ancient folk tools, dinosaur skeletons, taxidermy galore, uncountable biological, and mineralogical specimens, all stacked in glassy cabinets with typed cards and labels. It's supremely old-school and hugely satisfying. — KK

SFO Museum

For years the San Francisco airport has been accumulating and displaying stellar modern art throughout its four terminals. They now call this ongoing collection the SFO Museum. Though thinly dispersed, IMHO it's one of the better modern art museums today. It is well worth going to their website to discover where the works are and what is showing. Most are in post-security areas, so it's convenient if you have extra time once checked in, or are in transit. I've been seeking them out with great pleasure. — KK

SF interactive exhibit museum

Since I live in the San Francisco metro area, I get a lot of out-of-town visitors. My favorite place to take them is the Exploratorium, along the bayside waterfront. It is the original hands-on science museum, and still the world's best hands-on learning experience. Many of the interactive exhibits now common at science museums around the world began here; the Exploratorium has all of them and many more found nowhere else. This sprawling temple of innovation and maker-goodness can easily occupy me — even after my 50th visit — for four hours or more. (I normally get saturated after only one hour in other museums.) Of course while it is perfect for kids of all ages, every Thursday evening it's reserved for adults, and crowded with innovators and artists of all types. — KK

Scale of our War

The Te Papa Museum in Wellington, New Zealand has a permanent exhibit, Scale of Our War, that is almost worth going to New Zealand to see, and should certainly be on a must-visit list if you happen to travel there. Weta Workshops, the folks who made all the props and special effects in the Lord of the Rings movies and other Peter Jackson productions, created a set of sculptures to mourn the disaster of the WWI battle of Gallipoli, Turkey, which was the seminal trigger for New Zealand independence. Weta created 2X lifesize versions of soldiers and nurses in the war that are hyperreal in their detail, from each hair on their arms, to flies on their frayed jackets, the 2X scale of threads in the cloth, and uncannily realistic flesh and faces, all at twice the size. You are looking up, in the embrace of these large beings, like a child in the arms of its parent. I've seen statues and art, ancient and modern, around the world, and no sculpture has been so emotionally potent as these. Worth going out of your way to see. — KK

TRAVEL TIPS

40 tourist scams around the world

One reason I like traveling to Japan is that no one there has ever tried to pull a scam on me.

Not so in Europe, Mexico, and the United States, where I've experienced at least a few of the 40 scams presented in this infographic. A few are obvious, but there are always some surprising scams worth knowing about. Read this list to prepare yourself the next time you travel. — MF

All the travel info you need

The Basetrip provides essential information you need when traveling internationally. Just enter your country of origin and your destination and the site will tell you the currency exchange rate, mobile phone service options, the crime

rate, electrical outlets, drug and prostitution laws, and more. For an extra $5 per trip, you'll get passport & visa information, travel advisories, and language phrases with audio pronunciation. — MF

Offline travel guides

Guides by Lonely Planet was so helpful on my recent trip through Central Europe.
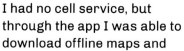
I had no cell service, but through the app I was able to download offline maps and

navigate to points of interest (bars, shops, sights) while learning more about the cities I visited. Also invaluable was the currency converter, tipping etiquette, and local phrasebook. — CD

Automate travel itineraries

Google Trips is an app (for iOS and Android) that scans my Gmail for travel and

dining reservations to build an itinerary and offer things to do at your destination. It's worked like a charm so far, identifying every upcoming trip I have planned. It even created summaries for past trips. — MF

DIY guidebook

The cheapest bargain of any overseas vacation is the $25 for the travel guidebook, so I always get the latest version. And I have no qualms about cutting it up. I get the large country-scale guide, and then with a razor blade knife I excise only the portions I could possibly use. Then I staple and bind with clear packing tape for very durable, and lightweight, thin booklets. — KK

AIR TRAVEL

Airfare price drop alerts

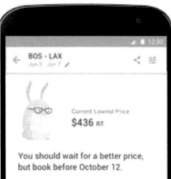

Hopper is a smartphone app that predicts when airfare to a desired destination will be the cheapest. I've set up an alert for Chiang Mai, Thailand. About once a month Hopper sends me a message with the best price it can find, telling me to "wait" or "buy." The price recently dropped from the $900s to the $500s and Hopper said "buy." — MF

Cheap flights

Scott's Cheap Flights is a free newsletter that finds amazingly inexpensive flights all over the world. The newsletter includes Google Flights and Momondo links, so you can book the flight yourself. The latest newsletter has a roundtrip flight from Los Angeles to Stockholm for $343. — MF

All the flights possible

I am often frustrated when trying to fly from one obscure place to another obscure place with as few stops in between. Most flight sites want you to keep the journey on the same airline. What I want is "show me ALL the flights from this airport," and I'll figure out a route on my own. No surprise, there's a site for that, called appropriately enough FlightsFrom.com. I can assemble a route, sometimes with obscure airlines, that won't show up elsewhere. — KK

Easy flight-delay compensation

My international flight to Los Angeles was delayed for 10 hours. The airline didn't tell me I was eligible for compensation, but a friend told me about an app called AirHelp. I entered my name and confirmation number. Instantly, AirHelp told me the airline was obligated to pay me about $700. AirHelp did all the work, and about a week later I got the money, minus a 25% commission for AirHelp, which was a small price to pay for not having to do anything. — MF

Real reason planes are late

Airlines are reluctant to tell passengers the real reason a plane is late, or how long 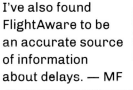 a delay will actually last. But if you go to your airline's special cargo website, you're more likely to get the real story. I've also found FlightAware to be an accurate source of information about delays. — MF

How to pick your seat

Would you like to improve your chance of having an empty middle seat when you fly on Southwest? Here's a trick I've started to use that works. When I board, I look for a 3-seat row of chairs where a very large person is sitting in the window or aisle seat. I will sit in that row, either in the aisle seat or window seat. As the plane starts to get full, passengers will be reluctant to sit in the middle seat because the big person is encroaching on the space. One time when I did this, the guy sitting in the seat (he was probably 6'5" and weighed 300 pounds) leaned over and said conspiratorially, "No one will sit here. It's always the last seat they take." — MF

Avoid luggage fees

Certain airlines offer very low prices on flights, and then charge for things most airlines include. On Frontier, a carry-on bag is $35-$60. I avoided the fee by using luggage that was small enough to be considered a "personal item" (it has to be under 14" high, 18" wide, 8" deep). A lot of backpacks will meet the size requirements. I have a Swissgear rolling bag, similar to this one. It held enough summer clothes for a 4-night trip, plus a gadget case, a toiletries bag, and my 13-inch laptop with charger. — MF

Second passport

I have two US passports, both valid and official. Because I travel overseas so much, I often have my passport tied up in getting a visa somewhere, so I have the second passport available. This gives me some breathing room. It's also useful if you are traveling to countries that don't recognize Israel and you have an Israel stamp in your passport. To get a second US passport you apply as if you are renewing your passport by mail and add a letter requesting a second passport. Instructions here. — KK

Qualify for TSA Pre-check

A Global Entry pass is a true bargain if you do any international travel. You don't need to wait in line for immigration at reentry to the US. But it also serves as validation for the TSA Pre-check short-cut for security screening at most major US airports. Much shorter lines. To get in, the program requires an appointment to get fingerprinted and $100 every five years. Well worth it. — KK

Global Entry guide

As I previously recommended, Global Entry membership is a great bargain if you fly a lot. Not just homecoming international travel but for TSA-Precheck domestically. With it I rarely wait in line in US airports. Here is a very complete, free, third-party, comprehensive guide to evaluating its perks (some premium credit cards will pay for it), and navigating its bureaucratic hurdles (the best airports to get an interview), the kind of info you won't find on the government webpage. — KK

Secure travel docs

I stow PDF scans of my passport, visas, itinerary and key travel docs in my Dropbox, which show up in the Dropbox app on my phone so I always have them in case of loss while traveling overseas. — KK

My travel packing list

Here's the latest version of my travel packing list. It's a PDF that can be edited in Adobe Illustrator (because I don't expect anyone to pack the same things I do). As you can see, my list is broken down into sublists of different bags: charger bag, meds bag, tool bag, etc. I keep the stuff in these excellent Japanese mesh zipper bags . Now I don't forget important things any more like I used to. I recommend that you make a similar packing list for yourself. — MF

Duplicate travel items

I have found it useful to purchase a duplicate set of cords, cables, chargers, desktop items, earphones, etc. that I carry in a dedicated bag just for travel. Increasingly I've added duplicate articles of clothing, shoes, and hats to my carry-on luggage. They never leave. That way I don't have to pack, but more importantly, I don't ever forget anything. The cost of duplication is minimal for the benefits. – KK

Traveling with tubes

Most tubes of toothpaste, hair gel, and lotion have sharp corners on the crimped end. The sharp corners easily slice through the plastic bag I keep my gels and liquids in when flying. I started snipping the corners with nail clippers. I even fillet the corners of tubes at home to prevent them from jabbing my fingers when I reach for them in a drawer. Just be careful not to cut the corners so much that it causes a leak. — MF

Free filtered water at hotels

I once walked into a hotel room and saw a large bottle of water on the desk. After I took a swig I noticed the $9 sticker on the bottle. Not wanting to pay the same price again, I started refilling the bottle from the cooler in the fitness center. Now when I travel I bring a bottle with me and head straight for the fitness center. — MF

Forgot your charger?

If you lose or forget to bring a cable, adapter or charger, check with your hotel. Most hotels now have a drawer full of cables, adapters and chargers others have left behind, and probably have the one you are missing. You can often claim it after borrowing it. — KK

Best way to book China travel

China is so vast that the only way to get around is either by high speed train or plane. But because of its language barrier it's really hard for foreigners to book tickets for either. The best way to book a flight in China is via the English language site Trip, which I use. Easy to make reservations, changes, and refunds. I can skype a call to them if needed. For trains I use the English language site Travel China Guide. — KK

Climbing the firewall in China

While traveling in China, the government will prevent you from accessing Google, Gmail, Google Maps, Facebook, YouTube, Twitter, Snapchat, Instagram, *The New York Times*, and many other news sites. If any of these services are important to you, you need to use a very good VPN to circumvent the censoring. (China is able to block some VPNs that work elsewhere). The best VPN for China is the ExpressVPN app, which you can load on your phone and laptop. Once

TRAVEL TO ASIA

loaded it's pretty seamless and unnoticeable. You can reach any site with fine speed. There's a monthly subscription of $8.32, but it's worth it compared to cheaper and free VPNs. It's useful anywhere in the world sites are blocked. Even in the West, if I am accessing a public wifi spot for my mail I'll turn it on as an added layer of privacy. — KK

Bullet trains in China

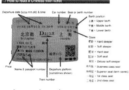

Japan has had a network of extremely high-speed bullet trains for 50 years. (The US has zero.) China now has an even more impressive network of high-speed bullet trains that cover great distances and are easy to ride. A popular route is Beijing to Shanghai in 4 hours, going 350 km/h (217 mph). Another great long trip is Beijing to Guangzhou (near Hong Kong) in 8 hours (averaging 305 km/h the whole way), which is the longest high-speed route in the world, a trip I

made with joy recently. Flying is faster and, depending on class, cheaper, but you get an intimate and revealing glimpse of this vast country slicing through at ground level. Booking tickets online is complicated but doable. As always, head to the Man in Seat 61 for the best advice on how to do this. — KK

Japanese transit

Japan is one of the most convenient places in the world to travel. Public transit — both local and long distance — is ubiquitous, frequent, fast, insanely prompt, safe, and reliable. However its ubiquity means there is a labyrinth of so many routes that your journey can be an impenetrable puzzle — not to mention the real hurdle of the language barrier. To the rescue comes Google Maps. If you choose the transit option for directions it will provide you with brilliantly designed color-coded instructions on which subway/bus/trains to take, exactly where to catch each leg, which line, how many stops, how many minutes you need to walk between, the price, and all the

alternative routes, in English. Since Japanese transit runs like clockwork, all this precision turns you into a relaxed native traveller. (Google Maps provides similar instructions all over the world, but for Japan's maze of transit, this is game changing.) — KK

Cheap fast wireless for travel to Japan

I spent almost five weeks in Japan this summer. My T-Mobile plan includes international data but it is pretty slow so I rented a Pocket WiFi from eConnect. I ordered it in advance and picked it up at the post office at Narita Airport. I bought the 50GB plan for about $125. When I came close to running out (our traveling party of five used it pretty much non-stop on their phones and laptops), I bought more data for about $1 per GB. It was very fast and worked everywhere we went, including the remote mountain town of Koya-san. At the airport on the way home I put it in the return mailer and dropped it off at the post office. — MF

Translate this, always

I am finding the new Google Translate mobile app to be indispensable when traveling. About 100 languages are available, including Kazakh, Igbo, Maori, etc. About 60 of those languages can be downloaded to your phone so you can translate offline when your phone is off, not working in the country, or out of cell range. (Instructions here.) The offline translation is text only, but surprisingly smart enough for touring needs. Having a language downloaded offline (about 40MB) also seems to help when translation is online as well (like using your phone camera to read menus and signs.) It's all free and one of the best bargains in the world. — KK

Learn celsius

Part 1: Here's an easy way to approximately convert Centigrade to Fahrenheit: "double the Centigrade temp, subtract the first digit of the result from the result and add 32." Example: 16 C = (32-3)+32 = 61 F. (This tip is from Fodor's Travel website.) — MF

Part 2: Recomendo reader Don wrote to tell us, "Your Centigrade to Fahrenheit conversion works 'sorta' as long as the result of doubling the C number is a two-digit number. I've always doubled the C number and subtracted 10%, then added 32. Most folks can figure out 10% and subtract it. Also, this doesn't result in an approximation, but the correct result." — MF

Part 3: The US is basically the only country in the world not using metric. It's not that hard to learn a rough sense of how many kilometers in a mile, or pounds in a kilo. But it is very hard to convert temperatures between Centigrade and Fahrenheit. The solution is to convert all your thermometers to Centigrade: on your phone, in or outside of your house, on websites. Have any digital device display only Celsius, so you can't cheat. In about a year, you'll have a reliable and native sense of what's cool and warm in degrees C. This is supremely handy if you travel anywhere outside of the US. — KK

Favorite hotel-booking website

I travel in other countries a lot, often in remote places, and when I do I prefer smaller

hotels, hostels, guesthouses, homestays, inns and Airbnb. Over the past decade I've used many apps and sites for booking smaller places in Asia, Latin America and Europe, but in the last 3 years I've settled on Booking.com as my go-to. It has a unified interface to 1.1 million hotels and guesthouses worldwide, with the widest coverage and selection, accurate prices and info. It is also high-reliability (if they say you have a reservation, you do) and they make it very easy to change or cancel. If I can, I will always book through Booking.com rather than the hotel direct. — KK

Tip for Hotwire Users

I've used Hotwire to book hotel rooms. On the plus side, they have good deals, on the minus side, you don't know which hotel you are reserving until after you've paid the non-refundable fee. But here's a video on "How ANYONE Can Get 50% Off Hotels" that shows you how to find out which hotel HotWire is offering before you commit. — MF

MAPS

Google Map tips

Here are 12 really great tips for using Google Maps on your phone. How to share your current location, or share your trip progress, remember a parking space, invoke street view, estimate trip duration by departure time, or send a map search from your computer to your phone. I had no idea I had these powers. — KK

Offline Google Maps

My friend Star Simpson tweeted this useful travel tip: "Not enough people know that Google Maps has an Easter egg. If you type 'ok maps' into the search field it will download a map for offline use. Great if you might not have awesome cell reception where you're going, is now a step on my packing checklist." (For some reason it doesn't work for Tokyo.) — MF

Terrain maps

On Google Maps: in between the standard street view, and the realistic satellite view, lies another hidden view called Terrain. Terrain is an

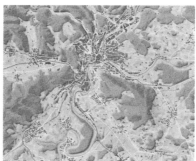

almost artistic rendering of a physical place without all the distractions of an aerial photograph. Its crisp clarity is tremendously useful as a base map — and beautiful. To get to Terrain mode, go to the "hamburger" (stack of 3 lines) in the upper left corner of Maps in a browser, and click on Terrain in the pull-down menu. — KK

Where were you on October 21, 2012?

I'm not surprised that Google has been tracking my every move since 2009. I'm sure I allowed it when I accepted its terms of service at some point. What is surprising is being able about to browse this timeline of my location on a world map. This Google page has day-by-day reports of where you where, the paths you traveled, the restaurants and stores you visited, and any geotagged photos you took on

any given day. You can even edit the information if its incorrect. Wow! — MF

Precise memorable addresses

What3Words divides the world into 3 x 3-meter squares and gives each square a unique, unalterable sequence of three random words. For instance, the location of my writing desk is "smile.rocket.gates." This global address is really handy for sending a delivery person to the right part of a building, or meeting someone on at trail head, or locating a home in the large parts of the developing world that have no operational address. It's better than a lat/long sequence because you can remember it. Works in multiple languages. The phone app version integrates into Google Maps, etc. — KK

Best travel credit card

My first choice for getting money when traveling overseas is to use a credit card with no foreign exchange transaction fees. Credit cards give me the best exchange rates, and it reduces how much cash I carry. (If a card is not accepted, my second choice is local cash issued from an ATM, using a debit card without transaction costs. I don't bother with Travelers Checks; they are unusable these days. And traditional money exchanges have unfavorable rates.) For a credit card without foreign transaction fees, I use a Chase Sapphire Reserve which has lots of other perks, but a high annual fee. Another good option is the Capital One Venture for $60 per year, but less perks. For the current lowdown on the best travel cards and their perks see ThePointsGuy, a free blog full of travel advice. — KK

Best exchange rates

It's been true for a while, but some travellers don't realize that the best currency exchange rates you'll get will be at a local ATM, even with a fee. It is also by far the most convenient way to change money. I've gotten local currency from my debit card in every country I have visited (though not every local ATM will accept foreign cards — look for American credit card logos on the machine as a sign that it will.) I raised the limit on the ATM card to its max since this is my only source of currency. — KK

Rental car special

Hertz rental cars have an option called "Manager's Special." You agree to take whatever car they give you at below Economy car rates. You'll get at least an economy car, but usually a bigger car, maybe even a nice car. — KK

Where's the gas tank?

When you rent or borrow a car and you pull up to a gas station to fill it up, what side is the gas tank on? Look down. In the gas gauge on your dashboard there's a little arrow to the side of the fuel pump icon. Its direction — left or right — will accurately point to the gas tank side. — KK

Travel tip for Starbucks people

Here's a tip I haven't tried yet, but it sounds like a great idea. When you're leaving a foreign country and still have some of the local currency, take it to a Starbucks and load it onto a gift card. You can use the card later in the UK, USA, Canada, Australia, Mexico, and the Republic of Ireland. — MF

Another use for Starbucks cards

(This tip comes from Recomendo reader Andy Kegel) "More and more rebates come as prepaid credit/debit cards. It's hard to find something for exactly the face amount, so I feel like I'm always gifting back part of the rebate via unspent residuals. So now I put the whole amount on a Starbucks card or similar and I can spend the entire face value." — MF

INDEX

INDEX

INDEX

INDEX

Made in the USA
Middletown, DE
13 December 2020

27780724R00122